6. ^{55}

Child
Learning

Child
Learning

SECOND EDITION

Through
Elementary
School
Physical Education

James H. Humphrey
University of Maryland

With the Collaboration of
JOY M. HUMPHREY

WM. C. BROWN COMPANY PUBLISHERS
Dubuque, Iowa

PHYSICAL EDUCATION

Aileene Lockhart
Texas Woman's University

PARKS AND RECREATION

David Gray
California State University, Long Beach

HEALTH

Robert Kaplan
Ohio State University

Copyright © 1965, 1974 by Wm. C. Brown Company Publishers

Library of Congress Catalog Card Number 73—83790

ISBN 0—697—07256—8

Printed in the United States of America

Contents

Preface

The decision to revise and rewrite CHILD LEARNING THROUGH ELEMENTARY SCHOOL PHYSICAL EDUCATION has been based largely on the vast changes and numerous research findings in the field. It is because of these rapid changes and recent discoveries that a major revision has been undertaken.

Inasmuch as the original edition contained ten chapters, the author, in this revision, has enlarged on the material to sixteen chapters. The book not only introduces many new concepts, but a new format as well.

Each chapter presents objectives stated in either an interrogative or declarative form in line with a systems approach designed to assist the reader to understand better the material in the chapter.

The book has been divided into three distinct but interrelated and interdependent parts, with each part identifying and detailing a branch of physical education.

In Part One, *Curricular Physical Education,* nine chapters are devoted to this basic branch which depicts physical education as a valuable and worthwhile subject with the same status given other courses in the elementary school. The introductory chapter presents a general overview of elementary school physical education. Chapter 2 develops the concept of growth and development through physical education. In Chapter 3 a thorough discussion of the function of the teacher and teacher behavior is presented, while Chapter 4 discusses recent trends in curriculum development. Chapter 5 takes into account teaching and learning in physical education with emphasis placed on principles of learning as they apply to the specific area of physical education. Movement and skills are discussed in detail in Chapter 6, and curriculum content in the form of game activities, rhythmic activities, and self-testing activities comprise Chapters 7, 8, and 9.

In Part Two, which involves *Cognitive Physical Education,* Chapter 10 gives an overview of the basic theory underlying this important branch. Chapters 11, 12, and 13 are devoted to physical education as a medium for learning in reading, mathematics, and science.

Part Three is concerned with *Compensatory Physical Education* and goes into some detail with regard to perceptual-motor development and media used in perceptual-motor training.

James H. Humphrey

Part One

Curricular
Physical
Education

Chapter 1

Orientation to Elementary School Physical Education

The material in this book has been prepared on the premise that the curriculum area of physical education has a vast potential contribution to make to the lives of children of elementary school age. The point of view is taken that this potential contribution can be realized only when there is a full understanding of all of the various facets and ramifications of physical education.

The purpose of this initial chapter is to give the reader a general overview of the area of elementary school physical education. This will be done through:

1. A presentation of a brief historical background of physical education in the elementary school.
2. A discussion of current status and trends.
3. An identification of certain branches of physical education, and the role of these branches in the modern elementary school.

Historical Background

In order to present a clearer picture of the place physical education occupies in the modern elementary school, it seems appropriate to discuss briefly its historical development. Moreover, if we can see how the past has challenged the present, there is a strong likelihood that we may be able to understand more fully how the present might challenge the future.

There is a widespread notion among some people at the present time that physical education at the elementary school level is something new. This idea is probably prompted by the fact that physical education at this level has been receiving more attention in recent years and by the further fact that more emphasis is being put on it in some school systems.

Contrary to this general belief, physical education at the elementary school level is not of recent origin. In fact, educators and philosophers as far back as the early Greeks felt that physical education activities might be a welcome adjunct to the total education of children. For instance, over 2,300 years ago Plato suggested that all early education should be a sort of play and develop around play situations.

In the seventeenth century, Locke, the English philosopher, felt that children should get plenty of exercise and learn to swim early in life. Rousseau, the noted French writer, held much the same opinion, believing that learning should develop from the activities of childhood. These men, along with numerous others, influenced to some extent the path that elementary school physical education was to follow through the years.

Throughout the ages physical education programs have been caught between mere preparation of the body for combat and a recognition of the essential unity of mind and body in the educative process. In addition, there have been periods when any type of physical education program was abandoned purely on the basis that body pleasure of any sort must be subjugated because this activity was associated with evildoing. The early American pioneers more or less typified this kind of puritanical thinking because there was no emphasis on physical education for the pioneer child as far as formal education was concerned. Although physical education received no attention in the early American elementary schools, a series of factors over a period of a few years were instrumental in effecting a radical change, such as Western expansion, wars, application of inventions which revolutionized travel and communications, and the concentration of population, all having an influence on the growth of the early common schools. Although the early grade schools of the mid-nineteenth century were concerned predominantly with the academic subject matter of reading, writing, and arithmetic, the need for physical activity as a part of the school day was becoming evident. As a result, some time for physical exercise was allotted in the school programs of Boston as early as 1852. St. Louis and Cincinnati followed this procedure in 1855 and 1859, respectively. Interest on the state level began to appear and a state law requiring physical education was passed in California in 1866. The fact that the public was becoming conscious of the play needs of children was indicated by the establishment of the first playground in Boston in 1885.

A short time later in 1889, in that same city, an interesting development occurred at a "Conference in the interest of physical training." School administrators were beginning to feel the pressure and need for some kind of formal physical activity as a genuine part of the school program. Acting in a conservative manner at this conference, some school administrators proposed that a "physical training" program might be introduced as a part of the school day, but that it must consume only a short period of time, minimal expenditure of money, and take place in the classroom. The Swedish pedagogical system of gymnastics, which was designed to systematically exercise the entire body in a single lesson, was proposed since this system satisfactorily met the criteria established by the school administrators. On June 24, 1890, the Boston School Committee voted that this system of gymnastics be introduced in all of the public schools of Boston. Although this proposal was a far cry from a well-balanced elementary school physical education program as we understand it today, it nevertheless served as a formal introduction of organized physical activity into the elementary school on the recommendation of school administrators. It should be mentioned, however, that the main objective of physical education in the eyes of school administrators of that day was that it should serve as a release for prolonged periods of mental fatigue. It was believed that the main purpose of engaging in physical activity was to provide children with a "break" in the school day so that they would approach their studies more vigorously.

This condition existed until such time that there was more widespread acceptance of the theory of mind-body relationship and the education of the *whole* person. John Dewey, one of the early exponents of this principle, introduced the concept of a balanced physical education program while at the University of Chicago Laboratory School at the turn of the century. Rather than only the more or less formalized gymnastics program, this school began to include games and dancing as a part of physical education for children. Some years later Dewey commented that "Experience has shown that when children have a chance at physical activities which bring their natural impulses into play, going to school is a joy, management is less of a burden, and learning is easier."[1]

However, up until the first World War physical education programs for elementary school children, where they did exist, consisted mainly of the formalized gymnastic and/or exercise types of program. The period between the two World Wars saw more attempts at balancing physical education programs at the elementary school level with more emphasis being placed upon games and rhythmic activities.

After World War II a number of factors developed which were to bring attention to the importance of physical education for young children. One estimate indicated that from the period of 1945 to 1955 more published

---

[1]John Dewey, *Democracy and Education,* An Introduction to the Philosophy of Education (New York: The Macmillan Company, 1919), pp. 228-229.

material appeared relating to elementary school physical education than was the case in the preceding fifty years. In addition, many areas of the country began to provide elementary school physical education workshops and other in-service education devices for elementary school personnel. In 1948, at its annual convention, the American Association for Health, Physical Education, and Recreation inaugurated an Elementary School Physical Education Section, and in 1951 the first National Conference on Physical Education for Children of Elementary School Age was held in Washington, D.C.

The two decades from 1950 to 1970 saw a continuation of the foundation that had been laid in the preceding years. Numerous national conferences, the appointment of an Elementary School Consultant by the American Association for Health, Physical Education, and Recreation, upgrading of teacher preparation, and the recent "discovery" of the importance of *movement* in the lives of children have all contributed to better elementary school physical education programs.

It should appear evident from this short historical background that elementary school physical education has traveled a strange and sometimes hazardous road in reaching the level of importance that is attributed to it in modern education. However, in spite of various pitfalls this area of education has forged ahead to the point where there has been almost unbelievable and unparalleled progress in the past few years. This does not mean that the proponents for this area of education can become lethargic. Much needs to be done to continue to interpret the place and function of physical education in the modern elementary school curriculum, as well as to provide ways and means whereby physical education learning experiences can become even more valuable in the total growth and development of the elementary school child.

Current Status and Trends

Current interest in elementary school physical education is without doubt at its greatest peak in history. The Elementary Education Consultant of the American Association for Health, Physical Education, and Recreation, Dr. Margie R. Hanson, has suggested that this interest is evidenced by the following factors.[2]

---

[2]Margie R. Hanson, "Elementary School Physical Education Today, Promising Practices in Elementary School Physical Education," *Report of the Conference for Teachers and Supervisors of Elementary School Physical Education,* American Association for Health, Physical Education, and Recreation, Washington, D.C., October 2-5, 1968.

1. An increasing demand for elementary school physical education teachers.
2. An increased number of clinics, institutes, and workshops.
3. Record-breaking attendance at conferences, conventions, and meetings devoted to the topic of physical education in the elementary school.
4. Requests for assistance received at the National headquarters office of the American Association for Health, Physical Education, and Recreation, and in the offices of the state departments of education.
5. The number of colleges now seeking to provide either a major or special area of concentration in elementary school physical education.
6. An increased interest in preschool programs where motor activity is a very important aspect of the problem.
7. The interest shown by disciplines outside the profession of physical education. (Many elementary education groups have met with physical education personnel to share ideas and to plan publications.)

As educators have become increasingly aware of the importance of a good physical education program in the elementary school, more emphasis has been placed on this area of the curriculum; and, as attention has been focused upon the potential value of physical education on the total growth and development of children, a number of relatively new developments have emerged into certain trends. Among others, these include:

1. With a better understanding of the importance of movement in the life of the young child, more emphasis is being placed upon these experiences at the preschool level.
2. Due to a greater awareness of some of the causes of learning disability, more attention is being directed to the perceptual-motor development of children.
3. Physical education is becoming a more important integral part of the experiences of the mentally retarded and physically handicapped children.
4. Many important and long-needed changes are being made in the area of curriculum development in elementary school physical education.
5. More physical education teachers are keeping abreast with learning theory and making a greater attempt to apply these valid principles of learning to methods of teaching.
6. More and more teachers are recognizing the value of the use of physical education as a learning medium in the development of skills and concepts in such areas as reading and language, mathematics, science, and social studies.

(Many of these trends will be the subject of detailed discussions in subsequent chapters.)

Branches of Physical Education

Over the years the term "physical education" has suggested different
things to different people. To some outside the field of education it may be
thought of only as a series of "setting-up" exercises. To others it means
only scoring touchdowns or hitting home runs. Even many educators are
not entirely sure of its meaning, and oftentimes people in the field of physical education itself attach different meanings to it.

The time is long since past when physical education should be thought
of only as a complete entity. For this reason, and for means of better communication, it seems necessary to identify certain branches of it. It should
be understood that the branches of physical education suggested here are
purely arbitrary. Some people may wish to add others or subclassify some
of those indicated here. Others may wish to give different names to the
branches suggested here, and, in the absence of anything resembling
standardized terminology, it is their prerogative to do so. With this idea in
mind the classifications that we prefer to use are: (1) *curricular* physical
education; (2) *cognitive* physical education; and (3) *compensatory* physical education.

Curricular Physical Education

This basic branch implies that physical education should be a subject
in the curriculum in the same manner that mathematics is a subject or science is a subject, and so on. Such factors as sufficient facilities, adequate
time allotment, and above all good teaching should be provided so as to
carry out the most desirable physical education learning experiences for
children. A curriculum that is child-oriented and scientifically developed
should be provided as would be the case with the language arts curriculum
or the social studies curriculum or any other curriculum in the school. It
is in this branch that the child should learn to move efficiently and effectively and to learn the various kinds of locomotor and manipulative skills
needed for satisfactory performance in games, rhythms, and self-testing
activities.

Two natural subclassifications of the curricular branch could be *adap-
tive* physical education and *extraclass* physical education. The term "adap-
tive" means that special kinds of activities are adapted for use with children who have some sort of physical impairment. The extraclass program
which would consist of the two broad categories of intramural activities

(within the school) and interscholastic activities (between schools) should be a natural outgrowth of the regular physical education class program.

With some of the recent new developments in the whole area of physical education, some individuals have lost sight of this most important branch, and in some cases parts of curricular physical education have been curtailed. Madeline Hunter, principal of the University Elementary School at the University of California at Los Angeles, has wisely cautioned against this by stating:

> In our zeal, generated by new knowledge from the perceptual-motor field, we must not lose sight of the fact that a good physical education program should exist in its own right because it makes important contributions to the learner over and beyond what such a program may contribute to his academic learning. Physical education is one of the few areas where we can confidently assume that the learner's needs will not markedly change by the time he reaches adulthood. We are told that motion pictures will replace reading as the most important medium of communication and information, that libraries, as we know them, will become obsolete, that paper and pencil computation already is archaic, but to date no one is assuming a major change in design and functioning of the human body. Consequently, facility, efficiency, and expertness in the use of one's body is predictably useful throughout the learner's life.[3]

Cognitive Physical Education

This branch of physical education, which considers its use as a learning medium in other curriculum areas, might well be considered a relatively recent innovation. In essence, this procedure involves the selection of a physical education activity in which a specific skill or concept of a given subject-matter area has a relatively high degree of inherency. The physical education activity is taught to the children and used as a learning activity in developing the skill or concept in the specific subject area.

It should be pointed out here that in recent years some educational psychologists have identified this approach as *the total physical response technique of learning*. In regard to our work in this area, one learning theorist has commented as follows:

> The work that comes closest to total physical response motor learning is Humphrey's investigations of learning through games in which, for example, the acquisition of certain reading skills was significantly accelerated when the learning task occurred in the context of a game involving the entire body.[4]

[3]Madeline Hunter, "Implications of Perceptual-Motor Programs for Physical Education," *Proceedings of the Perceptual-Motor Conference*, American Association for Health, Physical Education, and Recreation, Washington, D.C., 1971
[4]James J. Asher, "The Total Physical Response Technique of Learning," *Journal of Special Education*, Fall, 1969.

An example of a physical education activity and inherent *number* concept suitable for use with first-grade children follows:

Physical Education Activity: The Huntsman

The children stand in a circle and a leader is chosen to be the Huntsman. He walks around the outside of the circle and asks each of a given number of children to go hunting with him. All of these children fall in behind the Huntsman and do as he does. Suddenly the Huntsman calls out, "Bang!" On this signal the children who were following run back to try to get to their original place in the circle. The first one back may be selected as the Huntsman for the next time.

Concept Inherent in the Activity: Counting starts with one and enlarges the groups by successive ones.

The game starts with *one* person, the Huntsman, and he keeps *adding* to his hunting party *one* by *one* until he has the decided *number*. The children have the opportunity to count each time a new person is invited to go along on the "hunt" and realize that there is *one* more person each time.

These procedures presuppose that young children tend to learn better when the learning takes place through pleasurable physical activity; or, in other words, when the *motor* component operates at a maximal level in concept development in school subject areas predominantly oriented to *verbal* learning. This is *not* to say that "verbal" and "motor" learnings are two mutually exclusive kinds of learning, although it has been suggested that at the two extremes the dichotomy appears justifiable. It has been recognized that in verbal learning which involves almost complete abstract symbolic manipulations there are, among others, such motor components as tension, subvocal speech, and physiological changes in metabolism which operate at a minimal level.[5] It is also recognized that in an area such as physical education where the learning is predominantly motor in nature, verbal learning is in evidence, although at a minimal level. For example, in teaching a physical education activity there is a certain amount of verbalization involved in developing a kinesthetic concept of the particular activity.

It seems appropriate to take into account what might be considered some very important precautionary measures when using this branch of physical education. This approach should be considered as only *one* aspect of physical education and certainly not the major purpose of it. As mentioned previously, we should consider physical education to be a subject "in its own right" in the elementary school curriculum, with the

[5]G. B. Johnson, *Science and Medicine of Exercise and Sports,* ed. Warren R. Johnson (New York: Harper and Bros., 1960) p. 601.

natural corollaries of good teaching, sufficient facilities, and the like. Consequently, the use of physical education as a learning medium in other subject areas should not ordinarily occur during the regular time allotted to physical education. On the contrary, this approach should be considered a learning activity in the same way other kinds of learning activities are used in a given subject area. This means that, for the most part, this procedure should be used during the time allotted to the particular subject area in question. Moreover, the classroom teacher would ordinarily do the teaching when this approach is used. The function of the physical education teacher could be to furnish the classroom teacher with suitable physical education activities to use in the development of concepts. This is to say that the classroom teacher is familiar with the skills and concepts to be developed, and similarly the physical education teacher should know those activities that could be used to develop the skills and concepts. For example, let us say that the classroom teacher might be attempting to develop an understanding of *alphabetic sequence*. After explaining this to the physical education teacher, he or she should be able to provide a physical education activity for the classroom teacher to use as a learning activity.

Compensatory Physical Education

While compensatory physical education and cognitive physical education are essentially based on the same concept, the manner in which these two approaches are used should not be confused. It could be said that compensatory physical education is essentially concerned with education *of* the physical, while cognitive physical education is concerned with education *through* the physical.

Compensatory physical education seeks to correct various types of child-learning disabilities which may stem from an impairment of the central nervous system and/or have their roots in certain social or emotional problems of children.

This branch of physical education, most often through the medium of *perceptual-motor training*, involves the correction, or at least some degree of improvement, of certain motor deficiencies, especially those associated with fine coordination. What some specialists have identified as a "perceptual-motor-deficit" syndrome is said to exist with certain neurologically handicapped children. An attempt may be made to correct or improve fine motor control problems through a carefully developed sequence of motor competencies which follow a definite hierarchy of development. This may occur through either structured or unstructured programs. The structured type of program is more or less dependent upon a series of systematic physical exercises, while the unstructured program is more creative in nature and has a greater degree of flexibility.

The main thrust of this book is in the direction of curricular physical education (Part One). It will also be a primary function of the text to deal in some detail with cognitive physical education (Part Two). Although it is not a major concern of the book to go into detail with regard to compensatory physical education, nevertheless Part Three will be devoted to this particular branch.

Over the years physical education programs have often been encumbered by lack of facilities.

Chapter 2

Growth and
Development Through
Physical Education

In order to make a valid exploration of the area of physical education in the elementary school curriculum, it becomes necessary to consider the guiding philosophy and purpose of the elementary school as a whole. The necessity for this consideration lies in the fact that the basic philosophy which guides the entire educational program should also apply to physical education.

If one were to analyze the various statements of the purpose of elementary education which have been made by responsible educational groups, it would be a relatively easy matter to identify a constantly emerging pattern. These statements through the years have gradually evolved into a more or less general agreement among present-day educational leaders that the goal of elementary education is to stimulate and guide the growth of an individual so that he will function in life activities involving vocation, citizenship, and enriched leisure; and further, so that he will possess as high a level of physical, social, mental, and emotional health as his individual capacity will permit. More succinctly stated, the purpose of elementary education in our modern society should be in the direction of *total growth and development* of the child during the formative years which include kindergarten through sixth grade. The ensuing sections of this chapter should be read with this general frame of reference in mind. This is to say that if it is a valid assumption that the purpose of elementary education is to attempt to insure total growth and development of children, then it is incumbent upon teachers to explore the growth and development processes as they relate to physical education.

When it is considered that growth and development of children bring about needs and that these must be met satisfactorily, the importance of understanding of growth and development is readily discerned. When an understanding of the various elements is accomplished, the teacher is in a better position to provide improved methods for meeting the needs of each individual child. This implies that teachers might well be guided by what could be called a developmental philosophy if they are to meet with any degree of success in their dealings with children.

The purpose of this chapter is to give consideration to questions such as the following:

1. What is meant by "total personality"?
2. Why is the physical aspect of personality more concrete than the social, emotional, and intellectual aspects?
3. What are some of the problems encountered when attempting to evaluate any of the various aspects of personality?
4. How can physical education experiences contribute to intellectual development of children?
5. Why is it important to consider concepts of development in planning the physical education program?
6. How are the objectives of physical education compatible with the objectives of elementary education?

The Meaning of Total Growth and Development

As mentioned previously, total growth and development are the fundamental purposes of the education of children. All attempts at such education should take into account a combination of physical, social, emotional, as well as intellectual aspects of human behavior. A great deal of clinical and experimental evidence indicates that a human being must be considered as a whole and not a collection of parts. For our purpose here we would prefer to use the term "total personality" in referring to the child as a unified individual or total being. Perhaps a more common term is the "whole child." The term "total personality," however, is commonly used in the fields of mental health and psychology and recently has been gaining more usage in the field of education. Moreover, when we consider it from a point of man existing as a person, it is interesting to note that "existence as a person" is one rather common definition of personality.

What then comprises the total personality? Anyone who has difficulty in formulating his views with regard to what the human personality actually consists of can take courage in the knowledge that many experts who spend their time studying it are not always in complete agreement as to what it is or how it operates. Indeed, one of the greatest mysteries which confronts man in our modern society is man himself. If one were to analyze the literature on the subject, he would find generally that the total personality consists of the sum of all the physical, social, emotional, and intellectual aspects of any individual. The total personality is *one thing* comprising these various major aspects. All of these components are highly interrelated and interdependent. All are of importance to the balance and health of the personality because only in terms of their health can the personality as a whole maintain a completely healthy state. The condition of any one aspect affects each other aspect to a degree and hence the personality as a whole.

When a nervous child stutters or becomes nauseated, a mental state is *not* causing a physical symptom. On the contrary, a pressure imposed upon the organism causes a series of reactions which include thought, verbalization, digestive processes, and muscular function. Mind does not cause the body to become upset; the total organism is upset by a situation and reflects its upset in several ways, including disturbances in thought, feeling, and bodily processes. The whole individual responds in interaction with the social and physical environment. And, as the individual is affected by his environment, he, in turn, has an effect upon it.

However, because of long tradition during which physical development *or* intellectual development, rather than physical *and* intellectual development, has been glorified, we oftentimes are still accustomed to dividing the two in our thinking. The result may be that we sometimes pull human beings apart with this kind of thinking.

Traditional attitudes which separate mind and body tend to lead to unbalanced development of the child with respect to mind and body and/or social adjustment. To understand better the concept of total personality the human organism can be seen in terms of the following triangle: (Figure 2.1)

The three sides—physical, emotional, and intellectual aspects of the total personality—form a single figure, with the physical as a base. An arrow, extending from the center of the triangle upward through one of the sides, is designated "social" to represent interpersonal relationships. The arrow is pointed at both ends to suggest a two-way operation: The individual is affected by those around him, and he affects them. The whole figure, the triangle, is dependent upon a balance of all its parts, and if one part of the triangle is changed, the entire triangle is affected.

The foregoing statements have attempted to point out rather forcefully the idea that the identified components of the total personality—physical, social, emotional, and intellectual—comprise the unified individual. The fact that each of these aspects might well be considered as a separate entity should also be taken into account. As such, each aspect should warrant a

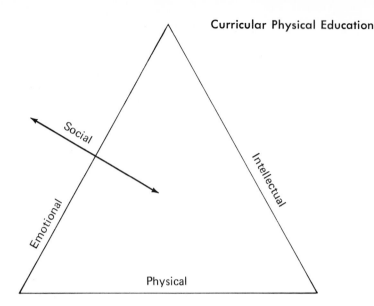

Figure 2.1

separate discussion. This appears extremely important if one is to understand fully the place of each aspect as an integral part of the whole personality. The following discussions of the physical, social, emotional, and
intellectual aspects of personality as they relate to physical education
should be viewed in this general frame of reference.

Physical Education and the Physical
Aspect of Personality

One point of departure in discussing the physical aspect of personality
could be to state that "everybody has a body." Some are short, some are
tall, some are lean, and some are fat. Children come in different sizes but
all of them have a certain innate physical capacity which is influenced by
the environment.

It might be said of the child that he *is* his body. It is something he can
see. It is his base of operation—what we previously referred to as the
"physical base." The other components of the total personality—social,
emotional, and intellectual—are somewhat vague as far as the child is
concerned. Although these are manifested in various ways, the child does
not actually see them as he does the physical aspect. Consequently, it becomes all important that the child be helped early in life to gain control
over the physical aspect, or what is known as basic body control. The
ability to do this, of course, will vary from one child to another. It will de-

pend upon the status of physical fitness of the child. The broad area of physical fitness can be broken down into certain components, and it is important that the child achieve to the best of his natural ability as far as these components are concerned. There is not complete agreement as far as identification of the components of physical fitness is concerned. However, the following information provided by the President's Council on Physical Fitness and Sports considers three components to be basic as follows:[1]

1. *Muscular strength.* This refers to the contraction power of the muscles. The strength of muscles is usually measured with dynamometers or tensiometers which record the amount of force particular muscle groups can apply in a single maximum effort. Man's existence and effectiveness depend upon his muscles. All movements of the body or any of its parts are impossible without action by muscles attached to the skeleton. Muscles perform vital functions of the body as well. The heart is a muscle; death occurs instantly when it ceases to contract. Breathing, digestion, and elimination are impossible without muscular contractions. And, these vital muscular functions are influenced by exercising the skeletal muscles: the heart beats faster, the blood circulates through the body at a greater rate, breathing comes deep and rapid, and perspiration breaks out on the surface of the skin.

2. *Muscular endurance.* Muscular endurance is the ability of muscles to perform work. Two variations of muscular endurance are recognized: *isometric,* whereby a maximum static muscular contraction is held; *isotonic,* whereby the muscles continue to raise and lower a submaximal load, as in weight training or performing push-ups. In the isometric form, the muscles maintain a fixed length; in the isotonic form, they alternately shorten and lengthen. Muscular endurance must assume some muscular strength. However, there are distinctions between the two; muscle groups of the same strength may possess different degrees of endurance.

3. *Circulatory-respiratory endurance.* Circulatory-respiratory endurance is characterized by moderate contractions of large muscle groups for relatively long periods of time during which maximal adjustments of the circulatory-respiratory system to the activity are necessary, as in distance running and swimming. Obviously, strong and enduring muscles are needed. However, by themselves, they are not enough; they do not guarantee well-developed circulatory and respiratory functions.

In addition to the basic three above, other components of physical fitness to be considered are:

[1]*Physical Fitness Research Digest,* President's Council on Physical Fitness and Sports, Washington, D.C., Series 1, No. 1, July, 1971.

1. *Muscular power:* ability to release maximum muscular force in the shortest time. Example: standing broad jump.
2. *Agility:* speed in changing body positions or in changing direction. Example: dodging run.
3. *Speed:* rapidity with which successive movements of the same kind can be performed. Example: 50-yard dash.
4. *Flexibility:* range of movement in a joint or a sequence of joints. Example: touch fingers to floor without bending knees.
5. *Balance:* ability to maintain position and equilibrium both in movement (dynamic balance) and while stationary (static balance). Examples: walking on a line or balance beam (dynamic); standing on one foot (static).
6. *Coordination:* working together of the muscles and organs of the human body in the performance of a specific task. Example: throwing or catching an object.

The components of physical fitness and hence the physical aspect of personality can be measured with calibrated instruments, as in the case of measuring muscle strength mentioned above. Moreover, we can tell how tall a child is or how heavy he is at any stage of his development. In addition, we can derive other accurate data with measurements of blood pressure, blood counts, urinalysis, and the like.

What Should Physical Education Do for the Child Physically?

There is an abundance of scientific evidence to indicate that well-planned physical activity is a stimulant to physical growth. Moreover, it has been established that participation in a well-balanced physical activi-´ ties program is one of the best known ways of maintaining optimum health. In reality, then, a well-balanced elementary school physical education program should be instrumental in helping the child gain strength, endurance, agility, coordination, and flexibility commensurate with the energy required for a successful and happy present and future life. A program of this nature implies that every child be given the opportunity to develop to the optimum of his individual physical capacity in skill and ability. This is essential if each individual is to get full benefit and optimum enjoyment from participation in physical education activities.

If the inherent physical values mentioned here are to accrue from physical education, it becomes essential that the program be planned on the basis of the physical needs of all children. Some elementary school physical education programs as now operated cannot be justified in terms of their contribution to the physical growth and development of all children. For example, it has been observed that on some elementary school playgrounds the children best endowed physically are the only pupils who are benefiting from the program. Reference is made here to the type of program that is known generally as "free play" which, if allowed to become the dominating activity, becomes a more or less "survival of the fittest" program. This is to say that there is gross neglect of the development of physical skill in all children and as a consequence each child does not have the opportunity to participate in terms of his potential ability.

In those schools where a concentrated effort is being made to develop programs to suit the physical needs of all children, it is likely that desirable contributions are being made to the physical growth of every child. This condition exisits in too few instances at the present time, however, and as a result there has been criticism of physical education by school people and laymen alike. In many cases this criticism has been due to misunderstanding on the part of lay people regarding the ultimate objectives of the physical education program.

Physical Education and the Social
Aspect of Personality

Human beings are social beings. They work together for the benefit of society. They have fought together in time of national emergencies in order to preserve the kind of society they believe in, and they play together. While all this may be true, the social aspect of personality still is perhaps a nebulous and confusing quality as far as the child is concerned.

It was a relatively easy matter to identify certain components of physical fitness such as strength, endurance, and the like. However, this does not necessarily hold true for components of social fitness, particularly as far as children are concerned. The components of physical fitness are the same for children as for adults. On the other hand, the components of social fitness for children may be much different from the components of social fitness for adults. By some adult standards children might be considered social misfits because certain behavior of children might not be socially acceptable to some adults. This is conversely true as well.

To the chagrin of some adults, parents as well as others, young children are uninhibited as far as the social aspect of personality is concerned. In this regard we need to be concerned with social maturity as it pertains to the growing and ever-changing child. This is to say that we need to give consideration to certain characteristics of social maturity and how well they are dealt with at the different stages of child growth and development.

Perhaps we need to ask ourselves such questions as these: Are we help-ing children to become self-reliant by giving them independence at the proper time? Are we helping them to be outgoing and interested in others rather than themselves? Are we helping them to know how to satisfy their own needs in a socially desirable way? Are we helping them to develop a wholesome attitude toward themselves and others?

Social maturity and hence social fitness might well be expressed in terms of fulfillment of certain social needs. In other words, if certain social needs are being adequately met, the child should be in a better position to realize social fitness. Among the needs we must give consideration to are: (1) the *need for affection* which involves acceptance and approval by per-sons; (2) the *need for belonging* which involves acceptance and approval of the group; and (3) the *need for mutuality* which involves cooperation, mutual helpfulness, and group loyalty.

When it comes to evaluating the social aspect of personality we do not have the same kind of objective and calibrated instruments that are avail-able in computing the physical attributes of the child. Mainly for diag-nostic purposes in their dealings with children, some teachers have suc-cessfully used some of the sociometric techniques. At best, however, the social aspect of personality is difficult to appraise objectively because of its somewhat nebulous nature.

What Should Physical Education Do for the Child Socially?

The elementary school physical education laboratory should present ideal surroundings for the social development of children. In fact, it is doubtful that there is any other laboratory that has greater potential pos-sibilities for operating on the basis of democratic principles. Cooperating for the benefit of the whole team, meeting the other children and the teach-er on a more or less informal basis, and other social factors inherent in physical education have been considered important in helping to make each individual a socially acceptable member of the group. It must be borne in mind, however, that the social values to be derived from physical education will not accrue automatically. For example, there is some ob-jective evidence which indicates that children who perform physical feats most proficiently are most popular with other children. It therefore should follow that if each child has the opportunity to develop optimum physical skill and ability, he should have greater opportunity for social acceptance among his peers.

Although the area of physical education presents a setting for an ideal social environment, at the same time there are situations in which children are likely to suffer social rejection. For example, open methods of selecting groups or teams by pupil choice can possibly result in situations where someone must be selected last, and sometimes reluctantly, by his group. In addition, faulty grouping of children for physical education classes can result in a kind of social ostracism because one child cannot run fast enough or throw a ball far enough to keep up with his group. These factors and numerous others must be taken into consideration by the teacher in elementary school physical education program planning if the best social values are to be obtained.

Physical Education and the Emotional Aspect of Personality

In introducing the subject of emotion we are confronted with the fact that for many years it has been a difficult concept to define and, in addition, there have been many changing ideas and theories in its study.

Obviously, it is not the purpose of a book of this nature to attempt to go into any great depth on a subject that has been one of the most intricate undertakings of psychology for many years. A few general statements relative to the nature of emotion do appear to be in order, however, if we are to understand more clearly this aspect of personality as it concerns physical education.

One of the most meaningful definitions of emotion we have come across is that "emotion is the response an individual makes when confronted with a situation for which he is unprepared, or which he interprets as a possible source of gain or loss to him."[2]

If an individual is confronted with a situation and does not have a satisfactory response, the emotional pattern of fear is likely to result. If a person finds himself in a position where his desires are frustrated, the emotional pattern of anger may occur.

In general, emotions might be classified in two different categories—those which are *pleasant* and those which are *unpleasant*. For example, joy would be considered a pleasant emotional experience while fear would be an unpleasant one. It has been suggested that "the pleasantness or unpleasantness of an emotion seems to be determined by its strength or intensity; by the nature of the situation arousing it; and by the way the individual perceives or interprets the situation."[3] Emotions tend to be more

---

[2]Frieda Kiefer Merry and Ralph Vickers Merry, *The First Two Decades of Life*, 2d ed. (New York: Harper & Bros., 1958) p. 356.

[3]Ibid., p. 355.

intense in children than in adults. If an adult is not aware of this aspect of child behavior, he will likely not understand why a child may react rather violently to a situation that to the adult seems somewhat insignificant. The fact that different individuals will react differently to the same type of situation also should be taken into account. For example, something that might anger one person might have a rather passive influence on another individual. In this regard it is interesting to observe the effect that winning or losing a game has on certain children.

What Should Physical Education Do for the Child Emotionally?

We are aware of the fact that all children manifest emotional behavior as well as ordinary behavior. Differences in the structure of the organism and in the environment of children will largely govern the degree to which the individual child expresses emotional behavior.

There appears to be one very outstanding way in which physical education experiences can help to make the child more secure and emotionally stable. This way consists of a means of releasing aggression in a socially acceptable manner. For example, kicking a ball in a game of kickball, bating a softball, or engaging in a combative stunt affords a socially acceptable way of releasing aggression. Indeed, the very atmosphere that should prevail in the physical education situation provides a unique setting for a feeling of emotional well-being in terms of a happy situation free from stress and fear.

Although physical education theoretically provides an ideal setting for children to react in terms of ordinary behavior instead of highly emotional behavior, this situation does not always prevail. For instance, in cases where children are under stress in highly competitive situations over prolonged periods, there may be a strong possibility of a detraction from, rather than a contribution to, their emotional stability.

Physical Education and the Intellectual Aspect of Personality

Individuals possess varying degrees of intelligence, and most people fall within a range of what is called "normal intelligence." In dealing with this aspect of personality we should perhaps give attention to what might be considered as some elements of intellectual fitness. We might regard this from two different points of view: first, from a standpoint of intellectual needs and second, from a standpoint of how certain things affect intelligence. We might say that if a person's intellectual needs are being met, then perhaps we could also say he is intellectually fit. From the second point of view, if we know how certain factors influence intelligence, then we might understand better how to contribute to intellectual fitness.

There appears to be rather general agreement on the intellectual needs of children. Some of these include: (1) a need for challenging experiences at their own level; (2) a need for intellectually successful and satisfying experiences; (3) a need for the opportunity to solve problems; and (4) a need for opportunity to participate in creative experiences instead of always having to conform.

Some of the factors which tend to influence intelligence are health and physical condition, emotional disturbance, and social and economic factors.

When teachers have a realization of intellectual needs and the factors influencing intelligence, perhaps then, and only then, can they deal satisfactorily with children in helping them in their intellectual pursuits.

It was mentioned that an important intellectual need for children is the opportunity to participate in creative experiences. This need is singled out for special mention because the opportunities for creative experiences are perhaps more inherent in the physical education situation than in any other single aspect of the elementary school curriculum.

What Should Physical Education Do for the Child Intellectually?

Of the contributions that physical education might make to the total education of the child, the one concerned with intellectual development has been subjected to a great deal of criticism by some general educators. Close scrutiny of the possibilities of intellectual development through physical education reveals, however, that a very desirable contribution can be made through this medium. This belief is substantiated in part by the affirmations made by such eminent philosophers and educators as Plato, Locke, Rousseau, Pestalozzi, and numerous others, Plato's postulation that learning could take place better through play, Locke's thoughts on a sound mind and sound body, Rousseau's belief that all children should receive plenty of wholesome physical activity early in life, and Pestalozzi's observations that children approach their studies with a greater amount of interest after engaging in enjoyable physical activity, have all contributed to the modern idea that physical education and intellectual development are closely associated.

With regard to the last-mentioned individual, Johann Heinrich Pestalozzi (1746-1827), it has been suggested that this famous Swiss educator perhaps laid the foundation for modern teaching. He is considered one of the great pioneers concerned with the importance of child study as a basis for helping children learn. It has been reported that while observing his own child, Pestalozzi noticed that after playing for a time the boy tended to concentrate on his studies for an unusually long period.

It is a matter of historical fact that many of the early elementary schools in this country were patterned after the philosophy of Pestalozzi. In view of this, one could be tempted to rationalize that when physical education was first introduced into the elementary schools of the United States, its primary purpose was in the direction of contributing to intellectual pursuits of children.

In a well-taught physical education lesson there are numerous opportunities for children to exercise judgment and resort to reflective thinking in the solution of various kinds of problems. In addition, in a well-balanced elementary school physical education program children must acquire a knowlege of rules and regulations in various games. It is also essential for effective participation that children gain an understanding of the various fundamentals and strategy involved in the performance of physical education activities.

Moreover, recent research has indicated that physical education activities provide a desirable learning medium for the development of concepts in other subject areas of the elementary school curriculum. As mentioned in Chapter 1 this is one of the major themes of this text and will be dealt with in detail in later chapters.

Indeed, physical education need not be considered an "all brawn and no brain" segment of the elementary school curriculum when it is realized that the various factors mentioned contribute substantially to the intellectual development of children.

Some Concepts of Development and Their Meaning for Physical Education

There has been a great deal of observation and research dealing with the growth and development of children. This information is most important to teachers in that it provides them with an understanding of how children might grow and develop in a way that is appropriate to their innate capacities and the environment in modern society.

Child development specialists have formulated what are termed concepts of physical, social, emotional, and intellectual development. A few examples of some of these are given here together with suggestions of their meaning for physical education. (It should be understood that only a partial list of these concepts is submitted and that the interested reader can resort to appropriate sources for a more detailed listing.)

Concepts of Physical Development

1. *Physical development and change are continuous.* In the early years physical education programs might well be characterized by large muscle activities. As the child develops, more difficult types of skills and activities can be introduced so that physical education experiences progress in a way that is compatible with the child's development.

2. *Physical development is controlled by both heredity and environment.* The physical education program should be planned in a way to meet the innate capacities of each child. The teacher should attempt to establish an environmental climate where all children have an equal opportunity for wholesome participation.

3. *Differences in physical development occur at each age level.* This implies that there should be a wide variety of activities to meet the needs of children at various developmental levels. While gearing activities to meet the needs of a particular group of children the teacher should also attempt to provide for individual differences of children within the group.

4. *Sex differences in development occur at different ages.* At the early levels of the elementary school, perhaps in grades one and two, boys and girls can participate satisfactorily together in most activities. As sex differences involving such factors as strength and endurance occur, provision might well be made for the separation of boys and girls in certain types of activities.

5. *Needs of a physical nature must be satisfied if a child is to function effectively.* Physical education lessons should be planned to provide an adequate activity yield. At the same time the teacher should be aware of fatigue symptoms so that children are not likely to go beyond their physical capacity. Physical education programs should be vigorous enough to meet the physical needs of children and at the same time motivating enough so that they will desire to perpetuate the physical education experience outside of school.

Concepts of Social Development

1. *Man is a social being.* Opportunities should be provided for children to experience followership as well as leadership. The teacher should capitalize upon the social skills that are inherent in most physical education activities.

2. *Interpersonal relationships have social needs as their basis.* All children should be given an equal opportunity in physical education par-

ticipation. Moreover, the teacher should impress upon children their importance to the group. This can be done in connection with the team or group effort that is essential to successful participation.

3. *A child can develop his self-concept through undertaking roles.* A child is more likely to be aware of his particular abilities if he is given the opportunity to play the different positions in a team game. Rotation of such responsibilities as squad or group leaders tends to provide opportunity for self-expression of children through role playing.

4. *There are various degrees of interaction between individuals and groups.* The physical education laboratory provides an excellent setting for the child to develop interpersonal interaction. The teacher has an opportunity to observe the children in a movement situation rather than in only a sedentary situation; consequently, he is in a good position to guide integrative experiences by helping children see the importance of satisfactory interrelationships in a physical education group situation.

5. *Choosing and being chosen, an expression of a basic need, is a foundation of interpersonal relationships.* As far as possible, children should be given the responsibility for choosing teammates, partners, and the like. However, great caution should be taken by the teacher to see that this is carried out in an equitable way. The teacher should devise ways of choice so that certain children are not always selected last or left out entirely.

Concepts of Emotional Development

1. *An emotional response may be brought about by a goal's being furthered or thwarted.* The teacher should make a very serious effort to assure successful experience for every child in his physical education activities. This can be accomplished in part by attempting to provide for individual differences within given physical education activities. The physical education setting should be such that each child derives a feeling of personal worth through making some sort of positive contribution.

2. *Self-realization experiences should be constructive.* The opportunity for creative experience inherent in many physical education activities affords the child an excellent chance for self-realization through physical expression. Teachers might well consider planning with children to see that activities are meeting their needs and as a result involve a constructive experience.

3. *As the child develops, his emotional reactions tend to become less violent and more discriminating.* A well-planned program and pro-

gressive sequence of physical education activities can provide for release of aggression in a socially acceptable manner.

4. *Depending on certain factors, a child's own feelings may be accepted or rejected by the individual.* The child's physical education experience should make him feel good and have confidence in himself. Satisfactory self-concept seems closely related to body control; therefore, physical education experiences might be considered as one of the best ways of contributing to it.

Concepts of Intellectual Development

1. *Children differ in intelligence.* Teachers should be aware that poor performance of some children in physical education activities might be due to the fact that they have not understood the directions. Differences in intelligence levels as well as in physical skill and ability need to be taken into account in the planning of physical education lessons.

2. *Mental development is rapid in early childhood and slows down later.* Children want and need challenging kinds of physical education experiences. Physical education lessons should be planned and taught in much the same way as other subjects of the elementary school curriculum. This precludes a program that is devoted entirely to what has been called "nondirected play."

3. *Intelligence develops through the interaction of the child and his environment.* Movement experiences in physical education involve a process of interacting with the environment. There are many problem-solving opportunities in the well-planned physical education environment and hence the child can be presented with challenging learning situations.

4. *Situations which encourage total personality development appear to provide the best situation for intellectual development.* The potential for total personality development is more evident in physical education than in any other single subject area in the elementary school curriculum. If one were to analyze each of the subject areas for its potentialities for physical, social, emotional, and intellectual development, it is doubtful that any one of these areas would compare with the potential that is inherent in the physical education learning situation.

Objectives of Physical Education

It should be readily discerned that the component elements of total growth and development become the objectives of physical education in the elementary school. These elements have been expressed in terms of physical, social, emotional, and intellectual growth and development of children of elementary school age, and as such become the physical, social, emotional, and intellectual objectives of elementary school physical education.

The Physical Objective

This objective should imply the development of skill and ability in a variety of physical education activities together with organic development commensurate with vigor, vitality, strength, balance, flexibility, and neuromuscular coordination.

The Social Objective

This objective should imply satisfactory experiences in how to meet and get along with others, development of proper attitudes toward one's peers, and the development of a sense of values.

The Emotional Objective

This objective should imply that sympathetic guidance should be provided in meeting anxieties, joys, and sorrows, and help given in developing aspirations, affections, and security.

The Intellectual Objective

This objective should imply the development of specific knowledge pertaining to rules, regulations, and strategies involved in a variety of worthwhile physical education learning experiences. In addition, this objective should be concerned with the value of physical education as a most worthwhile learning medium in the development of concepts and understandings in other curriculum areas.

Physical education contributes to total growth and development of children.

Chapter **3**

Professional Preparation
Characteristics of Good Teachers
Qualifications of Teachers
    Understanding the Child
    Competencies and Experiences
Children's Attitudes Toward Physical Education Teachers
Teaching Responsibility

The Teacher

The focal point of any teaching-learning situation is the teacher. Frequently, a communication medium appears which is heralded not only as a teaching aid but as a teacher substitute as well. The enormous expense of mass education, coupled with the need for high-quality teaching, has given rise to the wish that somehow a relatively few master teachers could direct the learning of large numbers of persons. In this way, it has been reasoned, both quantitative and qualitative problems of American education could be solved or at least minimized.

Several of the mass media of communication have been proposed with varying degrees of enthusiasm as the answer to this problem of educating large numbers of people well. Recordings, radio, films, television, teaching machines, and other mechanical and technical devices have been experimented with and widely used. In spite of their great value in education, all the mass media of communication have been found wanting when tried as teacher *substitutes* rather than as teaching *aids*, perhaps especially at the elementary school level. It is interesting to consider why.

In brief, the answer probably lies in the fact that although a teacher usually deals with a group of children, he or she must remain sensitive to the *individual*. The qualified teacher is aware that every child is almost incredibly unique and that he approaches all of his learning tasks with his own level of motivation, capacity, experience, and vitality. Moreover, such a teacher is aware that the individuals in a class must be *prepared* for a learning experience so that the experience may, in some way, be recognized by them as having meaning for them. Preparation of any class must be in terms of the particular individuals in that class. The teacher must then, by a combination of emotional and logical appeal, help each individual find his way through the experience at his own rate and, to some extent, in his own way. The teacher must also help the individual "nail down" the meaning of the experience to himself—help him to incorporate it and its use into his own life. The point of view reflected here is that there is no substitute for a competent teacher who, while necessarily teaching a *group*, is highly sensitive to the *individual* pupils involved.

The role of the teacher in providing physical education learning experiences for children differs little than in other teacher-learning situations. The essential difference is that the teacher deals with the children in movement experiences while in the other subject-matter areas the learning activities are more or less sedentary in nature.

The teacher's role should be that of a guide who supervises and directs desirable physical education learning experiences. In providing such experiences the teacher should constantly keep in mind how physical education can contribute to the physical, social, emotional, and intellectual well-being of every child. This implies that the teacher should develop an understanding of principles of learning and attempt to apply these principles properly in the teaching of physical education. (Information concerning principles of learning will be dealt with in detail in Chapter 5.)

It is important that the teacher recognize that individual differences exist among teachers as well as children, and that certain of these teacher differences will influence teaching method. Sometimes one teacher may have greater success than another with a method. This implies that there should be no specified resolute method of teaching elementary school physical education for all teachers. On the other hand, teachers should allow themselves to deviate from recommended conformity if they are able to provide desirable learning experiences through a method peculiar to their own abilities. This, of course, means that the procedures used should be compatible with conditions under which learning takes place best.

The subsequent discussions in this chapter are intended to help the reader deal more effectively with such questions as:

1. What are some of the important features of teacher preparation in elementary school physical education?
2. What are some of the basic characteristics of good teachers?
3. What are some of the qualifications and competencies needed by teachers of elementary school physical education?
4. What are some of the favorable and unfavorable attitudes that children have toward physical education teachers?
5. Who should be responsible for providing physical education learning experiences for children?

6. What kind of relationship should exist between the physical education teacher and classroom teacher?

Professional Preparation

An obviously important factor for the teacher is the quality of preparation received for the demanding, but most rewarding, task of providing physical education learning experiences for elementary school children.

Interest on a widespread basis in the employemnt of special teachers to teach physical education in elementary schools developed shortly after World War II. Although for several years some school systems had been using special teachers, for the most part this aspect of the elementary school curriculum had been the responsibility of the regular classroom teacher. In the late 1940's special teachers of physical education began to become more prevalent in the elementary schools, but most of these individuals had received their preparation predominantly in secondary school physical education.

Generally speaking, despite this expanded interest, teacher-preparation institutions did not tend to keep pace with the need. However, some institutions had been making it a practice for years to prepare personnel to teach at all levels from kindergarten through grade twelve. Nevertheless, most colleges and universities concentrated their efforts in the direction of preparing personnel to teach at the secondary school level.

In relatively recent years some teacher-preparation institutions have attempted to remedy the situation in a variety of ways. In a few instances there have been efforts to develop a major area of study in elementary school physical education. Some have worked along the lines of a combined major in elementary education and physical education. And still others have developed a minor or an area of emphasis in elementary school physical education. In addition, practically all institutions require at least one course for elementary education major students in view of the fact that these individuals are likely to be asked to assume various degrees of responsibility for elementary school physical education.

In spite of these efforts the present supply of properly prepared personnel to teach physical education in the elementary schools is far short of the needs. For example, one authoritative source has expressed it along the following lines.[1]

Currently there are about 5,000 elementary school physical education teachers identified on the membership rolls of the American Association

[1] Margie Hanson, "Professional Preparation of Elementary School Physical Education Teachers," Annual Workshop of the Society of State Directors of Health, Physical Education, and Recreation, Gull Lake, Michigan, Sept. 25, 1969.

for Health, Physical Education, and Recreation. It is estimated that there are another 10,000 who are not members, for a rough estimate of 15,000 available teachers in this area.

There are some 1,000,000 classrooms in the United States. If a physical education teacher were to be provided to see every child in a daily program with not more than 10 classes per day (and this is far too many), it would require 100,000 elementary school physical education teachers. If the standard is reduced to seeing children only one-half as often, 50,000 teachers would still be needed.

In the face of such a staggering deficit, it should be readily discerned that the profession of physical education faces a stern challenge. To meet this challenge it will be necessary to redevelop directions by focusing on the elementary school level and to influence the lives of millions of children by taking action to improve teacher preparation for the prospective elementary school physical education teacher as well as the prospective classroom teacher.

Characteristics of Good Teachers

Over the years there have been numerous attempts to identify objectively those characteristics of good teachers which set them apart from average or poor teachers. Obviously, this is a difficult matter because of the countless variables involved.

It is entirely possible for two teachers to possess the same degree of intelligence, preparation, and understanding of the subject they teach. Yet, it is also possible that one of these teachers will consistently achieve good results with children, while the other will not have much success. Perhaps a good part of the reason for this difference in success lies in those individual differences of teachers which relate to certain personality factors and how they deal and interact with children. Based upon the available research and numerous interviews with both teachers and children, we have found that the following characteristics tend to emerge most often among good teachers:

1. Good teachers possess those characteristics which in one way or another have a humanizing effect on children. An important factor which good teachers have that appeals to most children is a sense of humor. One third-grade boy put it this way: "She laughed when we played a joke on her."
2. In all cases good teachers are fair and democratic in their dealings with children and tend to maintain the same positive feelings toward the so-called "problem" child as they do with other children.

3. A very important characteristic is that good teachers are able to relate easily to children. They have the ability and sensitivity to *listen through children's ears and see through children's eyes.*
4. Good teachers are flexible. They know that different approaches need to be used with different groups of children as well as individual children. In addition, good teachers can adjust easily to changing situations.
5. Good teachers are creative. This is an extremely important factor because in movement experiences at the elementary school level teachers are dealing with a very imaginative segment of the population.
6. Good teachers have control. Different teachers exercise control in different ways, but good teachers tend to have a minimum of control problems probably because they provide a learning environment where control becomes a minimum problem.

Qualifications of Teachers

It might be said that there are certain *general* qualifications required for teaching in any of the subject-matter areas, and that teaching of elementary school physical education does not differ extensively from teaching in the other curriculum areas. On the other hand, it should be recognized that by the very nature of the content of some curriculum areas, *specific* abilities may be needed for teachers to be most successful in certain of these areas. This is no doubt true in the area of physical education. While an *understanding of the child* should certainly be a general requirement of all teachers, the need for it could be more pronounced in the area of physical education because the teaching content for this area is inherently involved in understanding the child and how he learns.

Understanding the Child

The previous chapter gave consideration to the potential contribution that desirable and worthwhile physical education learning experiences can make to the development of the child. The following discussion is intended to give the reader an overview of the behavior of children as they progress in their development.

As the child progresses through various stages in his growth and development, certain distinguishing characteristics can be identified which furnish implications for effective teaching and learning in physical education. (An extensive and detailed list of such characteristics appears in the Appendix.)

The range of age levels from 5 through 7 years usually includes pupils from kindergarten through Grade 2. During this period the child begins his formal education, although there is a definite trend at the present time to place a great deal more emphasis upon the preschool level. In our culture the child leaves the home and family constellation for a part of the day to take his place with a group of pupils of approximately the same chronological age. Not only is he taking an important step toward becoming increasingly more independent and self-reliant, but as he learns he moves from being a highly self-centered, egotistical individual to becoming a more socialized group member.

This stage is characterized by a certain lack of motor coordination, because the small muscles of the hands and fingers are not as well developed as the large muscles of the arms and legs. Thus, as he starts his formal education the child needs to use large crayons or pencils as one means of expressing himself. His urge to action is expressed through movement and noise. Pupils at these age levels thrive on vigorous activity. They develop as they climb, run, jump, hop, or keep time to music. An important physical aspect at this level is that the eyeball is increasing in size and the eye muscles are developing. This factor is an important determinant in the child's readiness to see and read small print, and thus involves a sequence from large print on charts to primer type in preprimers and primers. It is also an important factor for tracking an object, such as a ball in flight.

Even though he has a relatively short attention span,* he is extremely curious about his environment. At this stage the teacher capitalizes upon the child's urge to learn by providing opportunities for him to gain information from firsthand experiences through the use of the senses. He sees, hears, smells, feels, tastes, and of course *moves* in order to learn.

The age range of 8 and 9 years is the period which usually marks the time spent in the third and fourth grades. The child now has a wider range of interests and a longer attention span. While strongly individualistic, he is working from a position in a group. Organized team games can afford opportunities for developing and practicing skills in good leadership and followership, as well as body control, strength, and endurance. Small muscles are developing, manipulative skills (important in throwing, striking, and catching) are increasing, and muscular coordination is improving. The eyes have developed so that the children can, and do, read more widely. They are capable of getting information from books and are beginning to learn through vicarious experience. However, experiments

---

*The physiology of the short attention span in terms of basal metabolism is discussed in Chapter 10.

carry an impact for learning at this age by capitalizing upon the child's curiosity as he tests an hypothesis. This is the stage in his development when skills of communication (listening, speaking, reading, and writing) and the number system are needed to deal with situations both in and out of school.

At the age range of 10 through 12 most children complete the fifth and sixth grades. This is a period of transition for most, as they go from childhood into the preadolescent period of their growth and development. They may show concern over bodily changes, and are sometimes self-conscious about appearance. At this range of age levels children tend to differ widely in physical maturation and in emotional stability. Greater deviations in growth and development can be noted within the sex groups than between them. Rate of physical growth can be rapid, sometimes showing itself in poor posture and restlessness. Some of the more highly organized team games such as basketball, modified soccer, and the like, help to furnish the keen and wholesome competition ordinarily desired by these pupils. It is essential that the teacher recognize that at this level prestige among peers is more important than adult approval. During this period the child is ready for a higher level of intellectual skills involving reasoning, discerning fact from opinion, noting cause-and-effect relationships, drawing conclusions, and using various references to locate and compare the validity of information.

Thus, during the years between kindergarten and the completion of Grade 6, the child grows and develops (1) socially, from a self-centered individual to a participating member of a group; (2) emotionally, from a state manifesting anger outbursts to a higher degree of self-control; (3) physically, from childhood to the brink of adolescence; and (4) intellectually, from learning from firsthand experiences to learning from technical and specialized resources.

If the child is to be educated as a growing organism, aspects of growth and development need the utmost consideration of the teacher in planning and guiding physical education learning experiences which will be most profitable for the child at his particular stage of development.

Competencies and Experiences

One of the modern approaches in meeting the needs of teachers for proficiency in a given curriculum area involves the acquisition of certain *competencies* and *experiences* in that area. The following statement by Snyder and Scott some years ago lent insight to the meaning and relationship of the terms "competency" and "experience."

A competency is defined as a skill, insight, understanding, qualification, fitness, or ability which is used to meet a life situation. An experience is defined as the conscious interaction of the individual with the environment.[2]

The job of the teacher of elementary school physical education is a complex one. Many important competencies, abilities, and experiences are needed by the teacher in order to provide physical education learning experiences in the most desirable way. The material in this text is designed to help the prospective teacher or teacher in service acquire the skills, insights, understandings, and abilities which are so important to successful teaching in elementary school physical education.

Children's Attitudes Toward Physical Education Teachers

It should be advantageous for teachers to know that those things which they do will have either a favorable or unfavorable influence on the teaching-learning situation. Thus, in order to insure that certain teaching procedures are not detrimental to the development of favorable attitudes toward physical education, practices and behaviors should be investigated and clearly identified. With this general idea in mind an extensive study[3] conducted at the University of Maryland attempted to answer some of the following questions:

1. What are the critical behaviors of physical education teachers in the elementary school instructional program?
2. Which critical behaviors are considered to contribute to the development of favorable or unfavorable attitudes toward physical education at the elementary school level?
3. Do certain teacher behaviors contribute to a change in pupil attitudes toward physical education?
4. What are pupil attitudes toward physical education when they enter a particular grade?
5. Does the sex of the teacher play an important role in attitude development in physical education classes?
6. Is there any relationship between type of activity and attitude development?

The purpose of this study was to identify critical incidents in order to develop a checklist of requirements which could be utilized for the im-

---

[2]Raymond A. Snyder and Harry A. Scott, *Professional Preparation in Health, Physical Education, and Recreation* (New York: McGraw-Hill, Inc., 1954).
[3]Mehdi Zadeh Namazi, "Critical Teaching Behaviors Influencing Attitude Development of Elementary School Children Toward Physical Education," Ph.D. dissertation, University of Maryland, College Park, Maryland, 1969.

provement of teaching in relation to favorable attitude development toward physical education. The study employed the *critical incident technique*. This involves a set of procedures for collecting direct observations of human behavior in such a way as to facilitate their potential usefulness in solving practical problems and developing broad psychological principles.[4]

The subjects for study consisted of 1,170 fifth-and-sixth-grade children, 561 boys and 609 girls. Each child reported two critical incidents which affected his or her attitude toward physical education, both positively and negatively. All of the 1,170 children were able to recall 987 favorable critical incidents. From the 987 favorable incidents, 1,190 favorable teacher behaviors were extracted. The 692 unfavorable incidents yielded 995 unfavorable teacher behaviors.

Within the limitations of the study it was concluded that children of this age level were capable of identifying critical incidents that contributed to both favorable and unfavorable attitude development toward physical education. And further, based on these identifications, a checklist of critical requirements for improved teaching could be formulated and categorized.

As a result of the study a checklist was designed to be used by the physical education teacher as a means of self-evaluation. Such a checklist should be of value for purposes of becoming aware of one's strengths and weaknesses in relation to teaching procedures and interactional behaviors affecting attitude development.

Before presenting the checklist some comment should be made with regard to the *extraction of behaviors* from the critical incidents reported by the children. This study was more subjective than objective in nature; therefore, for the purpose of placing some degree of control over the subjectivity factor, the following steps were taken:

1. Initially a number of behaviors were extracted and paraphrased by the investigator.
2. A panel of experts was asked to check the ability of the investigator to extract behaviors. As there was close agreement in relation to the behaviors extracted, the remaining interview forms were analyzed.

The behaviors were extracted, paraphrased, and recorded on a blank lined form and a corresponding number code was placed on the original interview form, after which frequencies were tabulated. The following incident, reported as a favorable incident, is an example:

[4]John C. Flanagan, "The Critical Incident Technique," *Psychological Bulletin,* July 1954, p. 335.

Our teacher this year ordered some ropes to put in our multipurpose room. When the chorus goes and leaves about 20 sixth graders, he brings us down to the multipurpose room and shows us some "tricks" to do on the ropes in his spare time.

The following critical behavior was extracted from this critical incident reported:

Teacher did something extra to provide fun and enjoyment in physical education along with encouraging creativity by performing new and self-directed activities.

The pupils' feelings were expressed as having confidence during class and an increase in social interaction with other members of the class.

An example of an unfavorable incident is given below:

This incident always happened when we have sports such as soccer, football, baseball, and basketball. When we start these sports we go over basic skills the first couple of weeks, then the boys start to play the games but the girls still do basic things. For instance, when we play softball around the third week, we start playing but the girls must throw balls and hardly get a chance to play. I don't see how he expects the girls who don't play well to learn and the ones that do to do better.

From this critical incident, the following critical behavior was extracted.

Teacher did not provide equal opportunity for participation and displayed favoritism in dealing with pupils.

The pupil response was that the teacher did more for the boys, and that this was not fair to the girls.

A CHECKLIST OF CRITICAL TEACHING REQUIREMENTS FOR FAVORABLE ATTITUDE DEVELOPMENT IN ELEMENTARY SCHOOL PHYSICAL EDUCATION PROGRAMS

A. Positive attitudes and feelings toward physical education at the elementary school level are developed and enhanced when the physical education teacher:

1. Technical teaching procedures and operation
   _____ is well skilled and provides demonstration in the process of teaching different skills
   _____ gives instructions clearly and orderly
   _____ teaches skills and helps with skill development
   _____ has the ability to diagnose errors in pupil performance
   _____ pays attention to the slow learners and provides individual instruction after class.
   _____ utilizes audiovisual aids in teaching skills
   _____ utilizes whole-part-whole methods in his lesson plans

_____ follows the principles of progressive learning in teaching physical education activities

_____ allows pupil participation in planning and organizing class activities

2. Social interaction skills in teaching method

_____ encourages pupils to ask questions

_____ provides for pupil participation in class discussions

_____ utilizes modern innovations, creativity, and variety in class participation

_____ enhances learning by knowing when to participate in class activities

_____ explains rules and regulations of games clearly

_____ is aware of "teachable moments" and shows concern for individual growth in skill improvement

3. Class surroundings and atmosphere

_____ makes physical education period something to look forward to

_____ considers the interests of pupils and provides for fun and excitement in the class

_____ cautions students of different hazards inherent in activities and takes proper safety measures to eliminate them

_____ treats all pupils equally

4. Teacher's manner and general interpersonal relationships

_____ stimulates pupil interest in class activities

_____ encourages pupils to accomplish their best according to their capabilities

_____ understands pupils and exhibits patience

_____ shows concern for pupil if injured in class

_____ makes extra effort to provide fun and enjoyment in physical education

_____ guides and helps in solving problems in class

_____ exhibits sense of humor

_____ is informal and friendly

_____ provides leadership in class organization

_____ introduces and promotes physical education activities and sports in local communtiy

_____ shows concern for the pupil as a person

5. Organization, administration, and policy

_____ plans and organizes learning experiences according to the developmental stage of pupils

_____ arranges for competition on the basis of equal skill achievement

_____ uses advanced pupils to demonstrate skills and assist classmates

_____ uses class time efficiently and effectively

_____ allows some choice of partners

_____ provides and presents a variety of games and activities

_____ provides for free time activity and allows some choice of activities

_____ coordinates physical education with other subject matter

6. Teacher characteristics and personality traits

_____ is dedicated and has a genuine interest in teaching

_____ utilizes democratic processes in solving problems

_____ controls temper and maintains composure
_____ shows ability to guide and direct class activities effectively
_____ is in good health and physically fit
7. Interest and concern for pupil growth and recognition of pupil achievement.
_____ rewards winning teams for their accomplishments
_____ plans and organizes activities while considering individual differences
_____ provides for pupil participation regardless of level or degree of skill
_____ provides adequate time for active participation and skill practice
_____ gives special consideration in special circumstances
8. Evaluation procedures and grading policy
_____ establishes a sound policy in regard to grading
_____ sets standards and provides sound teaching to accomplish requirements
_____ is fair, honest, and grades pupils on class participation and skill achievement
B. Negative attitudes and feelings toward physical education at the elementary school level are developed when the physical education teacher:
1. Technical teaching procedures and operation
_____ is unprepared and disorganized in teaching skills
_____ is poorly skilled and unable to demonstrate different skills
_____ lacks the interest and ability to provide and present a variety of activities and learning experiences
_____ loses sequence in teaching physical education activities
_____ fails to follow up and provide practice time for the skills learned
_____ does not utilize audiovisual aids in teaching procedures
_____ uses lecture technique excessively and ineffectively
_____ neglects the principle of teaching progression in skill learning
2. Social interaction skills in teaching method
_____ leaves rules and regulations of games and sports unclear and unexplained
_____ shows lack of ability to explore and recognize errors in skill performance
_____ gives insufficient directions and causes confusion
_____ does not provide a friendly atmosphere in class to stimulate action without being afraid of getting embarrassed
_____ requires participation in all activities
_____ does not present an instructional program in skill development
_____ uses verbal negative reinforcement
3. Class surroundings and atmosphere
_____ forces pupils to participate in inclement weather
_____ does not provide for adequate safety measures
4. Teacher's manner and general interpersonal relationships
_____ does not provide equal opportunity for participation
_____ fails to show sincere concern for injured pupil in class
_____ disagrees with pupil judgment in class situation
_____ leaves things unfinished

_____assigns unclear tasks
_____displays favoritism in dealing with pupils
_____maintains poor control of class
_____ridicules and embarrasses pupils
_____uses physical punishment
_____expects too much from pupils
_____separates pupil from activity
_____does not show any interest in pupils
_____does not arrange and provide enough time for active participation
_____shouts at pupils and does not understand them

5. Organization, administration, and policy
   _____uses class time ineffectively and improperly
   _____makes physical education period monotonous and uninteresting
   _____presents a monotonous program with no provision for fun and enjoyment
   _____does not utilize advanced pupils in demonstrating skills
   _____dominates class activities by overparticipation
   _____fails to observe and practice necessary safety measures
   _____does not provide proper equipment and facilities

6. Teacher's characteristics and personality traits
   _____does not utilize and employ democratic processes in solving class problems
   _____is "bossy"
   _____is mean, unpleasant, and manifests poor personality characteristics
   _____"shows off"
   _____loses temper and uses profanity

7. Interest and concern for student growth and recognition of student achievement
   _____neglects individual differences in planning and organizing activities.
   _____fails to provide for individual instruction when it is needed most
   _____punishes pupils without sufficient reason
   _____accuses pupils of underachievement
   _____exhibits lack of concern for pupil accomplishments

8. Evaluation procedures and grading policy
   _____fails to establish a sound grading system
   _____lowers grade because of absence
   _____attaches little value to what is being done

Teaching Responsibility

The question of where to place the responsibility for providing desirable physical education learning experiences for elementary school children cannot be dealt with in a single pat answer. There does not appear to be "one best plan" of teaching that fits all conditions. Many postulations have been made with regard to the classroom teacher and the physical education teacher concerning which of them is in the better position to provide physical education learning experiences. It is a well-known fact that some individuals are staunch proponents of the use of either the classroom teacher or the physical education teacher in absolute form. It is also recognized that various arguments can be set forth which purport to show how any one plan is more effective than others.

In general, there are three possible ways in which the responsibility for the provision of physical education learning experiences for elementary school children can be delegated. These are:

1. Placing the responsibility with the classroom teacher. From 10% to 15% of the schools use this plan.
2. Placing the responsibility with the special teacher. Between 10% and 15% of the schools use this plan.
3. Various combinations utilizing both the classroom teacher and the specialist. From 70% to 80% of the schools use this plan.

Contemporary thought indicates that the classroom teacher and special teacher should be mutually involved. For example, a statement from a position paper of the American Association for Health, Physical Education, and Recreation suggests that:

> To assure that the most meaningful learning takes place, both the physical education teacher and the classroom teacher should work together to develop an understanding of the children and, through this understanding, should provide a program which is commensurate with the children's needs. Although the physical educator assumes the primary role in conducting the program, it is essential that he regard himself as one part of the total education process.[5]

The special teacher and classroom teacher need to pool and share their knowledge and abilities so that the most worthwhile learning experiences can be provided for children through physical education.

In summary, a few general considerations should be taken into account. The specific way of designating the responsibiliity for teaching will depend upon a number of factors. Among others these include: (1) the underlying philosophy of the local school; (2) preparation, experience, and interest of personnel; (3) facilities and time allotment for physical education; and (4) funds available for implementation of the program.

In the final analysis the plan of teaching employed must be compatible with the local situation and, above all, one that meets the needs of all of the

---

[5]American Association for Health, Physical Education, and Recreation, "Essentials of a Quality Elementary School Physical Education Program—A Position Paper," Washington, D.C., 1970.

children satisfactorily. For this reason it seems essential that all factors pertinent to local conditions be thoroughly appraised and evaluated before a particular plan of teaching is introduced. Moreover, any plan should be subjected to continuous evaluation so that desirable practices can be retained or modified and undesirable practices eliminated as the occasion demands.

Chapter 4

Curriculum
Development

Since there has been some confusion with regard to the meaning of "curriculum," it seems essential that the term be described at the outset of this chapter. Curriculum has been employed in a number of different ways over the years, and the result has been a misunderstanding as to just what the scope of the curriculum actually entails.

In the past, the curriculum in some instances has been confused with the course of study and as a result these two terms have been used interchangeably. It should be understood, however, that the curriculum is very broad in scope and that the course of study is actually an outgrowth of curriculum development.

For some time now, the curriculum as it pertains to elementary education has been regarded to include all of the school experiences which in one way or another influence the pupil. Of course these experiences should be guided, supervised, and directed in such a way that they are channeled toward the achievement of the objectives of the elementary school.

In order to keep pace with current advanced thinking in the whole area of education, physical education should accept the broad concept of the curriculum. This is particularly important since there are so many facets and ramifications which combine to make a satisfactory program of physical education. Moreover, there are a variety of factors which in one way or another tend to have an influence on the elementary school physical education curriculum. The fact that the scope of physical education is somewhat different from other areas in the elementary school necessitates an identification of some of the things upon which a successful elementary school physical education program may be dependent. Such factors as (1) the attitude of school administrators; (2) facilities and equipment; (3) teaching responsibility; and (4) time allotment, all play an important part in terms of the status that physical education may have in a particular elementary school.

Because of these influencing factors it is exceedingly difficult to have much uniformity of program among schools. Due to this fact some educators have tended to take a dim view of physical education because of its lack of standardized curriculum content in relation to other curriculum areas. It should be understood, however, that a fair comparison cannot be made between standardized curriculum content in other subject areas and physical education. This is substantiated by the fact that the aforementioned influencing factors have tended to preclude such a standardization of curriculum content.

Although there may be lack of standardization in specific physical education curriculum content from one elementary school to another, this does not imply that physical education will not contribute to the total purpose of the elementary school because of differences in physical education activity offerings. For example, teachers in one school may be meeting objectives through one group of activities while those in another school may be meeting objectives through another group of activities.

It is the purpose of this chapter to provide the reader with suggestions in dealing with questions such as the following that involve the elementary school physical education curriculum:

1. What are some of the current trends and changing ideas?
2. What are some valid principles of curriculum development and why is it important to establish such principles?
3. What are the criteria for the selection of curriculum content and how should application of these criteria be made?
4. Why is cooperative curriculum development important?
5. How can curriculum development take into account the individual differences of children?
6. What are some of the important factors to consider when using a Curriculum Guide?
7. How can curriculum revision be made a continuous process?

Current Developments and Trends in Curriculum Development

Over the years a most interesting paradox in the area of curriculum development for elementary school physical education has existed to the effect that the curriculum content in many schools has been incompatible with the objectives set forth in the program. This is to say that theoretically, while the purpose has been to help meet growth and developmental needs of children, the type of curriculum designed for this purpose has not always fulfilled its function. This has been due largely to the fact that more often than not curriculum development has not been approached scientifically. For the most part, it has been more or less haphazard, relying mainly on the "dead hand" of tradition and adult experiences rather than what is known about child growth and development.

In far too many instances the curriculum has focused upon certain physical education activities in the early school years without providing children with a basic foundation in movement and development of skills necessary for successful performance in these activities. This approach is analogous to giving a first-grade child a book to read before he has had any experience with sight words and word attack skills.

This should *not* be interpreted to mean that the physical education activities such as games, rhythms, and self-testing activities should be abandoned in the early elementary school years in favor of a program devoted entirely to basic movement and skill learning. On the contrary, it means that a child can and should engage in such activities when he is *ready* to move efficiently and effectively, commensurate with his innate capacity and the requirements of the activity.

An example of this is seen in the following recommendation by Boyer.[1] She rightfully contends that if a child has not learned how to run, he is not ready for the dodging-tagging required in running-chasing activities. She suggests a learning sequence where a child first learns to run on the balls of his feet, to stop on a signal, to stop on a line, to touch a line and turn, to dodge, and finally to tag. As he experiences each of the parts of the running skill, he should be given opportunity to use that particular part in activities in which only that part of the skill or a preceding one is used. In this way he runs with less falling and, in developing the overall skill of running, his confidence in himself increases. While learning the skill he is experiencing self-discovery—how he relates to another person and how together he and another affect each other. Thus, he is growing socially and emotionally.

In teaching movement skills essential to running and stopping, turning and stopping, dodging, and tagging activities, the child is given the opportunity to explore certain movement possibilities. Through such

[1] Madeline H. Boyer, "What makes a good physical education program?" *Physical Education for Children's Healthful Living*, Bulletin No. 23-A 1968 by Association for Childhood Education International, Washington, D.C.

exploration, knowledge and understandings about the skill tend to be discovered and developed. The skill when learned can then be used in a game.

The following illustrations point up the practical application of the above suggestions.

Running and Stopping

Explore: Children scatter over a play area. All run within this area and stop on a signal.

Teacher: "I can hear many different sounds of running. Who knows what I mean?"

Discover: The question leads to discussion of sound. The teacher heard a loud noise. What does this mean? Pounding feet. What's wrong with pounding feet? Recognition of the need to run lightly on balls of feet results from this question.

Teacher: "Why do you suppose some of you fell down on the signal to stop?"

Discover: Discussion leads to understanding of *balance*.

Explore: Children try various stopping positions to find one that will make them feel so steady that even when the teacher comes around and pushes them lightly, they seem solidly rooted.

Discover: To stop in *balance* you stop in a forward-stride position with weight placed equally between the two feet. Knees flexed to lower the weight helps balance.

Explore: After these discoveries, children continue to run and to stop so that the learnings may be firmly established.

Use: Squirrels in Trees. (See explanation of this activity in Chapter 7.)

Starting and Stopping

Explore: Children stand on one end line of the playing area and experiment with starting position for running games. They discover feet are in a forward-stride position with weight on forward foot; eyes are looking ahead. On a signal they run to opposite line and stop in balance; teacher comments that some have turned one way, some another.

Discover: On trying again, pupils discover correct way to turn is to touch the line with one foot and turn on the balls of both feet rather than the unsafe method of circling.

Use: Fire Engine. (See explanation of this activity in Chapter 7.)

Dodging and Tagging

Explore: Walk around a big area in different directions. How closely can you pass others without touching anyone?

Discover: How to avoid bumping into another person, how to dodge and move away to avoid collision.

Explore: Children repeat exploration, running instead of walking. The children tag the person they are dodging.

Discover: Good tagging is lightly touching another; pushing or holding is unnecessary.
Use: Animal Chase. (See explanation of this activity in Chapter 7.)

At the present time the curriculum in some cases is being structured *only* around movement experiences and skill learning. The fallacy of this approach is that the child does not have sufficient opportunity to make practical application of these experiences. In a sense, the movement experiences are being developed in isolation of the purpose for which they are intended. Relating this idea to the area of elementary school mathematics, it would be the same as having children spend all of their time drilling on arithmetic facts without using this information in practical situations. Many years ago mathematics' educators saw the weaknesses in this approach and changed learning experiences accordingly.

An interesting current trend in elementary school physical education curriculum development is that which is concerned with the intellectual need of children for the opportunity to participate in creative experiences rather than always having to conform. This is an extremely important development because one of the utmost concerns to educators in a modern democratic society is the problem of how to provide for creative expression so that a child may develop to the fullest extent of his potentialities. In fact, democracy is only beginning to understand the *power of the individual* as perhaps the most dynamic force in the world today. It is in this frame of reference that creativity should come clearly into focus because many of the problems in our complex society can be solved only through creative thinking.

While a variety of media including art, music, and writing are considered traditional approaches to creative expression, the very essence of creative expression is movement. Movement, as a form of creativity, utilizes the body as the instrument of expression. For the young child, the most natural form of creative expression is movement. Because of their very nature, children have a natural inclination for movement and they use this medium as the basic one for creative expression,

Another current development in elementary school physical education curriculum is concerned with what is generally known as the *conceptual* approach. This is not a *new* development as such. However, it is considered new to many physical educators because of its limited use in this field. Succinctly stated, the conceptual approach is concerned with "letting the children in" on the objectives. That is, teachers may know the concepts that they want the children to develop but at the same time the children may not be made aware of the concepts.

Several decades ago the idea emerged that the term "concept" could be considered to be the same as a teacher objective. The main job of the teacher was to provide a kind of learning environment where children would adopt the objectives as their own with the idea in mind that the concept would be developed. This approach, depending upon the skill of the teacher, has met with varying degrees of success in some of the subject areas, but its practice in physical education has been very limited.

One of the proponents of the conceptual approach to curriculum development, Dr. Ione G. Shadduck, has made some outstanding contributions in terms of its possibilities, and the interested reader is referred to her work in this area.[2]

It is gratifying to note that curriculum development in physical education is leaning more and more in the direction of curriculum theory and practice which has met with success in other subject areas. That is, learning experiences are tending to be classified more in a sequential order and based upon the physical, social, emotional, and intellectual traits and characteristics. (A detailed list of such traits and characteristics appears in the Appendix.)

In addition, in physical education curriculum development and planning, more attempts are being made to express objectives in behavioral terms, as suggested by the following comment by Hunter.

> Curriculum theory is also demanding that we build precision in our instruction by specifying in behavioral terms our instructional objectives. "Enjoying team games" or "learning motor skills" will no longer suffice as our educational destination in a physical education program. Such unassessable objectives must be replaced by precise and specific objectives expressed in behaviorable terms. "Catching a large ball when it is thrown with moderate force to a position between his waist and shoulders" or "catching eight out of ten baseballs thrown from any direction to his general position" tells the instructor the type of learning opportunity to plan and whether or not the objective has been achieved.[3]

When objectives are stated in behavioral terms there is a need to analyze activities for possible outcomes. The purpose of this is to try to determine how a given activity can contribute to the objectives. When a teacher analyzes a specific activity for possible outcomes it seems essential that certain criteria be devised in order to determine outcomes of the activity as accurately as possible. With this in mind the following criteria are suggested as a guide in analyzing an activity for outcomes.

---

[2]Ione G. Shadduck, Johnson research project—a curriculum based on concepts, *The Physical Educator,* October 1970, p. 107.

[3]Madeline Hunter, "The Role of Physical Education in Child Development and Learning," *Journal of Health, Physical Education, and Recreation,* May 1968.

Physical Outcomes. What are the essential motor skills involved in the activity? What parts of the body are especially developed as a result of engaging in the activity? Is the activity conducive to the best physical health of the child? Is the activity such that it imposes too great a physical strain on the child?

Social Outcomes. Does the activity provide for satisfactory group relationships? Does the activity provide a feeling of belonging for every child? Is the activity organized in such a way that some children might be placed in a position of rejection?

Emotional Outcomes. Does the activity provide for satisfactory release of stress and tension? Does the activity provide for release of aggression in a socially acceptable manner? Is the activity such that it places children under undue emotional stress?

Intellectual Outcomes. Does the activity provide opportunities for the application of judgment? Does the activity provide opportunities for the application of reflective thinking? Does the activity provide for intellectually challenging experiences? Does the activity provide for the opportunity to solve problems? Does the activity provide for the opportunity for creative thinking?

It should be clearly understood that every physical education activity will not satisfactorily meet all of the above criteria. Moreover, desirable behavioral outcomes will not accrue automatically. On the contrary, this will depend largely upon how well the activity is organized and taught, in addition to the nature of the activity itself.

The preceding discussion of current developments and trends in curriculum developments should not be interpreted to mean that the trends that have been designated as worthwhile are being practiced on a widespread basis. There are still far too many weak physical education curriculums at the elementary school level. One authority has expressed it this way.

There still is the type of watered-down secondary school program, such as one which puts a fourth-grade boy, or even a little girl, on a gymnasium floor with a man-sized basketball and a ten-foot hoop, because the teacher was prepared for secondary school teaching or for coaching and really doesn't know the needs of little children or how to meet them. And programs consisting mainly of conditioning exercises in long lines on command because of the belief that this is the best way to promote fitness and is the sole objective of many programs.[4]

[4] Margie R. Hanson, "Elementary School Physical Education Today," *Promising Practices in Elementary School Physical Education,* American Association for Health, Physical Education and Recreation, Washington, D.C., 1968.

Some Basic Principles of Curriculum Development

It is essential that those persons responsible for physical education curriculum development in the elementary school take into consideration certain guides to action. In those cases where physical education programs have developed on a more or less haphazard basis, it is likely that this practice could be avoided to some extent by establishing a sound set of principles of curriculum development.

The list of principles suggested here is not necessarily all inclusive nor is each principle a separate entity. It may be noticed that they overlap to some extent and, as a consequence, serve the purpose of the basic considerations essential to the success of the physical education program.

1. *The physical education curriculum should comprise all of the experiences that children have which are under the auspices of the school.* This principle implies that each component part of the program is interrelated with and dependent upon other parts. The point of view is taken that such activities as extraclass activities should be considered an outgrowth of the basic physical education activities program. In this way there should develop a more sound relationship among the various areas in the broad field of physical education.

2. *Physical education curriculum development should be based on a philosophy of equal opportunity for all children.* Physical education is the rightful heritage of all the children in all of the schools. If principles of democracy are to be practiced in the schools of America, physical education programs must be devised so that all children will have an equal opportunity to engage in wholesome activity.

3. *Physical education curriculum development should utilize all available appropriate resources.* Those persons responsible for curriculum development should survey each resource and evaluate its possible use in the program. Such factors as multiple use of facilities and wise placement of teaching personnel must be given consideration in curriculum development for the betterment of the program.

4. *Physical education curriculum development should be a cooperative enterprise.* It does not seem wise to place the development of the curriculum in the hands of a single individual. Supervisors, teachers, and others should share their knowledge and experience in an attempt to develop a program that will make a significant contribution to the optimum growth and development of children.

5. *Learning activities and experiences in the physical education curriculum should be selected by the application of valid criteria.* Although there is perhaps little in the way of scientific objective evidence to support

the placement of physical education activities at the various grade levels, there are, nevertheless, certain criteria sufficiently valid to justify their application.

6. *Physical education curriculum development should recognize indi--vidual differences in children.* In order to develop each individual to his ultimate capacity, physical education curriculum development should take into consideration the fact that children differ in physical ability as well as social, emotional, and intellectual characteristics. Such factors as organization of classes and classification of children must be regarded as highly significant if the school plans to assume a responsibility for the optimum physical development of each child.

7. *Physical education curriculum planning should be flexible.* The lack of standardization in the physical education curriculum makes it almost imperative that it be characterized by a degree of flexibility. Varying backgrounds of previous child experiences in physical education activities together with such factors as wide differences in facilities from school to school manifest the need for a curriculum which can be adapted to meet the specific needs of the children of a particular school.

8. *Physical education curriculum development should be continuous.* Since education is considered a continuous process, it naturally follows that physical education curriculum development should be continuous in order to meet the needs of a changing society. Paradoxically, in some instances physical education has been content to rest on past laurels. As a consequence, gaps have not always been bridged and in some cases physical education has not always been abreast with advanced thinking in general education. When this occurs it is indeed unfortunate since physical education is based primarily on motor activity and should be one of the last disciplines to fall into lethargic complacency. Continuous curriculum development should do much to alleviate this situation by taking up the necessary slack with regard to the needs of the concomitant culture.

Criteria for the Selection of Curriculum Content

It is of utmost importance that valid criteria be applied in the selection of physcial education learning activities and experiences. In this regard, the two most basic criteria are the *needs* and *interests* of children.

Needs of Children

In their efforts to develop a sound curriculum, teachers and others must take into consideration those physical education activities which can contribute to the needs of the individual and the group. Certain physiological and sociological principles based on a study of child growth and development readily point up some of the directions which might be taken when physical education activities are selected to meet children's needs.

Teachers, supervisors, and others working together on a cooperative basis can help to identify more clearly the needs of children of a particular community. In this way they will not only contribute to the wise selection of curriculum content but will be in a position to make suitable placement of learning experiences at the various grade levels.

Interests of Children

Although needs and interests of children may be closely related, there are differences which should be taken into consideration when activities are selected for the curriculum. While interests are, for the most part, acquired as products of the environment, needs, particularly those of an idivinual nature, are more likely to be innate. Herein lies one of the main differences in the two criteria as far as the selection of activities is concerned. For example, a child may demonstrate a temporary interest in an activity which may not contribute to his needs at a certain age level. This interest may perhaps have been aroused because of the child's environment. In other words, an older brother or parent might influence a child to develop an interest in an activity which might not contribute to his needs or which might possibly have a detrimental effect as far as his needs are concerned.

In selecting physical education activities, children's interests should be thoroughly explored. Sometimes when teachers are asked why a certain activity has not been included in the curriculum they may reply that the children are not interested in it and do not care to participate in it. This cannot be considered an entirely valid answer because children must be given a fair opportunity to develop an interest in an activity. For example, some people feel that children at certain age levels are reluctant to accept an activity like square dancing. After this activity has been introduced, however, children may show sufficient interest to justify inclusion of square dancing as a part of the program. (The Appendix includes a detailed list of physical, social, emotional, and intellectual traits and characteristics of boys and girls from ages 5-12. In a general way this list reflects needs and interests of children.)

Cooperative Curriculum Development

The construction of the elementary school physical education curriculum should be a project which involves all or a majority of the persons who can make a worthwhile contribution. The personnel involved might well include administrators, supervisors of physical education, supervisors of other subject areas, teachers, parents, and pupils.

The teacher is the key figure in supervising and guiding the learning of pupils. Furthermore, the success of the physical education curriculum depends largely on wise teacher leadership. Consequently, physical education curriculum development which utilizes teachers on a cooperative basis not only provides for creative teacher action, but serves as an outstanding means of inservice growth.

Any cooperative aspect of curriculum development requires the functioning of certain committees, the personnel of which should be representative of the entire staff. In this regard, the following committees, along with others as seem necessary, might be selected to provide for complete representation of all factions concerned:

1. Production committee
2. Horizontal committees
3. Vertical committees
4. Reviewing committee

Production committee. The production committee is actually made up of the chairmen of all other committees. In other words, each member may be responsible for a subcommittee. The production committee may sometimes be referred to as the steering or clearance committee.

Horizontal committees. These committees are made up of teachers at given grade levels. For example, one committee may consist of a group of first-grade teachers, another a group of second-grade teachers, and so on. These committees can work together for the specific needs and interests of children at a particular age and grade level.

Vertical committees. These committees concern membership of teachers for all grade levels. For example, there may be a committee with representatives for the primary grades, one for the upper elementary, and one for the combination of these. The importance of these committees lies in the attempts to develop a gradated curriculum in order to provide, insofar as possible, for sequential growth in the various physical education learning experiences throughout the elementary school years.

Reviewing committee. It is the function of this committee to review the material, raise questions, and make suggestions or recommendations for the improvement of the curriculum. Membership of this committee should perhaps include teachers, administrators, supervisors of other subject areas as well as someone outside the field of education. In the case of the latter, it might be well to have one or more parents appointed to this committee.

It will be the duty of some staff member, perhaps the supervisor of physical education if there is such a person, to coordinate all committee activities. This coordinator should perhaps act at least in an ex officio status on all committees where he is not actively engaged in the work of the committee.

Providing for Individual Differences

One of the most important features of modern curriculum theory is one which emphasizes individualized instruction based upon individual differences of children. At the same time recognition of this is one of the most neglected aspects of curriculum development in physical education in the elementary school.

It should be realized, however, that because of the nature of most physical education experiences, providing for individual differences is not an easy matter. In the more or less *passive* subject-matter areas such as reading and mathematics it may be less difficult to provide for individual differences. For example, in reading it is a common practice to group children so that they can proceed at their individual level of ability. Individual differences are being provided for here in a somewhat sedentary situation. However, in physical education activities where vigorous movement is involved, as in some of the game activities, provision for individual differences can become a relatively complicated manner, and teachers must exercise a great deal of ingenuity.

Two of the important factors to take into account with reference to individual differences of children as pertaining to physical education are sex differences and differences in skill and ability levels. Although boys and girls start out in life perceiving things differently, these differences are not pronounced enough to warrant segregation of the sexes for physical education in the early school years. Thus, segregation of the sexes does not need to be taken into account until about the middle of the third grade in school. At this time it appears advantageous to both sexes to separate them in those types of game activities that require certain kinds of skills where girls on the average will not be as proficient as boys. As boys begin to gain more than girls in strength, it is best to separate them for activities that involve strength, throwing ability, and the like. Of course they can participate satisfactorily together in rhythmic activities and in most self-testing activities at *all* grade levels.

Differences in skill and ability levels, however, need to be taken into account whether or not boys and girls are segregated. For example, boys of the same age sometimes will vary markedly in their ability to perform skills required in certain physical education activities. Obviously, these differences should be taken into account within the class.

How to Use a Curriculum Guide*

It should be understood that recommendations for use of activities in the average curriculum guide should be considered only as general suggestions. This means that the teacher should use the description of physical education activities in a curriculum guide as a *guide* and not as a *recipe*. That is, the teacher should select activities recommended generally for a given grade level or age range. Following this the activity should be analyzed for use with a particular group of children.

Ordinarily, the selection of a given physical education activity for a particular group of children is likely to depend upon the following three important factors.

1. What the children do in the activity.
2. The conditions under which the activity is performed.
3. What is used to perform the activity.

What the children do in the activity is concerned with those motor skills necessary for proficient performance. The teacher who is aware of the ability level of the class should be able to tell at once if the children will have difficulty in engaging in the activity.

The conditions under which the activity is performed involves the complexity of the rules and/or strategies necessary for successful conduct of the activity. Immediately the teacher should be able to determine whether or not such rules and strategies are within the realm of understanding and active participation level of the particular class.

What is used to perform the activity refers to the kind of materials and equipment needed for its execution. It may be that the activity calls for the use of a piece of equipment which the children are not ready to manipulate proficiently in order to perform the activity successfully.

After reading the description of a given activity the teacher can use the foregoing factors as criteria to determine whether or not the activity is suitable for a particular group. If teachers relate all of these factors to ability levels it should follow that they will meet with some degree of success in selecting activities for their children.

One very important consideration to take into account is that any single factor or all of the foregoing factors can be modified to make a given ac-

---

*This also pertains to textbooks and other sources containing directions for physical education activities for children.

tivity less difficult or more difficult to meet the needs and interests of a group of children. After the teacher has made a serious attempt, based on the preceding criteria, to modify the activity, it can then be presented to the children in an experimental way. As they participate in the activity the teacher should be able to discern quickly if it is suited to their needs and interests. It may be that the activity as modified is suitable for use of a majority of the pupils; however, due to differences in ability levels it may be too difficult for some and not challenging enough for others. When this situation arises it becomes necessary for the teacher to attempt to provide for the individual differences of some of the children.

Using the game of CALL BALL we might present an example of provision for individual differences. The game is played in the following manner.

> Six or more children form a circle. One child stands in the center of the circle holding a rubber ball. He tosses the ball into the air and at the same time calls out the name of one of the children. The child whose name is called attempts to catch the ball either on first bounce or on the fly, depending upon the ability of the children. If the player whose name is called catches the ball he changes places with the child in the center and the game continues in this manner. If the child whose name is called does not catch the ball, the thrower remains in the center of the circle and tosses the ball up again.

Rather than having a child throw the ball into the air from the center of the circle, the game could be controlled somewhat by the teacher's assuming this position. For those children who are not too adept at getting into the circle and catching the ball, the teacher might call a child's name and let a small amount of time elapse before releasing the ball. Similarly, for those children who react quickly and catch the ball well, the teacher might release the ball before calling the name. In this way the teacher can make the activity challenging for all children and provide a chance for all to succeed in relation to their individual ability.

It should be borne in mind that it takes a skillful teacher to conduct an activity in this manner. Insofar as possible the activity should be conducted in such a way that the teacher's actions are not too obvious. Unless the teacher handles this kind of situation skillfully, the child with lesser ability might feel inferior, while the more highly skilled child might feel that there is some degree of discrimination. Teachers should understand the children well enough to know how and when to avoid this kind of situation.

Curriculum Revision

In order to meet needs and changing conditions the physical education curriculum should be under continuous revision. This continuous process has a two-fold purpose. First, there is a greater possibility for providing more and better learning experiences, and second, teachers are kept on the alert to detect factors which will improve the program. With regard to the latter, teacher participation in curriculum revision is practically indispensable since the teacher is the key figure in the learning situation.

Problems concerned with grade placement of physical education activities make it all the more important that teachers be encouraged to analyze their own techniques and to experiment with their classes. Teachers can determine to a large extent what the reactions of children are to certain activities and how the activities are related to the needs and interests of children. However, the important factor is that such data be accumulated and put into use through curriculum revision. After information of this type is assembled, it must be studied and interpreted by teachers and supervisors so that the best possible revision can be effected.

It should be kept in mind that curriculum analysis and revision are not the responsibility of one person. On the other hand, the eventual improvement of the entire program will depend largely upon the cooperation of supervisors, teachers, and others in this enterprise.

Chapter 5

Teaching and Learning In Physical Education

The teaching-learning process is complicated and complex. For this reason it is most important that teachers have as full an understanding as possible of the role of teaching and learning in elementary school physical education. It will be the primary function of this chapter to assist the reader to deal efficiently with such questions as:

1. What are some of the basic considerations which should be taken into account with regard to teaching methods?
2. How are certain principles of learning applied to physical education?
3. What are the various phases of the physical education teaching-learning situation?
4. What important factors should be taken into account in the phase of the physical education teaching-learning situation which is concerned with *auditory input?*
5. What important factors should be taken into account in the phase of the physical education teaching-learning situation which is concerned with *visual input?*
6. What are some of the important factors to consider in the *participation* phase of the physical education teaching-learning situation?
7. What are some of the important factors to consider in the *evaluation* phase of the physical education teaching-learning situation?
8. What factors should the teacher take into account in planning physical education lessons?

Basic Considerations

The concepts of learning that an individual teacher or a group of teachers in a given school subscribe to are directly related to the kind and variety of physical education learning activities and experiences that will be provided for children. For this reason it is important for beginning teachers to explore some of the factors that make for most desirable and worthwhile learning. Among the factors which should help to orient the reader with regard to some basic understandings in the teaching of physical education are (1) an understanding of the meaning of certain terms; (2) an understanding of the derivation of teaching methods; and (3) an understanding of the various learning products in physical education.

Meaning of Terms

Due to the fact that certain terms, because of their multiple use, do not actually have a universal definition, no attempt will be made here to *define* terms. On the other hand, it will be the purpose to *describe* certain terms rather than attempt to define them. The reader should view the descriptions of terms that follow with this general idea in mind.

Learning. Without exception, most definitions of learning are characterized by the idea that learning involves some sort of change in the individual. This means that when an individual has learned, his behavior is modified in one or more ways. Thus, a valid criterion for learning would be that after having an experience a person could behave in a way in which he could not have behaved before having had the experience. In this general connection, many learning theorists suggest that it is not possible to *see* learning. However, behavior can be seen and when a change in behavior has occurred, then it is possible to infer that change and learning have occurred. Figure 5.1 depicts this concept.

Learning Can Be Inferred By A Change in Behavior[1]

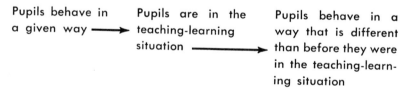

Pupils behave in a given way ⟶ Pupils are in the teaching-learning situation ⟶ Pupils behave in a way that is different than before they were in the teaching-learning situation

FIGURE 5.1

[1]James H. Humphrey, Alice M. Love, and Leslie W. Irwin, *Principles and Techniques of Supervision in Physical Education*, 3d ed. (Dubuque, Iowa: Wm. C. Brown Company Publishers, 1972), p. 61.

Teaching. Several years ago the author was addressing a group of teachers on the subject of teaching and learning. Introducing the discussion in somewhat abstract terms, the speaker asked, "What is teaching?" After a short period of embarrassing deliberation, one member of the group interrogated the following answer with some degree of uncertainty: "Is it imparting information?" This kind of thinking is characteristic of that which reflects the traditional meaning of the term "teaching." A more acceptable description of teaching would be to think of it in terms of guidance, direction, and supervision of behavior that results in desirable and worthwhile learning. This is to say that it is the job of the teacher to guide the child's learning rather than to impart to him a series of unrelated and sometimes meaningless facts.

Method. The term "method" might be considered as an orderly and systematic means of achieving an objective. In other words, method is concerned with "how to do" something in order to achieve desired results. If best results are to be obtained for elementary school children through physical education, it becomes necessary that the most desirable physical education learning experiences be provided. Consequently, it becomes essential that teachers use all of the ingenuity and resourcefulness at their command in the proper direction and guidance of these learning experiences. The procedures that teachers use are known as *teaching methods.*

Derivation of Teaching Methods

Beginning teachers often ask, "Where do we get our ideas for teaching methods?" For the most part this question should be considered in general terms. In other words, although there are a variety of acceptable teaching procedures utilized in the modern elementary school, all of these methods are likely to be derived from two somewhat broad sources.

The first of these involves an accumulation of knowledge of educational psychology and what is known about the learning process in providing physical education learning experiences. The other is the practice of successful teachers.

In most instances, undergraduate preparation of prospective elementary school classroom teachers and physical education teachers includes at least some study of educational psychology as it applies to the learning process and certain accepted principles of learning. With this basic information is expected that begining teachers have sufficient knowledge toe make application of it to the practicle situation.

It has been the observation of the present author over a period of years that many beginning teachers tend to rely too much upon the practices of successful teachers as a source of teaching methods. The validity of this procedure is based on the assumption that such successful practices are likely to have as their bases the application of fundamental psychological principles of learning. Nevertheless, it should be the responsibility of every teacher to become familiar with the basic psychological principles of learning and to attempt to apply these in the best possible way when providing the most desirable and worthwhile physical education learning experiences for children.

Learning Products in Physical Education

In general, three learning products can be identified which accrue from participation in physical education activities, namely, direct, incidental, and indirect. In a well-planned program these learning products should develop satisfactorily through physical education activities.

Direct learning products are those which are the direct object of teaching. For instance, running, dodging, jumping, throwing, and catching are some of the important skills necessary for reasonable degrees of proficiency in the game of dodge ball. Through the learning of skills more enjoyment is derived from participating in an activity than just the practice of the skills. For this reason the learning of skills is one of the primary direct objects of teaching. However, it should be understood that certain incidental and indirect learning products can result from direct teaching in physical education. The zeal of a participant to become a more proficient performer gives rise to certain of the incidental learning products. These may be inherent in the realization and acceptance of practices of healthful living which make the individual a more skilled performer in the activity.

Attitudes have often been considered in terms of behavior tendencies and as such might well be concerned with indirect learning products. This type of learning product involves such qualities as sportsmanship, appreciation of certain aspects of the activity, and other factors that involve the adjustment and modification of the individual's reactions to others.

Teachers who have the responsibility for providing physical education programs for elementary school children should give a great deal of consideration to these various kinds of learning products. This is particularly important if children are to receive the full benefit of the many physical education learning experiences which should be provided for them.

Some Principles of Learning Applied to Physical Education

There are various basic facts about the nature of human beings of which modern educators are more cognizant than educators of the past. Essentially these facts involve some of the fundamental aspects of the learning process which all good teaching should take into account. Older concepts of teaching methods were based largely upon the idea that the teacher was the sole authority in terms of what was best for children, and that children were expected to learn regardless of the conditions surrounding the learning situation. For the most part, modern teaching replaces the older concepts with methods which are based on certain accepted beliefs of educational psychology. Outgrowths of these beliefs emerge in the form of principles of learning. The following principles provide important guidelines for arranging learning experiences for children and they suggest how desirable learning can take place when the principles are satisfactorily applied to elementary school physical education:

1. *The child's own purposeful goals should guide his learning activities.*

In order for a desirable learning situation to prevail, teachers must consider certain features about purposeful goals which guide learning activities. Of utmost importance is the fact that the goal must seem worthwhile to the child. This will perhaps involve such factors as interest, attention, and motivation. Fortunately, in the recommended activities from which physical education learning experiences are drawn, interest, attention, and motivation are likely to be inherent qualities. Thus, the teacher does not always necessarily need to "arouse" the child with various kinds of motivating situations. On the other hand, the type of program that has body conditioning as its only objective may take a great deal of coercing on the part of the teacher to induce participation. In other words, engaging in a variety of setting-up exercises may not seem to be a worthwhile goal to the child.

The goal should not be too difficult for the child to achieve. While it should present something of a challenge, it should be something that is commensurate with his abilities and within his realm of achievement. By the same token, the goal should not be too easy or it will not be likely that the child will have the opportunity to develop to his greatest possible capacity. To be purposeful a goal should give direction to activity and learning. In substance, this implies that after a child has accepted a goal he should have a better idea of where he is going and what he should be able to accomplish in a given situation.

It is important that the child find and adopt or accept his own goals. This implies that he should not receive them directly from the teacher. If the most desirable learning is to take place, it is doubtful if one person can give another person a goal. This should not be interpreted to mean that goals may not originate with the teacher. On the contrary, the teacher can be of considerable help assisting the child to find his own goal. This can be done by planning the physical education learning environment in such a way that pupils with varying interests and abilities may find something which appears to be worthwhile. This procedure can be followed and still be in keeping with teacher's objectives. For instance, it may be a goal of the teacher to improve the social relationships of children in a given physical education class. This might be accomplished by providing a variety of self-testing activities with the children participating in groups, and requiring that each member of the group achieve a certain degree of proficiency in a given activity before the entire group is given credit for achievement. Experience has shown that this procedure has been most useful in welding together a group of children who have previously experienced some difficulty in getting along together. While the goal of obtaining better social relationships originated with the teacher, the experience was planned in such a way that the goal was eventually adopted by the children.

2. *The child should be given sufficient freedom to create his own responses in the situation he faces.*

This principle indicates that *problem solving* is the way of human learning, and that the child will learn largely only through experience, either direct or indirect. This implies that the teacher should provide every opportunity for children to utilize judgment in the various situations that arise in physical education activities, particularly the games aspect of the program. Even many of the lowly organized games present possibilities for problem-solving situations whereby children can employ judgment and resort to reflective thinking in connection with various kinds of game strategy that contribute to more satisfaction and enjoyment from participation in the game.

It should be borne in mind that although the child learns through experience this does not mean that experience will assure desirable learning, since it might possibly come too soon. For example, children at the first-grade level are not expected to learn some of the complex skill patterns involved in the highly organized game of basketball simply because at that level they are not ready for it.

When the child is free to create his own responses in the situation he faces, individual differences are being taken into consideration, and generally experience comes as the right time for desirable learning. This situation necessitates an activity area environment which is flexible to the extent that children can achieve in relation to their individual abilities.

In a sense this principle of learning refutes—and perhaps rightly so—the idea that there is a *specific* "problem-solving method" mutually exclusive from other methods. In other words, all methods should involve problem solving which actually means the application of this principle.

3. *The child agrees to and acts upon the learning which he considers of most value to him.*

Children accept as most valuable those things which are of greatest interest to them. This principle implies in part, then, that there should be a satisfactory balance between *needs* and *interests* of children as criteria for the selection of physical education learning experiences. Although it is of extreme importance to consider the needs of children in developing experiences, the teacher should not lose sight of the fact that their interest is needed if the most desirable learning is to take place.

While needs and interests of children may be closely related, there are nevertheless differences which should be taken into consideration when physical education learning experiences are selected. Interests are, for the most part, acquired as products of environment, while needs, particularly those of an individual nature, are more likely to be innate. Herein lies one of the main differences in the two criteria as far as the selection of physical education learning experiences is concerned. For instance, a child may demonstrate a temporary interest in an activity which may not contribute to his needs at a certain age level. This interest may be aroused because of the child's environment. Perhaps an older brother or a parent might influence a child to develop an interest in an activity which might not contribute to his needs or which might possibly have a detrimental effect on them. Despite the inevitability of such contingencies, interests of children may serve as one of the valid criteria for the selection of physical education learning activities. In this connection, it is interesting to note that there is a rather marked relationship between physical education learning experiences recommended by experts in the field of physical education and pupil interest in these same activities.

To a certain extent interests may be dependent upon past experiences of children. For instance, interests in certain physical education activities may stem from the fact that they are a part of the traditional background of the community, and as such have absorbed the interests of parents as well as pupils.

4. *The child should be given the opportunity to share cooperatively in learning experiences with his classmates under the guidance but not the control of the teacher.*

The point that should be emphasized here is that although learning may be an individual matter, it is likely to take place best in a group. This is to say that children learn individually but that socialization should be retained. Moreover, sharing in group activities seems an absolute essential in educating for democracy.

The physical education situation should present near-ideal conditions for a desirable balance between individualization and socialization. For example, the elements of an activity must be learned individually, but then they are combined by the entire group in a game situation. In the game of dodge ball each child learns how to perform the skills necessary for successful performance in the game situation. However, he may improve his skill, or application of skill, when he is placed in the actual game situation. Another example may be seen in the performance of certain stunt and tumbling activities. Although these are predominantly individual in nature, children oftentimes work together in small groups, assisting each other, and as a consequence are likely to learn from each other by pooling and sharing experience.

5. *The teacher should act as a guide who understands the child as a growing organism.*

This principle indicates that the teacher should consider learning as an evolving process and not just as instantaneous behavior. If teaching is to be regarded in terms of guidance and direction of behavior which results in learning, the teacher must display wisdom as to when to "step in and teach" and when to step aside and watch for further opportunities to guide and direct behavior.

The application of this principle precludes an approach which is teacher-dominated. On the other hand, the implementation of this principle is perhaps more likely to be realized in physical education classes where the teacher recognizes that numerous problem-solving situations are inherent in many physical education situations. For example, if a particular game is not going as it should, the teacher can stop the game and evaluate it with the children so that they can determine how the game may be improved. In other words, children are placed in a position to identify problems connected with the game and given the opportunity to exercise judgment in solving them. The teacher thus helps children discover direct pathways to meaningful areas of experience, and at the same time contributes to the children's ability to become self-directed individuals.

Phases of the Teaching-Learning Situation

There are certain fundamental phases involved in almost every physical education teaching-learning situation. These phases are (1) auditory input, (2) visual input, (3) participation, and (4) evaluation. Although these four features are likely to be weighted in various degrees, they will occur in the teaching of practically every physical education lesson regardless of the type of activity that is being taught. While the application of the various phases may be of a general nature, they nevertheless should be utilized in such a way that they become specific in a particular situation.

Depending upon the type of activity being taught—game, rhythm, or self-testing activity—the use and application of the various phases should be characterized by flexibility and awareness of the objective of the lesson.

Auditory-Input Phase

The term "auditory" may be described as stimulation occurring through the sense organs of hearing. In education, the term "input" is concerned with the use of as many media as are deemed necessary for a particular teaching-learning situation, including the teacher's behavior. The term "output" is concerned with behaviors, or reactions of the learner resulting from the various forms of input. Auditory input involves the various learning media which are directed to the auditory sense. This should not be interpreted to mean that the auditory-input phase of the teaching-learning situation is a one-way process. While much of such input may originate with the teacher, consideration should also be given to the verbal interaction among pupils and between pupils and teacher.

Physical education provides a most desirable opportunity for learning through direct purposeful experience. In other words, the physical education learning situation is one which involves "learning by doing" or learning through pleasurable physical activity. Although verbalization might well be kept to a minimum in teaching elementary school physical education, a certain amount of auditory input, which should provide for auditory-motor association, appears to be essential for a satisfactory teaching-learning situation. The quality of "kinesthetic feel," which might be defined as the process of changing ideas into muscular action, is of primary importance in the proper acquisition of physical education motor skills. It might be said that the auditory-input phase of teaching helps to set the stage for a kinesthetic concept of the particular activity that is being taught.

Listening experiences are, no doubt, among the most abstract of the learning media used with children. As such, this type of learning experience has been much maligned by some educators. However, it should be pointed out that the child first learns to act on the basis of verbal instructions by others. In this regard it has been suggested that later he learns to guide and direct his own behavior on the basis of his own language activities—he literally talks to himself, giving himself instructions.[2]

This point of view is supported by research, particularly that of Luria,[3] who has postulated that speech as a form of communication between

[2]S. Glucksberg, *Symbolic Processes* (Dubuque, Iowa: **Wm. C. Brown Company** Publishers, 1966).

[3]A. R. Luria, Development of the Directive Function of Speech in Early Childhood, *Word*, 1959, p. 15.

children and adults later becomes a means of organizing the child's own behavior. That is, the function which was previously divided between two people—child and adult—later becomes an internal function of human behavior.

Great care should be taken with the auditory-input phase in the physical education teaching-learning situation. The ensuing discussions are intended to suggest to the reader ways in which the greatest benefits can accrue when using this particular learning medium.

Preparing the Children for Listening

Since it is likely that the initial part of the auditory-input phase will originate with the teacher, care should be taken to prepare the children for listening. The teacher may set the scene for listening by relating the activity to the interests of the children. In addition, the teacher should be on the alert to help children develop their own purposes for listening.

In preparing children to listen the teacher should be aware that it is of extreme importance that the comfort of children be taken into consideration and that attempts should be made for any possible attention-distraction factors. Although evidence concerning the effect of environmental distractions on listening effectiveness is not in great abundance, there is reason to believe that distraction does interfere with listening comprehension. Moreover, it was reported a good many years ago that being able to see as well as hear the speaker is an important factor in listening distraction.[4]

All of these factors have a variety of implications for the auditory-input phase of the physical education teaching-learning situation. For example, consideration should be given to the placement of pupils when a physical education activity is being explained to them. This means, for instance, that if the teacher is providing auditory input from a circle formation, the teacher should take a position as part of the circle instead of speaking from the center of the circle. Moreover, if the group is large, it will perhaps be best to place the children in a small group for the auditory-input phase and then put them into formation for the activity. Also it might be well for teachers to consider that an object, such as a ball, can become an attention-distracting factor when an activity is being explained. The attention of children is sometimes focused on the ball and they may not listen to what is being said. The teacher might wish to conceal such an object until time for its use is most appropriate. With reference to the importance of the listener being able to see the speaker, teachers might exercise caution in the use of

[4]Edward J. Kramer, and Thomas R. Lewis, "Comparison of Visual and Non-Visual Listening," *Journal of Communication,* November 1951.

records for rhythmic activities which include instructions on the record. Particularly with primary level children it might be well for the teacher to use the instructions only for himself and the musical accompaniment for the children.

Teacher-Pupil and Pupil-Pupil Interaction

It was mentioned previously that the auditory-input phase is a two-way process. As such, it is important to take into account certain factors involving verbal interaction of pupils with pupils and pupils with teacher.

By "democracy" some people seem to mean everyone doing or saying whatever happens to cross his mind at the moment. This raises the question of control and it should be emphasized that *group discussions*, if they are to be democratic, must be in control. This is to say that if a group discussion is "to get somewhere" it must be under control; and let us stress that democracy implies discipline and control.

Children understand games. They soon realize that a game is no fun, that is, it gets nowhere if it is lacking in clearly defined rules which every player agrees, tacitly, to observe. A poor sport is unpopular with the other players of the game, not for "moral" reasons necessarily, but because he stops, interrupts, or impedes the flow of the game. So it is with verbal interactions of teacher and pupils in the group discussion.

Group discussion is a kind of sociointellectual exercise (involving numerous bodily movements of course) just as basketball is a kind of sociointellectual exercise (involving too, higher mental functioning). Both imply individual discipline to keep play moving and within bounds, and both require moderators (or officials) overseeing, though not participating in the play in a manner that is objective and aloof from the heat of competition. In brief, disciplined, controlled group discussion can be a training ground for living in a society in which both individual and group interests are profoundly respected—just as games can serve a comparable function.

Another important function in teacher-pupil verbal interaction is that which is concerned with time given to questions after the teacher has given an explanation. The teacher should give time for questions from the class, but should be very skillful in the use of questions. It must be determined immediately whether or not a question is a legitimate one. This implies that the type of questions asked can help to serve as criteria for the teacher to evaluate the auditory-input phase of teaching. For example, if numerous questions are asked, it is apparent that either the auditory input from the teacher was incomplete or the children were not paying attention.

Directionality of Sound

In summarizing recent findings concerned with the directionality of sound, Smith has pointed up a number of interesting factors which are important to the auditory-input phase.[5] She mentions that individuals tend to initiate movement toward the direction from which the sound cue emanates. For example, if a verbal cue is given that instructs the individual to move a body segment or segments to the left, but the verbal cue emanates from the right side of the individual, the initial motor response is to the right, followed by a reverse response to the left. Emphasizing the importance of this at the elementary school level, Smith recommends that when working on direction of motor responses with young children, one should make certain that sound cues come from the direction in which the motor response is made. The point is made that children have enough difficulty in discriminating left from right without confounding them further.

Visual-Input Phase

The term "visual" is concerned with images that are obtained through the eyes. Thus, visual input involves the various learning media which are directed to the visual sense.

Various estimates indicate that the visual sense brings us upwards of three-fourths of our knowledge. If this postulation can be used as a valid criterion, the merits of the visual-input phase in teaching physical education are readily discernible. In many cases visual input, which should provide for visual-motor association, serves as a happy medium between verbal symbols and direct participation in helping teachers further to prepare children for the kinesthetic feel mentioned previously.

In general, there are two types of visual input which can be used satisfactorily in teaching physical education. These are visual symbols and human demonstration (live performance).

Visual Symbols

Included among the visual symbols used in physical education are motion pictures and various kinds of flat or still pictures. One of the disadvantages of the latter centers around the difficulty in portraying movement with a still figure. Although movement is obtained with a motion picture, it is not depicted in the third dimension which causes some degree of ineffectiveness when this medium is used. One valuable use of visual

---

[5]Hope M. Smith, "Implications for Movement Education Experiences Drawn from Perceptual-Motor Research," *Journal of Health, Physical Education, and Recreation,* April 1970.

symbols is that which is concerned with employing diagrams to show dimensions of playing areas. This procedure may be useful when the teacher is explaining an activity in the classroom before going on to the outdoor activity area. Court dimensions and the like can be diagramed on the blackboard, providing a good opportunity for integration with other areas such as mathematics and drawing to scale.

Human Demonstration

Some of the guides to action in the use of demonstration follow:

1. If the teacher plans to demonstrate, this should be included in preparation of the lesson by practicing and rehearsing the demonstration.

2. The teacher does not need to do all of the demonstrating—in fact, in some cases it may be much more effective to have one or more pupils demonstrate. Since the teacher is expected to be a skilled performer, a demonstration by a pupil will oftentimes serve to show other children that one of their own classmates can perform the activity and that they might well be able to do it also. In addition, it may be entirely possible that the teacher may not be an efficient enough performer to demonstrate a certain activity. For example, it may be necessary for a teacher to call upon pupils to demonstrate some of the more complex stunt and tumbling activities.

3. If the teacher prefers to do the demonstrating in a given situation, it may still be advisable to use pupils to demonstrate in order to show the class that the performance of the activity is within its realm of achievement.

4. The demonstration should be based on the skill and ability of a given group of children. If it appears to be too difficult for them, they may not want to attempt the activity.

5. When at all possible, a demonstration should parallel the timing and conditions in which the demonstration will be put to practical application. However, if the situation is one in which the movements are complex or done with great speed, it might be well to have the demonstration conducted on a slower basis than that involved in the actual playing or performance situation.

6. The groups should be arranged so that everyone is in a favorable position to see the demonstration. Moreover, the children should be able to view the demonstration from a position in which it takes place. For example, if the activity is to be performed in a lateral plane, children should be placed so that they can see it from this position.

7. Although auditory input and demonstration can be satisfactorily combined in many situations, care should be taken that an explanation is not lost because the visual sense offsets the auditory sense. That is, one

should not become an attention-distracting factor for the other. It will be up to the teacher to determine the amount of verbalization that should accompany the demonstration.

8. After the demonstration has been presented it may be a good practice to demonstrate again and have the children go through the movements with the demonstrator. This provides for the use of the kinesthetic sense together with the visual sense, which makes for close integration of these two sensory stimuli.

9. Demonstrations should not be too long. Children are eager to participate and this opportunity should be provided as soon as possible after the demonstration.

Participation Phase

Direct, purposeful experience is the foundation of all education. Because physical education activities are essentially motor in character, there is a near-ideal situation for learning in this particular area of the elementary school curriculum. The child needs to get his hands on the ball, feel his body coordinated in the performance of a stunt, or dance the folk dance in order to gain a full appreciation of the activity. There is an opportunity in a well-taught physical education lesson for learning to become a part of the child's physical reality, providing for a pleasurable concrete experience rather than an abstract one. For this reason the following considerations should be kept in mind in connection with the participation phase of teaching.

1. The class period should be planned so that the greatest possible amount of time is given to pupil participation.

2. If the activity does not progress as expected in the participation phase, perhaps the fault may lie in the procedures used in the auditory- and visual-input phases. Participation then becomes a criterion for the evaluation of former phases.

3. The teacher should take into account the fact that the original attempts in learning an activity should meet with a reasonable degree of success.

4. The teacher should constantly be aware of the possibility of fatigue of children during participation, and should understand that individual differences in pupils create a variation with regard to how rapidly fatigue takes place.

5. Participation should be worthwhile for every pupil, and all pupils should have the opportunity to achieve. Procedures which call for elimination of participants should be avoided lest some individuals do not receive the full value from participation.

6. The teacher should be ever on the alert to guide and direct learning, thus making the physical education period a teaching-learning period.

7. During the participation phase the teacher should constantly analyze performance of children in order to determine those who need improvement in skills. Behaviorisms of children should be observed while they are engaging in physical education activities. For example, various types of emotional behavior might be noted in game situations that might not be indicated in any other school activity.

8. Problems involved during participation should be kept in mind for subsequent evaluation of the lesson with the children.

Evaluation Phase

Evaluation is a very important phase of the physical education teaching-learning situation and yet perhaps one of the most neglected aspects of elementary school physical education lessons. For instance, it is not an uncommon procedure to have the physical education class period end at the signal of the bell, with the children hurrying and scurrying from the activity area without an evaluation of the results of the lesson.

Children should be given the opportunity to discuss the lesson and to suggest ways in which improvement might be effected. When this procedure is followed, children are placed in a problem-solving situation and desirable learning is more likely, with the teacher guiding learning rather than dominating the situation in a direction-giving type of procedure. Also more and better continuity is likely to be provided from one lesson to another when time is taken for evaluation. In addition, children are much more likely to develop a clearer understanding of the purposes of physical education if they are given an opportunity to discuss procedures involved in the lesson.

Ordinarily the evaluation phase should take place at the end of the physical education lesson. Experience has shown that a satisfactory evaluation procedure can be effected in from three to six minutes, depending upon the nature of the activity and upon what actually occurred during a given lesson. Under certain circumstances if an activity is not proceeding well in the participation phase of the lesson, it may be desirable to stop the activity and carry out what is known as a spot evaluation. This does not mean that the teacher should stop an activity every time the situation is not developing according to plan. A suggestion or a hint to children who are having difficulty with performance can perhaps preclude the need for having all of the children cease participation. On the other hand, if the situation is such that the needs of the group will best be met by a discussion concerning the solution of a problem, the teacher is indeed justified in stopping the activity and conducting an evaluation "on the spot."

Teachers should guard against stereotyping the evaluation phase of the physical education lesson. This implies that the teacher should look for developments during the participation phase of the lesson that might well serve as criteria for evaluation at the end of the lesson. If the evaluation phase is always started with the question, "Did you like the game?" this part of the lesson soon becomes meaningless and merely time-consuming as far as the children are concerned. Depending upon what actually occurred during the participation phase of the lesson, the following general questions might be considered by the teacher when beginning the evaluation phase with the children:

1. Should we review briefly what we learned today?
2. What are some of the things that we learned today?
3. What do we have to do or know in order to be a good performer in this game?
4. What did today's activity do for our bodies? Did it help us to have better control over our feet and legs? Did it improve our ability to throw? Did you find that you had to breathe much faster when you played this game?
5. What were some of the things you liked about the game we played today?
6. Can you think of any ways that we might improve the dance we learned today?

Questions such as these place children in a problem-solving situation and consequently provide for a more satisfactory learning situation. Moreover, this procedure is likely to provide a better setting for a child-centered physical education lesson because the children have an opportunity to discuss together ways and means for improvement in the performance of activities.

A very important feature of the evaluation phase is that the teacher has an opportunity to evaluate teaching procedures with a given group of pupils. In other words, she should have a better understanding of how well the lesson was taught when she is able to hear firsthand the expressions of the children who participated.

Planning Physical Education Lessons

The term "lesson plan" is the name given to a statement of achievements together with the means by which these are to be attained as a result of the physical education activities participated in during a specified amount of time that a group spends with the teacher.

The success of any elementary school physical education program will depend to a large extent upon the daily physical education experiences of children. This implies that lessons in physical education should be carefully planned the same as in other subject matter areas. However, the fact that many classroom teachers look upon physical education as consisting of free play only has detracted from lesson planning on the same basis as in other subject areas where the classroom teacher has the responsibility of teaching.

Physical education lesson planning should take into account those factors that indirectly as well as directly influence the teaching-learning situation. This means that the teacher must consider class organization as a very important factor when daily lessons are planned, because various conditions associated with it can have an indirect influence on the physical education learning situation. For example, it will be desirable for the teacher to effect a plan of class organization that (1) is conducive to carrying out the objectives of the lesson, (2) provides sufficient activity for each child, and (3) provides for efficient and optimum use of available facilities and equipment. After sufficient consideration has been given to ways and means of class organization in developing the physical education lesson, the teacher should take into account the essential characteristic features that directly influence the teaching-learning situation. In this regard it is strongly emphasized that teachers might well devise their own lesson outlines or patterns. This procedure appears to be essential if teachers are to profit by the flexibility that is inherent in a plan that fits their own needs. With this idea in mind, the following lesson-plan outline, indicating some of the features that might be incorporated into a physical education plan, is submitted as a guide for the teacher:

1. *Objectives*: A statement of goals that the teacher would like to see realized during the lesson.
2. *Content*: A statement of the physical education learning experiences in which the class will engage during the lesson.
3. *Class Procedures*: A brief commentary of procedures to be followed in conducting the lesson, such as (a) techniques for initiating interest and relating previous teaching-learning situations to the present lesson, (b) auditory input, (c) visual input, (d) participation, and (e) evaluation.
4. *Teaching Materials:* A statement of essential materials needed for the lesson.

If the teacher is to provide physical education learning experiences that contribute satisfactorily to the broad objectives of elementary education, there must be a clear perspective of the total learning that is expected from the area of physical education. This implies that in order to provide for progression in physical education activities there must be some means of preserving continuity between class periods. Consequently, each individual lesson becomes a link in the chain of physical education learnings that contribute to the total education of the elementary school child. Experience has shown that the implementation of this theory into reality can be most successfully accomplished by wise and careful lesson planning.

Evaluation of a physical education activity after participation is an important aspect of learning.

Chapter 6

Clarification of Terminology Used in Movement and Skills
    Movement Education
    Movement Exploration
    Locomotor Movements
    Axial Movements
Factors Involved in Movement
Movement As a Basis for Physical Education
Skills
Factors Involved in Skill Teaching and Learning
Locomotor Skills
    Walking   Hopping
    Running   Galloping
    Leaping   Skipping
    Jumping   Sliding
Axial Skills
Auxiliary Skills
    Starting   Pivoting
    Stopping   Landing
    Dodging   Falling
Skills of Propulsion and Retrieval
    Throwing
    Striking
    Kicking
    Catching

Basic Movement
and
Fundamental Skills

One of the most important characteristics of life is movement. Whatever else they may involve, all of man's achievements are based upon his ability to move. Obviously, the very young child is not an intelligent being in the sense of abstract thinking, and he only gradually acquires the ability to deal with symbols and intellectualize his experience in the course of his development. On the other hand, the child is a creature of movement and feeling. Any effort to educate the child must take this dominance of movement in the life of the child into account.

For the young child, being able to move as effectively and efficiently as possible is directly related to the proficiency with which he will be able to perform the various fundamental motor skills. In turn, the success that he will have in physical education activities requiring certain motor skills will be dependent upon his proficiency of performance of these skills. Thus, effective and efficient movement is prerequisite to the performance of basic motor skills needed for success in most physical education activities.

The purpose of this chapter will be to help the reader gain an understanding of the following:

1. The terminology used in *movement* and *skills.*
2. The various factors involved in movement.
3. The importance of movement as a basis for physical education.
4. The various factors involved in skill learning.
5. Performance of locomotor skills.
6. Performance of axial skills.

7. Performance of certain auxiliary skills.
8. Performance of skills of propulsion and retrieval.

Clarification of Terminology Used in Movement and Skills

There has been a great deal of confusion in recent years with regard to terminology used in the general area of movement. As a consequence, communication has become something of a problem, not only with persons outside the field of physical education, but within the discipline itself. An attempt will be made here to clarify the meaning of some of the terms used and to make recommendations that may result in better communication.

As far as human motion is concerned, the term *motor* pertains to a muscle, nerve, or center that effects or produces movement. That is, a nerve connecting with a muscle causes the impulse for motion known as *motor impulse*. The term *motion* or *movement* simply means a change in body position. The human organism interacts with its environment through changes in position of the body and/or its segments through movement.

Movement Education

It is difficult to fix an exact date when the term *movement education* was introduced into the United States. However, it appears that this area was beginning to become known in this country in the mid-1950's, having its origin in England. What was eventually to be called "movement education" was introduced to educators in England by Rudolph Laban, an outstanding expert in human movement who had come to England from Germany. Laban's early work involved free and individual exploratory movements particularly pertinent to the dance.

Whether or not one accepts the term *movement education* as a valid one, depends largely upon the philosophy that one has toward human movement generally. For example, if it is the belief that *movement* is the term which is most characteristic of the body of knowledge and subject matter in physical education,* then the term movement education does not appear to be a valid one.

To make an analogy, a majority of psychologists use either of the terms *behavior* or *cognition* as most descriptive of the body of knowledge and subject matter in psychology. However, psychologists would not consider the term *behavior education* or *cognition education*. To be more specific, the educational psychologist tends to identify the term *learning* as best describing the body of knowledge and subject matter in educational psy-

---

*Our surveys of physical educators indicate that a majority subscribe to this notion.

chology. Yet, educational psychologists do not subscribe to the term *learning education*. In any event, according to some authorities,[1] the use of the term *movement education* appears to be waning in favor of the term *basic movement* which seems to have emerged as the accepted terminology which actually identifies the content.

Movement Exploration

Whereas the term *movement education* has been used with reference to content, the term *movement exploration* is said to be concerned with method. The proponents for movement education have tended to consider movement exploration as a method of approaching movement education through a creative problem-solving process. It is questionable, however, if the term *movement exploration* is a valid one when used in this context. Actually, the movement exploration idea is simply the application of a particular principle of learning, rather than a method. This specific principle of learning which is "the child should be given sufficient freedom to create his own responses in the situation he faces," was discussed in the previous chapter. It was mentioned at that time that this principle of learning refutes the idea that there is a specific problem-solving method exclusive of all other methods, and that all methods should involve problem solving.

The movement exploration idea was perhaps derived from the so-called "discovery method," which has been used in elementary school mathematics. The idea of this was that the child arrived at his own solution of a problem in his own way, rather than having to conform to a specific way of arriving at a solution. This idea is fine as long as it is profitable to the child. For example, one child might arrive at the answer of the problem of ten 2's being 20 by adding a column of ten 2's. If this procedure was followed in entirety this particular child would not derive the value of the process of *multiplication* which is, in reality, a shorter method of *addition*. In other words it would be more profitable to him to learn the process of multiplication in arriving at the answer of ten 2's equaling 20.

Some teachers, in attempting to apply movement exploration as a method to movement experiences of children, have actually engaged in malpractice by not fully applying the principle of learning that is implied in so-called movement exploration. This has been brought about by these teachers relying too much on the child discovering his own responses without sufficient teacher guidance. This is to say that in too many instances

[1]Margie R. Hanson, "Developing Creativity Through Physical Education," presented at the Elementary, Kindergarten, Nursery Education Workshop, St. Paul, Minnesota, June 30, 1967.

the child has been left too much on his own to "explore" without the teacher getting into the teaching-learning situation at the proper time to guide and direct learning that results in the most profitable behavior for the child.

Locomotor Movements

Locomotor movements involve changes in body position which propel the body over the surface area with the impetus being given by the feet and legs. There are five basic types of these movements, namely, walking, running, leaping, jumping, and hopping, and three combination movements which are galloping, skipping, and sliding. The first five of these are performed with an even rhythm and the last three are done with an uneven rhythm. When these movements are done with some sort of accompaniment, such as a drum or music, they are ordinarily referred to as fundamental rhythms. In Chapter 8, these movements will be dealt with in detail with respect to their performance to rhythmical accompaniment. The term *locomotor skills,* an area to be discussed in depth later in this chapter, is concerned with the proficiency of performance of these locomotor movements.

Axial Movements

Axial movements, or nonlocomotor movements, refer to bending and stretching and twisting and turning, and the like. As in the case of locomotor skills, the skill performance of axial movements will be discussed in an ensuing section of the chapter.

Axial movements are ordinarily performed with a part of the body remaining as a fixed base to the surface area. However, they can be done with parts of the body or the whole body in gross movement. For example, twisting can be combined with a locomotor movement to avoid being hit in a game such as dodge ball.

Factors Involved in Movement

Generally speaking, in every body movement the following factors should be taken into account:

1. *Time.* Time is concerned with how long it takes to complete a movement. For example, a movement can be slow and deliberate such as a child attempting to create his own body movement to depict a falling snowflake. On the other hand, a movement might be made with sudden quickness such as starting to run for a goal on a signal.

2. *Force.* Force needs to be applied to set the body or one of its segments in motion as well as to change its speed and/or direction. Thus, force is concerned with how much strength is required for movement. Swinging the arm in an axial movement requires less strength than attempting to propel the body over the surface area with a standing broad jump.

3. *Space.* In general, there are two factors concerned with space. These are the amount of space required to perform a particular movement and the utilization of available space. With regard to the latter it has been suggested that young children during nonstructured self-initiated play seem to reveal differences in the quantity of space they use, and that these differences may be associated in important ways with other aspects of the child's development. At least one study tends to support the concept that space utilization of the young child in active play is a relatively stable dimension of his patterned behavior.[2]

4. *Flow.* All movements involve some degree of rhythm in their performance; thus, flow is concerned with sequence of movement involving rhythmic motion.

The above factors are included in all body movements in various degrees. The degree to which each is used effectively in combination will determine the extent to which the movement is performed with skill.

Movement As a Basis for Physical Education

Just as the perception of symbols is concerned with reading readiness, so is basic movement an important factor in readiness to perform in various kinds of physical education activities. Since proficient performance of physical education activities is dependent upon skill of body movement, the ability of the child to move effectively should be readily discerned.

Professor Naomi Allenbaugh, of the Ohio State University, a modern authority in the area of movement, lends considerable support to this notion.[3] She has maintained that sometimes at a very early age a child may discover and use combinations of movements which in reality are (or will eventuate into) specialized motor skills normally used in the complex organization of a game or a dance. In this sense the child is becoming ready for direct skill teaching and learning. With proper teacher guidance the basic movements that he has developed on his own can be improved in terms of proper principles of body mechanics and commensurate with his natural ability. The important factor is that in the early stages the child

[2]Frederick A. Mulhauser, "Relationships of Space Utilization by Children with Selected Aspects of Behavior," *Research Quarterly,* March 1972.
[3]Naomi Allenbaugh, "Learning About Movement," *NEA Journal,* March 1967.

has been made to feel comfortable with the way he moves and thus be in a better position to learn correct performance of skills.

Skills

It was mentioned previously that skill is concerned with the degree of proficiency with which a given body movement is performed. This is to say that skills are concerned with the scientific way to move the body and/or its segments in such a way as to expend a minimum of energy requirement, but achieve maximum results. One prominent neurophysiologist[4] has suggested that skill is the putting together of simple natural movements, of which we have only about two hundred, in unusual or complex combinations to achieve a given objective. Performance of specific skills has been arrived at by scientific insight from such fields as anatomy and kinesiology which suggest to us how the body can move to achieve maximum efficiency.

Other things being equal, the degree of proficient performance of a skill by any individual is directly related to his innate capacity. That is, each individual is endowed with a certain amount of native ability. Through such factors as good teaching, motivation, and the like, attempts are made to help the child perform to the best of his particular ability, or to attain his highest *skill level.*

Factors Involved in Skill Teaching and Learning

Because of the importance of the development of certain kinds of motor skills for best performance in physical education activities, one would think that this area of teaching in physical education would receive a great amount of attention. On the contrary, the teaching of physical education skills is one of the most neglected phases of the entire elementary school physical education program. This is indeed a paradoxical situation because the successful performance and resultant enjoyment received from a physical education activity depends in a large measure upon how well the child can perform the elements involved. Yet at a time in the child's life that is ideal for learning physical education motor skills, we find that in far too many instances this important phase is left almost entirely to chance.

---

[4]Elizabeth B. Gardner, "The Neuromuscular Base of Human Movement: Feedback Mechanisms," *Journal of Health, Physical Education, and Recreation,* October 1965.

Although each child is born with a certain potential capacity, teachers should not subscribe to the notion that skills are a part of the child's inheritance. Physical education skills must be learned. In order that a child can participate satisfactorily with his peers, he must be given the opportunity to learn the skills under careful guidance of competent teachers.

The elementary school has long been considered the educational segment in an individual's life that provides the best opportunity for a solid educational foundation. The need for the development of basic skills in reading, writing, and arithmetic has seldom been challenged as an essential purpose of the elementary school. Why, then, should there be a neglect of such an important aspect of learning as that existing in the development of physical education motor skill?

It was previously mentioned that perhaps the ideal time to learn motor skills is in childhood. The muscular pliability of the elementary school-age child is such that there is a desirable setting for the acquisition of various kinds of motor skills. He is at a stage in life when he has a great deal of time for practice—a most important factor because he needs practice in order to learn—and at this age level he does not seem to become weary of repeating the same thing over and over again. In addition, the elementary school-age child has a limited number of established skills to obstruct the learning of new skills. Skill learning therefore should be facilitated, provided competent teaching in the area of physical education motor skills is available. There should be little or no future problem of "unlearning" skills that the child might have had to learn incorrectly "on his own."

Experimental research on the influence of specific instruction on various kinds of physical education motor skills is somewhat limited. More and more scientific evidence is being accumulated, however, which appears to indicate that children in the early elementary years are mature enough to benefit by instruction in such skills as throwing and jumping. Unfortunately this type of instruction is lacking in far too many elementary school physical education programs.

Following are some suggested guidelines that teachers might take into account in the teaching of skills:

1. The teacher should become familiar with the skills involved in the various physical education activities. This means that it will be necessary for the teacher to analyze each activity to determine the extent of the skill requirements.

2. In considering the teaching of physical education skills, the teacher should recognize that skills include the following three components: (a) preparing for the movement, (b) executing the movement, and (c) follow-

ing through. For example, in throwing a ball the individual prepares for the movement by assuming the proper position to throw; he completes the actual throwing of the ball; and finally there is a follow-through action of the arm after the ball leaves his hand. All of these elements are essential to satisfactory performance of this particular skill.

3. The skill should be taught correctly from the beginning; otherwise children may have to do a considerable amount of "unlearning" at a later stage of development.

4. When an error in skill performance is observed, it should be corrected immediately. This can be done under the guidance of the teacher by evaluating the child's performance with him. Correction of errors in skill performance is essential, first because continued repetition may formulate the faulty practice into a habit, and second because the child will have less difficulty learning more complex skills if he has previously learned easier skills correctly. Teachers should recognize that while there are general patterns for the best performance of skills, individual differences must be considered. This implies that a child should be permitted to deviate from a standard if he is able to perform a skill satisfactorily in a manner peculiar to his individual abilities.

5. The greatest amount of time should be spent on skill learning that involves immediate application. In other words, the child should have use for the physical education skills being taught so that he can properly apply them commensurate with his stage of development.

6. There is some indication that rhythmic accompaniment is important in the learning of skills. Although evidence is not definitive and clear cut, various studies tend to support this contention. For example, it was found in one study on the development of selected sport skills at the fifth-grade level, that a conventional method of instruction supplemented by rhythmic accompaniment was superior to the conventional method without such accompaniment.[5]

Locomotor Skills

In the previous discussion of locomotor movements it was indicated that the proficiency of performance of these movements concerns the degree of skill involved in the execution of such movements. Thus, the term "locomotor skills" requires a certain amount of strength and the development of the important sensory-motor mechanics that are concerned with

---

[5]Donald M. Megale, "Rhythmic Accompaniment as a Teaching Aid in the Development of Elementary School Sport Skills," *Research Abstracts*, American Association for Health, Physical Education, and Recreation, Washington, D.C., 1972.

balance. They also require various degrees of neuromotor coordination for
proficient performance.

All of the locomotor skills should be learned by the elementary school
child. The reason for this is that these skills comprise the basic requirements for proficiency of performance in the activities contained in a well-
planned physical education program. Teachers should have certain basic
knowledge about the locomotor skills so that they will be alert to improve
performance of these skills. The following generalized information is intended for this purpose.

Walking

Walking is the child's first experience with bipedal locomotion. He
starts out to propel himself over the surface area with uneven full sole
steps (flatfootedness). He is generally referred to as a "toddler," a term
which is perhaps derived from the word "tottering." He appears to be tottering to keep in an upright position which is indicative of the problems he
is having with balance and the force of gravity. At about four years of age,
on the average, the child's pattern of walking approximates that of an
adult.

Ordinarily, when the child is learning to walk, his only teachers are his
family members. Because of this he is not likely to benefit from instruction
on correct procedure. As a result, the very important aspect of foot position
is overlooked. Possibly because of this many children enter school walking
in the "toeing out" position rather than pointing the toes straight ahead.
Poor walking habits, if allowed to persist, can place undue amounts of
strain on certain body parts which in turn can contribute to lack of proficiency in body movement.

Walking involves transferring the weight from one foot to the other.
The walk is started with a push-off backward against the surface area with
the ball and toes of the foot. After this initial movement the leg swings
forward from the hip, the heel of the other foot is placed down, the outer
half of the foot next, and then the next push-off is made with toes pointing straight ahead. Walking is used in such physical education activities
as walking to rhythmical accompaniment, combining the walk with other
movements in various dance activities, walking about in singing games,
and walking around a circle preparatory to the start of a circle game activity.

Running

At about 18 months of age the average child develops a movement that
appears to be in between a walk and a run. This is to say that the walking

pattern is accelerated but does not approximate running form. Usually, it is not before age five or six that the child's running form becomes like that used by an adult. As the child gets older he is able to increase his speed of running as well as to be able to run greater distances.

As in the case of walking, running involves transferring the weight from one foot to the other, but the rate of speed is increased. The ball of the foot touches the surface area first and the toes point straight ahead. The body is momentarily suspended in the air when there is no contact with the surface area. This differs from the walk in which contact with either foot is always maintained with the surface area. In the run there is more flexion at the knee which involves a higher leg lift. There is also a higher arm lift with flexion at the elbow reaching a point of about a right angle. In running there is more of a forward body lean than in walking and in both cases the head points straight ahead. In many instances the child who has not been taught to run correctly will violate certain mechanical principles by having a backward rather than forward lean, by carrying the arms too high, and by turning the head to the side rather than looking straight ahead. The teacher should be alert to correct these violations.

Running is probably the most used of all of the locomotor skills in physical education, particularly as far as most game activities are concerned.

Leaping

Leaping, like walking and running, is performed with an even rhythm, and is like a slow run with one essential difference. That is, the push-off is up and then forward, with the feeling of suspension "up and over." The landing should be on the ball of the foot with sufficient flexion at the knee to absorb the shock.

Although leaping is not used frequently as such as a specific locomotor skill in many physical education activities, there are certain reasons why it is important that children become proficient in this skill. For example, the leap can be combined with the run to leap over an object so as not to deviate from the running pattern. In addition, in retrieving a ball that has been thrown or hit high, a leap for the ball can help the child catch it "on the run" and thus continue with the running pattern, rather than having to stop his movement.

Specific uses of leaping consist of its performance by children in creative rhythms where they move like the music makes them feel like moving, or in the case of a game like "Leap the Brook," where the object is to leap over an area while gradually increasing the distance.

Jumping

In a sense, jumping is somewhat like walking and running as far as a movement pattern is concerned. However, jumping requires elevation of the body off the surface area and thus more strength is needed to apply force for this purpose. Usually, the child's first experience with a movement approximating jumping occurs when he steps from a higher to a lower level as in the case of going downstairs. Although there are many variations in the jumping performance of children, generally speaking, they tend to improve their performance as they get older, with improvement tending to be more pronounced for boys than for girls.

Jumping is accomplished by pushing off with both feet and landing on both feet, or pushing off with one foot and landing on both feet. Since absorption of shock is important in the jump, the landing should be with flexed knees and on the balls of the feet.

Games such as basketball and volleyball require skill in jumping for success in such activities. The jump becomes a complete self-testing activity in itself when children compete against their own performance in individual jumping. This can be done with the standing broad jump (taking off and landing on both feet) or the long jump (running to a point and taking off on one foot and landing on both feet).

Hopping

While hopping is the least difficult of the *even* rhythmic locomotor skills to describe, at the same time it is perhaps the most difficult to execute. Hopping involves taking off and landing on the same foot. Thus, hopping is a more complex aspect of the jump because the body is elevated from the surface area by the action of only one foot. Not only is greater strength needed for the hop, but also a more refined adjustment of balance is required because of the smaller base of support.

Hopping, as such, is not used frequently as a specific skill in many physical education activities. Exceptions include such dance steps as the schottische which involves a pattern of "step-step-step-hop-step-hop-step-hop," or the hopping relay in which children hop to a point on one foot and return on the other foot. In addition, it should be obvious that such games as hopscotch require skill in the ability to hop.

Even though hopping is not a specific skill used in most physical education activities, one of the more important reasons why children should become proficient in this locomotor skill is that it can help them regain balance in any kind of activity where they have temporarily "lost their footing." When this occurs, the child can use the hop to keep his balance and remain in an upright position while getting the temporarily incapacitated foot into action.

Galloping

The skill of galloping is a combination of the basic patterns of walking and leaping and is performed with a uneven rhythm. Since an uneven rhythmic movement requires more neuromotor coordination, the ability to gallop is developed later than those locomotor movements requiring an even rhythm. The child is likely to learn to gallop before he learns to skip and about one-half of the children are able to perform a galloping movement by about the age of four. Between the ages of 6 and 7 most children can perform this movement.

Galloping can be explained by pretending that one foot is injured. A step is taken with the lead foot, but the "injured" foot can bear very little weight and is brought up only behind the other one and not beyond it. A transfer of weight is made to the lead foot, and thus a fast limp is really a gallop.

Galloping is a skill that does not have prevalent use as a specific skill in most physical education activities. One very important exception is its use as a fundamental rhythm when the children become "galloping horses" to appropriate rhythmical accompaniment. One of the most important factors about learning how to gallop is that it helps children to be able to change direction in a forward or backward plane more easily. Backward galloping can be done by starting with the lead foot to the back. If a child is proficient in galloping, he will likely be more successful in game activities that require a forward and/or backward movement for successful performance in that particular activity.

Skipping

Although skipping requires more coordination than galloping, some children will perform variations of the skip around four years of age. With proper instruction a majority of children should be able to accomplish this movement by age six.

Skipping can be taught from the walk. A strong push-off should be emphasized. The push-off should be such a forceful upward one that the foot leaves the surface area. In order to maintain balance a hop is taken. The sequence is step, push-off high, hop. The hop occurs on the same foot that was pushing off, and this is the skip. The two actions cause it to be uneven as to rhythm, with a strong or long action (step) and a short one (hop).

The skill of skipping is rarely used as a specific locomotor skill in many physical education activities. It does find limited use, however, as a fundamental rhythm when children skip to a musical accompaniment, when used in certain singing games and dances, and when skipping around a circle preparatory to the start of certain circle games.

Sliding

Sliding is much the same as the gallop, but movement is in a sideward direction. One foot is drawn up to the lead foot; weight is shifted from the lead foot to the drawing foot and back again. As in the case with the other locomotor skills that are uneven in rhythm, sliding is not used frequently as a specific skill in most physical education activities. The one main exception is its use in many of the social or ballroom dance patterns.

The important feature of gaining proficiency in the skill of sliding is that it helps the child to be able to change direction skillfully in a lateral plane. Many games involving guarding an opponent such as in basektball require skill in sliding for success in the game. When a child has developed the skill of sliding from side to side he does not have to cross his feet and thus can change direction laterally much more rapidly.

Axial Skills

It was mentioned previously that axial movements are nonlocomotor in nature. They can be performed with some parts of the body remaining in contact with the surface area or the body as a whole in gross movement. Included among the axial skills are swinging, bending, stretching, pulling, pushing, and the rotation movements of turning and twisting.

Each of these movements is required at one time or another in the performance of practically all physical education activities. Proficiency of performance of the axial skills will improve performance in locomotor skills; for example, the importance of arm swinging in running. When children can perform the axial skills with grace and facility there is a minimum expenditure of energy and better performance results.

The axial skills can be practiced independently particularly as a part of creative rhythms such as arms *swinging* like trees in a breeze or *stretching* tall to "grow" like a flower.

Auxiliary Skills

There are certain skills that are not ordinarily classified as either locomotor or axial. However, they are most important in the successful performance of most physical education activities. These skills are arbitrarily identified here as *auxiliary skills*. Among some of the more important of this type of skill are: starting, stopping, dodging, pivoting, falling, and landing.

Starting

In games that require responding to a stimulus such as running to a goal on the word "go," a quick start is an important contribution to success. How well a child will be able to "start" depends upon his reaction time and speed of movement. Reaction time is the amount of time that it takes from the time a signal is given until the initial movement. Speed of movement is concerned with how fast a person completes the initial movement. Although the factors concerned with starting are innate, they improve with age and they can be improved with practice. When a teacher observes children as being "slow starters," additional help should be given to improve this skill.

Stopping

The skill of stopping is very important because all locomotor movements culminate with this skill. Numerous game activities require quick stopping for successful performance.

The two ways of stopping are the *stride* stop and the *skip* stop. The stride stop involves stopping in running stride. There is flexion at the knees and there is a slight backward lean to maintain balance. This method of stopping can be used when the performer is moving at slow speed. The skip stop should be used when there is fast movement and the performer needs to come to a quick stop. This is accomplished with a hop on either foot with the other foot making contact with the surface area almost simultaneously. Because of the latter movement, this method of stopping is sometimes called the *jump* stop because it appears that the performer is landing on both feet.

Starting and stopping can be practiced in a game situation with the game "Start and Stop." In this game the children are in a straight line with the teacher at a goal line some distance away. The teacher calls "Start" and on this signal all children run forward. The teacher calls "Stop!" and anyone moving after the signal must return to the starting line. This procedure is continued until one or more children have reached the goal line. The teacher should be alert to detect starting and stopping form.

Dodging

Dodging involves changing body direction while running. The knees are bent, and the weight is transferred in the dodging direction. This movement is sometimes referred to as "veering" or "weaving." After a dodge is made, the performer can continue in the different direction with a push-off from the surface area with the foot to which the weight was previously transferred.

The importance of skill in dodging is seen in game activities where getting away from an opponent (tag games) or an object (dodge ball) is concerned.

Pivoting

Whereas dodging is used to change direction during body movement, pivoting is employed to change direction while the body is stationary. One foot is kept in contact with the surface area, while the other foot is used to push off. A turn is made in the desired direction with the weight on the foot that has maintained contact with the surface area. The angle of the pivot (turn) is determined by the need in the particular situation. This angle is seldom over 180 degrees as might be the case in pivoting away from an opponent in basketball.

Theoretically, the pivot is executed on only one foot; however, a *reverse turn* is sometimes referred to as a "two-foot" pivot. In this case a complete turn to the opposite direction is made with both feet on the surface area. With one foot ahead of the other, the heels are raised and a turn is made with the weight equally distributed on both feet.

Pivoting is important in the performance of many kinds of physical education activities such as various forms of dance, and game activities where quick movements are necessary while the body remains stationary. This is particularly true in games like basketball and speedball where a limited number of steps can be taken while in possession of the ball.

Landing

Landing is concerned with the body coming to the surface area from a height or distance. Absorption when landing is accomplished by bending the knees. The weight is on the balls of the feet and there is flexion at the ankle and knee joints. After landing, the performer comes to an upright position with the arms in a sideward position so as to keep the body in balance.

Many game activities such as basketball, volleyball, and touch football require the performer to leave the surface area which makes the skill of landing important. In addition, vaulting over objects in apparatus activities requires skill in landing, not only for good performance, but for safety as well.

Falling

In those activities that require keeping in an upright position, emphasis, of course, should be on maintaining this position. Nevertheless, there are occasions when a performer loses balance and falls to the surface area. Whenever possible, a fall should be taken in such a way that injury is least likely to occur. One way to accomplish this is to attempt to "break the fall" with the hands. Relaxation and flexion at the joints that put the performer in a "bunched" position are helpful in avoiding injury when falling to the surface area. Practice in the correct ways to make contact with the surface area when falling can take place in connection with the various rolls in tumbling activities.

Skills of Propulsion and Retrieval

Skills which involve propelling and retrieving objects, in most cases a ball,* are used in many types of game activities. It will be the purpose of the ensuing sections of this chapter to provide the reader with knowledge which is important to an understanding of such propelling and retrieving skills as throwing, striking, kicking, and catching.

Throwing

The skill of throwing involves the release of a ball with one or both hands. In general, there are three factors concerned with success in throwing. These are the accuracy or direction of the throw, the distance which a ball must be thrown, and the amount of force needed to propel the ball.

Any release of an object from the hand or hands could be considered as an act of throwing. Thought of in these terms, the average infant of six months is able to perform a reasonable facsimile of throwing from a sitting position. It has been estimated that by four years age, about twenty percent of the children show at least a degree of proficiency in throwing. This ability tends to increase rapidly, and between the ages of five and six, over three-fourths of the children have attained a reasonable degree of proficiency as previously defined here.

Sex differences in the early throwing behavior of children tend to favor boys. At all age levels boys are generally superior to girls in throwing for distance. There is not such a pronounced sex difference in throwing for accuracy, although the performance of boys in this aspect tends to exceed that of girls.

*Hereafter in this discussion the object retrieved or propelled will be referred to as "the ball."

There are three generally accepted throwing *patterns*. These are the (1) underarm pattern; (2) sidearm pattern; and (3) overarm pattern. It should be noted that although the ball is released by one or both hands, the term "arm" is used in connection with the various patterns. The reason for this is that the patterns involve a "swing" of the arm.

Underarm Throwing Pattern

The child ordinarily begins the underarm throwing pattern by releaseing the ball from both hands. However, he is soon able to release with one hand, especially when the ball is small enough for him to grip.

At the starting position the thrower stands facing in the direction of the throw. The feet should be in a parallel position and slightly apart. The right arm* is in a position nearly perpendicular to the surface area. To start the throw, the right arm is brought back (back swing) to a position where it is about parallel with the surface area. Simultaneously, there is slight rotation of the body to the right with most of the weight transferred to the right foot. As the arm comes forward (front swing) a step is taken with the left foot. (Stepping out with the opposite foot of the swinging arm is known as the *principle of opposition*.) The ball is released on the front swing when the arm is about parallel with the surface area. During the process of the arm swing, the arm is straight, prescribing a semicircle with no flexion at the elbow. The right foot is carried forward as a part of the follow-through after the release.

The underarm throwing pattern is used in bowling, and in games that involve passing the ball from one person to another over a short distance. It is also used for pitching in the game of softball.

Sidearm Throwing Pattern

Aside from the direction the thrower faces and the plane of the arm swing, the mechanical principles applied in the sidearm throwing pattern are essentially the same as the underarm throwing pattern.

The thrower faces at a right angle to the direction of the throw, whereas in the underarm throwing pattern he faces in the direction of the throw. The arm is brought to the backswing in a horizontal plane, or a position parallel to the surface area. Body rotation and weight shift is the same as in the underarm pattern. The arm remains straight and a semicircle is prescribed from the backswing to the release of the ball on the front swing.

---

*All of the descriptions involving the skills of propulsion and retrieval are for a right-handed child. In the case of the left-handed child, just the opposite should apply.

The sidearm throwing pattern will ordinarily be used to propel a ball that is too large to grip with one hand. Thus, on the backswing the opposite hand helps to control the ball until there is sufficient momentum during the swing. Greater distance can be obtained with the sidearm throwing pattern with a ball too large to grip, but accuracy is more difficult to achieve.

Overarm Throwing Pattern

Again the basic body mechanics of the overarm throwing pattern are essentially the same as the two previous patterns. The thrower faces in the same direction as for the sidearm throwing pattern; that is, at a right angle to the direction of the throw. An essential difference in the overarm throwing pattern is in the position of the arm. Whereas in the two previous patterns the arm was kept straight, in the overarm throwing pattern there is flexion at the elbow. Thus, on the backswing the arm is brought back with the elbow bent and with the arm at a right angle away from the body. The arm is then brought forward and the ball is released with a "whiplike" motion at about the height of the shoulder. Foot and arm follow-through is the same as with the underarm and sidearm throwing patterns. This pattern is used for throwing a ball that can be gripped with the fingers in games such as softball where distance as well as accuracy are important.

Striking

Striking involves propelling a ball with a part of the body, ordinarily the hand, as in handball, or with an implement such as a bat in softball. The object to be struck can be stationary (as batting a ball from a batting tee) or moving (as batting a pitched ball in softball).

Some motor development specialists have identified a reasonable facsimile of striking in infancy associated with angry children throwing "nothing" at each other or an adult.[6]

There is some evidence to support the notion that as early as the age of three, verbal direction to the child will educe a sidearm striking pattern with a plastic paddle when a tennis ball is suspended in a stationary position at about waist high. In addition, it has been found that at age three the child will have a degree of success with the sidearm throwing pattern in striking a light ball when tossed slowly to him.[7]

[6]Anna S. Espenschade and Helen M. Eckert, *Motor Development* (Columbus, Ohio: Charles E. Merrill Books, Inc., 1967).

[7]Lolas E. Halverson and Mary Ann Robertson, "Motor Pattern Development in Young Children," *Research Abstracts,* American Association for Health, Physical Education, and Recreation, Washington, D.C., 1966.

As far as principles of body mechanics are concerned, striking patterns are essentially the same as the three previously mentioned throwing patterns, that is, underarm, sidearm, and overarm. The same movements are applied, but in order to propel an object by striking, greater speed is needed with the striking movement. For example, greater speed of movement is needed in the underarm striking pattern when serving a volleyball than in releasing a ball with a short toss in the underarm throw.

Kicking

Kicking involves propelling a ball with either foot. As early as age two the average child is able to maintain his balance on one foot and propel a stationary ball with the other foot. At this early stage the child is likely to have limited action of the kicking foot with little or no follow-through. With advancing age, better balance is maintained and with greater increments of strength, by age six the child can develop a full leg backswing and a body lean into the kick with a stationary ball.

In kicking, contact with the ball is made with the (1) inside of the foot, (2) outside of the foot, or (3) with the instep of the foot. With the exception of these positions of the foot the mechanical principles of kicking are essentially the same. The kicking leg is swung back with flexion at the knee. The leg swings forward with the foot making contact with the ball. As in the case of the skill of striking, contact with the ball in kicking can be made when the ball is either stationary or moving.

There is not complete agreement in terms of progression in the skill of kicking. The following sequence is recommended by the present author:

1. *Stationary.* The ball and the kicker remain stationary. That is, the kicker stands beside the ball and kicks it. The kicker is concerned only with the leg movement and it is more likely that he will keep his head down with his eyes on the ball at the point of contact.

2. *Stationary and run.* This means that the ball is in a stationary position and that the kicker takes a short run up to the ball before kicking it. This is more difficult as the kicker must time and coordinate his run to make proper contact with the ball.

3. *Kick from hands.* This is referred to as "punting" as in football, soccer, and speedball. The ball is dropped from the hands of the kicker and he takes one or two steps and kicks the ball as it drops. He is kicking a moving ball but he has control over the movement of the ball before kicking it.

4. *Kicking from a pitcher.* This means that another person pitches or rolls the ball to the kicker as in the game of kickball. This is perhaps the

most difficult kick because the kicker must kick a moving ball that is under the control of another person.

Catching

Catching with the hands is the most frequently used retrieving skill although, as previously mentioned, a ball can be retrieved with the feet as in "trapping" the ball in soccer.

One of the child's first experiences with catching occurs at an early stage in life when he sits with his legs in a spread position and another person rolls a ball to him. By four years of age about one-third of the children can retrieve a ball in aerial flight thrown from a short distance. Slightly over half of them can perform this feat by age five, and about two-thirds of them can accomplish this by age six.

Generally speaking, it has been observed that children achieve the same skill level sooner in catching with a larger ball than they do with a smaller ball. However, the reason for this may lie in the way the child tries to catch the ball, as suggested in a study by Victors.[8] She selected 20 boys for inclusion in a cinematography study. On the basis of a predetermined catching performance score and the subjective ranking of the physical education teacher, the five most successful and the five least successful boys were selected from each level. Each child was filmed during four consecutive catching attempts, two with a three-inch and two with a ten-inch ball. It was found that ball size did not generally differentiate between success and failure in catching. Size of ball, however, did make a difference in the type of catch utilized by the children. The arms and body were used more frequently with the larger ball, resulting in a "basket catch." There was evidence of more hand closure success with the smaller ball.

In recent years studies have been conducted in an attempt to determine effects of velocity, projective angle, and time of ball in flight. One such study by Bruce[9] using second-fourth-and sixth-grade boys and girls indicated that catching performance improved with grade level; that boys were superior to girls in catching performance; that younger, lesser skilled children showed poorer performance as ball velocity increased; and that changes in vertical angle of projection had little effect on catching per-

[8]Evelyn Victors "A Cinematography Study of the Catching Behavior of Selected Nine and Ten Year Old Boys," Ph.D. dissertation, University of Wisconsin, Madison, Wisconsin, 1968.

[9]Russell D. Bruce, "The Effects of Variations in Ball Trajectory Upon the Catching Performance of Elementary School Children," Ph.D. dissertation, University of Wisconsin, Madison, Wisconsin, 1966.

formance. It was further indicated that variation in time of ball flight had no significant effect on catching performance.

There are certain basic mechanical principles that should be taken into account in the skill of catching. It is of utmost importance that the catcher position himself as nearly "in line" with the ball as possible. In this position he will be better able to receive the ball near the center of gravity of the body. Another important factor is hand position. A ball will approach the catcher (1) at the waist, (2) above the waist, or (3) below the waist. When the ball approaches at about waist level, the palms should be facing each other with fingers pointing straight ahead. The "heels" of the hands should be close together depending upon the size of the ball. That is, closer together for a small ball and farther apart for a large ball. When the ball approaches above the waist the palms face the ball and the fingers point upward with the thumbs as close together as necessary. When the ball approaches below the waist the palms still face the ball but the fingers point downward with the little fingers as close together as seems necessary, depending again upon the size of the ball. When the ball reaches the hands it is brought in toward the body. That is, the catcher "gives" with the catch in order to control the ball and absorb the shock. The position of the feet will likely depend upon the speed with which the ball approaches. Ordinarily, one foot should be in advance of the other in a stride position, with the distance determined by the speed of the approaching ball.

Chapter 7

Game Activities

For purposes of discussion in this chapter, we will consider games as *active interactions of children in competitive and/or cooperative situations.* This description of games places emphasis on *active* games as opposed to those that are *passive* in nature. This is to say that games in physical education are concerned with a total or near total physical response of children as they interact with each other.

Games not only play a very important part in the school program but in society in general. The unique quality of games and their application to situations in everyday living have become a part of various colloquial expressions. In many instances descriptive word phrases from games have become part of daily vocabulary and appear frequently in news articles and other written material. These words and phrases are used to describe a situation that is so familiar in a game situation that they give a clear meaning to an event from real life.

Many of us have used, at one time or another, the expression "that's the way the ball bounces" to refer to a situation in which the outcome was not as desirable as was anticipated. Or, "that's par for the course," meaning that the difficulty was anticipated and the results were no better or no worse than expected. When we are "home free" we tend to refer to having gotten out of a tight situation, with results better than expected. The expression "the bases are loaded" describes a situation in which a critical point has been reached and there is much at stake on the next event or series of events. If you have "two strikes against you," you are operating at a grave disadvantage, and if someone "strikes out," he has failed.[1]

[1]James H. Humphrey and Anne Gayle Ingram, *Introduction to Physical Education for College Students* (Boston: Holbrook Press, 1969), p. 56.

It is interesting to consider how the game preferences of a particular country give insight into their culture, and this has been an important area of study and research by sociologists in recent years. The national games, the popular games, and the historical games in which the people of a nation engage provide insight into their culture. They are as much a cultural expression as their books, theater, and art.

The value of games as an important intellectual influence in the school program has been recognized for decades. For example, as far back as 1909, Bancroft observed that as a child's perceptions are quickened, he sees more quickly that the ball is coming toward him, that he is in danger of being tagged, or that it is his turn; he hears the footsteps behind him, or his name or number called; he feels the touch on the shoulder; or in innumerable other ways he is aroused to quick and direct recognition of, and response to, things that go on around him.[2]

The physiological value of games has often been extolled because of the vigorous physical nature of many game activities in which children participate. And in more recent years a great deal of credence has been put in the potentialities for modifying human behavior within a social frame of reference which many games tend to provide. For instance, it has been suggested that the game is probably the child's first social relationship with strangers and his first testing of self against others.[3]

It is a well-known fact that there exists literally scores of sources regarding games and their suitable use for children of elementary school age. Obviously, it would be impossible to deal with all the facets of active games in a single chapter. However, the major purpose of this chapter will be to provide at least an overview of the following information for the reader:

1. An insight into the various types of game classifications.
2. An understanding of some of the factors involved in the organization of game activities.
3. An idea of some progressive sequences for game activities.
4. Some suggested teaching procedures for games.
5. Some representative examples of games suitable for use with elementary school children.

Competition and Cooperation in Games

It should be recalled that our description of active games previously given took into account both cooperative and competitive situations. In

---

[2]Jessie H. Bancroft, *Games* (New York: The Macmillan Company, 1909).
[3]Eli M. Bower, "Play's the Thing" *Today's Education NEA Journal,* September 1968.

view of the fact that there has been a considerable amount of interest in competitive activities for children of elementary school age, it seems appropriate that we discuss this, particularly as it relates to games.

It is interesting to note that the terms *cooperation* and *competition* are antonymous; therefore the reconciliation of children's competitive needs and cooperative needs is not an easy matter. In a sense we are confronted with an ambivalent condition which, if not carefully handled, could place children in a state of conflict. Horney recognized this many years ago when she indicated that on the one hand everything is done to spur us toward success, which means that we must not only be assertive but aggressive, able to push others out of the way. On the other hand, we are deeply inbued with ideals which declare that it is selfish to want anything for ourselves, that we should be humble, turn the other hand, be yielding.[4] Thus, modern society not only rewards one kind of behavior (cooperation) but its direct opposite (competition). Perhaps more often than not our cultural demands sanction these rewards without provision of clear-cut standards of value with regard to specific conditions under which these forms of behavior might well be practiced. Hence, the child is placed in somewhat of a quandary as to when to compete and when to cooperate.

In generalizing on the basis of the available evidence with regard to the subject of competition, it seems justifiable to formulate the following concepts:

1. Very young children in general are not very competitive but become more so as they grow older.
2. There is a wide variety in competition among children; that is, some are violently competitive, while others are mildly competitive, and still others are not competitive at all.
3. Boys tend to be more competitive than girls.
4. Competition should be adjusted so that there is not a preponderant number of winners over losers.
5. Competition and rivalry produce results in effort and speed of accomplishment.

In the elementary school physical education teaching-learning situation teachers might well be guided by the above concepts. As far as active games are concerned they are not only a good medium for the various aspects of growth and development of children but, under the guidance of skillfull teachers, they can also provide for competitive needs of children in a pleasurable and enjoyable way.

[4]Karen Horney, *The Neurotic Personality of Our Times* (New York: W. W. Norton & Company, Inc., 1937).

Classification of Games

Within the broad category of active games there are various ways in which these activities might be classified. Ordinarily, game classifications center around certain constant elements which are inherent in the games in a given classification, Among others, some of these elements include organization, contest mode, formation, materials, function, place, and type. It should be borne in mind that precise classification is most difficult and that there is likely to be unavoidable overlapping from one classification to another.

Organization

In classifying games by organization, it is a standard practice to consider two broad classifications—*low* organization and *high* organization. Games of low organization are those with a few simple rules and they do not require a high level of skill. On the contrary, games of high organization have definite and fixed rules. Highly organized games ordinarily require well-developed skill in their performance as well as the use of various kinds of tactics and strategy in playing the game.

Contest Mode

Contest mode refers to how the game is organized as far as individual participants are concerned. Included in this type of classification are team games, individual sports and games, and the like.

Formation

Games classified by formation pertain to the kind of alignment necessary for playing the game. For example, among others there may be a circle formation, line formation, or file formation.

Materials

A broad classification of games in the use of materials would be those requiring the use of equipment and those not requiring it. A more specific classification in terms of materials would be ball games, net games, and the like.

Function

This classification refers to body function and more specifically to body skills, such as running, throwing, and striking games.

Place

The two broad classifications as far as place is concerned are indoor and outdoor games. More specific classifications would take into account such kinds as playground games, gymnasium games, and classroom games.

Type

Examples of classification of games by type are the dodge ball type where the objective is to strike another with an object and for the opponent to dodge the object, and the baseball type played on a facsimile of a baseball diamond with a home base and one or more other bases.

Recently the author examined over 100 pieces of literature published over a thirty-year period which pertained to games and their classifications. This information yielded the following classifications:

1. Active games
2. Athletic-type games
3. Ball games
4. Catching-throwing games
5. Catching-throwing-kicking games
6. Chasing and fleeing games
7. Circle games
8. Classroom games
9. Combative games
10. Competitive games
11. Constructed games
12. Dual games
13. Games of imitation
14. Games of pursuit
15. Goal games
16. Highly organized games
17. Hunting games
18. Individual games
19. Indoor games
20. It games
21. Jumping-hopping games
22. Kicking games
23. Large group games
24. Lead-up games
25. Limited area games
26. Lowly organized games
27. Mass games
28. Net games
29. Outdoor games
30. Playground games
31. Play party games
32. Relay games
33. Sensory games
34. Sidewalk games
35. Singing games
36. Small group games
37. Snow and ice games
38. Tag games
39. Team games
40. Water games

The above information should give the reader an idea of the various possibilities as far as classification of games is concerned. It is recommended that if teachers wish to do so, they might consider devising their own system of classification compatible with their own individual needs.

Organization of Game Activities

The benefits that can be derived from participation in game activities are more likely to accure when these activities are properly organized. The following discussions will focus upon general organization, signaling, scoring, organization of classroom games, and organization of relays.*

General Organization

Many games begin from certain standard formations which include circles, lines, and files. In a *circle* formation children ordinarily stand facing inward toward the center. The teacher should be a part of the circle rather than in the center of it so as to be able to see and be seen by all children. Forming a circle of young children for the first time can be done by the teacher taking the hand of one child and then each child in turn taking the hand of another. The teacher can "circle around" and take the hand of the last child to form the circle. After the children understand the concept of a circle the teacher can ordinarily just simply tell them to arrange themselves in a circle. Circles may be made larger by each child taking a specified number of steps backward, and smaller by taking steps forward.

In some cases games played from a circle formation have been much maligned on the basis that there is too much inactivity of children just standing in a circle. It is doubtful if such criticism is entirely justified because the skillful teacher can conduct this type of activity in such a way that there will be equal opportunity for participation. Teachers should guard against having a circle too large in those kinds of games that involve only two children as principal performers at one time. Small circles afford many more turns.

Some teachers feel that the circle formation has a positive psychological effect in that it tends to provide a spirit of unity among the participants. That is, each player can see and become aware of the performance of other players in the group. An example of a circle game is Ball Pass (page 122).

In a *line* formation the children stand side by side to form the line. When they have learned the idea of a line the teacher can get them into this formation by merely telling them to make as many lines as are needed after the class has been divided into the appropriate number of groups for a given activity. Hill Dill (page 124) is an example of a game which begins from a line formation.

---

*Some individuals prefer to have a separate broad category of *relays,* while others refer to these activities as *relay games.* In this discussion relays are considered as games and are classified as such.

The children stand one behind the other in one or more columns to form a *file* formation. Most relays are performed from this formation.

In any kind of formation the teacher should be alert to a lack of interest on the part of the participants. This is usually observed when some children are not afforded the opportunity to participate because of too large a number of players. This situation can be avoided to a certain extent by such practices as having several runners and/or chasers rather than just one, and putting more than one ball into play when practical where directions for play call for only one ball.

It is well for the teacher to have some method of keeping a game going when the object such as a ball used in the game inadvertently gets away from the immediate activity area. For example, in the game Circle Soccer (page 132) the teacher should have another ball ready to put into play immediately in case the ball is kicked away from the immediate area. In this way play can continue while a player retrieves the ball.

Signaling

As in any kind of human endeavor, every game has a beginning and an ending. All games begin with some sort of signal, but there are different ways in which a game can end. For example, a game can be played for a specified amount of time or it can continue until a particular objective has been accomplished. In some instances it may be necessary to stop a game before its completion and this requires some sort of signal.

Generally speaking, signals used for games can be broadly classified as *natural* signals and *mechanical* signals. An example of a natural starting signal would be in a game such as Hill Dill (page 124). The signal to start this game is "Hill Dill run over the hill." The first few words tend to get the attention of the players and the last word "hill" starts the game.

If a game does not have a particular statement or saying to get it started, the teacher or a pupil can get it started by simply saying, "Ready! Go!" The word "ready" gets the attention and the word "go" starts the game.

Mechanical signals require some sort of device and can be further subclassified into *sight* and *sound* signals. An example of a sight signal is the use of a flag or piece of cloth. Sometimes such sight signaling devices can be of different colors and waved in different ways so as to have specific meaning for children.

The most common of the sounding devices is a whistle, although signaling with a horn or a bell can also be used. Ordinarily, the use of mechanical signals can be kept to a minimum for starting and stopping games for elementary school children. If a sounding device such as a whistle is used at all, it is perhaps best to use it only for *stopping* activities. Children then become accustomed to associating the sound of the whistle with stopping activity. If a whistle is used both to start and stop games, confusion can sometimes result.

Scoring

By their very nature and purpose some games require scoring while others do not. In a baseball type game the purpose is to score as many runs as possible and thus a winner is declared on the basis of the higher score. Other games such as Lions and Tigers (page 124) do not recommend scoring in the directions for play. In such a game a person when tagged goes to the other side. Sometimes in games of this nature some sort of scoring method may be desirable in that it would be possible that a child could either be just a runner or a chaser throughout the game rather than having the opportunity to be both a runner *and* a chaser. In a game like Lions and Tigers the group could be kept intact and when a person is tagged a point could be scored for the other side.

When scoring is used it seems advisable to have as many children score as possible. This can be done by "breaking down" the scoring. For instance, in a baseball type game a score is ordinarily made only when a player has made a complete circuit of the bases. More children could get involved in the scoring by having a score for reaching each base. That is, one for reaching first base, two for reaching second base, and so on.

In some games the directions call for eliminating players such as certain tag games where if one is tagged he is out of the game. In cases such as this the rule can be changed to use a scoring system that would keep children in the game. For example, if a child is tagged it could count a point against him or a point for the child who tagged him. In this way he would still remain in the game.

Organization for Classroom Games

On occasion it is necessary to confine game activities to the limited area of the regular classroom when no other space is available. At first glance this might appear impossible. Nevertheless, with wise planning and effective organization it is possible to conduct certain game activities within the limited confines of the average classroom. Although chasing and fleeing games may not be adaptable to the classroom, games of circle formation, stationary relays, and other games that require little space afford much enjoyment for children.

The following discussion of organization for participation in classroom games need not be thought of only in terms of game activities. This is to say that the suggestions that follow can also apply to the use of rhythmic activities and self-testing activities in the classroom situation. With this general idea in mind the following discussion will focus upon ways to prepare the classroom for activities.

The way in which one organizes for classroom activities will depend generally upon such factors as the kinds of activities to be taught and time required to arrange the room before and after activity. The following suggestions for preparing the classroom for activity have certain advantages and disadvantages, and for this reason the above factors need to be taken into account. In all of the following plans is is expected that a system will be devised whereby the children will be able to prepare the room effectively and efficiently under the guidance of the teacher.

1. *Clear the room of all furniture.* The obvious advantage of this plan is that a maximum amount of space is provided for activity. However, an inordinate amount of time may be required to get the furniture in and out of the room. In addition, furniture in the hall outside the room can possibly cause an obstruction.

2. *Move furniture to one side.* This procedure will provide for a little more than half of the room space for activity. It has the advantage of not being time consuming for room preparation.

3. *Place furniture on all sides around the walls.* With this plan all space is available for utilization with the exception of three or four feet taken up by furniture around the walls. An advantage of this setup is that children who are not participating due to lack of space are in a good position to observe those who are participating. With this arrangement, however, it is not always as easy to get the furniture back to its original position as quickly as when the furniture is placed at the side of the room. In this regard some plan of organization should be effected, regardless of how the room is prepared, to get children in and out of activities with little loss of time.

4. *Place furniture in center of room.* This plan is useful when circle games are to be used if there is no need to have performers within the circle. The circle is arranged around the furniture and thus is not an encumbrance. This arrangement also provides for the possibility of having children in as many as four small groups in each corner of the room. This is particularly useful for individual activities such as self-testing activities.

5. *Leave the room as it is.* This, of course, depends on the original arrangement of the furniture. For example, if it is arranged in rows, relays can be conducted using the aisles between the rows as paths to run the relays.

Organization for Relays

Relay activities are those in which each of the participants perform the same feat. That is, in a relay race each performer travels the same distance. One of the good features about relays is that every child has the same equal opportunity to participate.

Relay activities are sometimes criticized on the basis that they do not provide enough activity because of the period of time children must wait for their turn. However, this is often due to faulty organization, with particular reference to the number of performers on a team. For example, if 40 children were divided into ten relay teams of four children each, they could perform five times as many relays in the same amount of time than if the 40 children were divided into only two teams of 20 each.

Relays can be worthwhile activities for about any age level if properly organized. The creative teacher can devise various kinds of relays to meet the needs and interests of most children. Also children themselves can use their own imagination in making up relays.

Two important factors to take into account in the organization of relay activities are (1) a consideration of some of the various *types* of relays, and (2) an understanding of certain relay *formations*.

Types of Relays

Three types of relays will be described here. These are (1) Travel and Return, (2) Travel, Return, and Pass Object, and (3) Stationary.

1. The *travel and return* type of relay means that each member of the relay team in his turn will move across the surface area with some form of locomotor movement to a given distance and will then return to the original starting position to "touch off" the next participant.

2. In the *travel, return, and pass object* type the first person on each team has an object such as a ball which is passed back by team members to the last person. The last person then travels to a designated point and returns and this procedure is continued until all have had a turn. This type of relay takes longer than the travel and return but it is a little less difficult to control. The reason for this is that each team must align itself to pass back the object every time a child takes a turn.

3. In the *stationary* type relay no one leaves the immediate area of the relay teams. That is, there is no traveling to a point and returning. The only distance traveled is the length of the relay column. In this type of relay, ordinarily an object such as a ball is passed back such as a ball rolled between the legs of the team members. The last person receives the ball, goes to the front of the relay column and rolls it back. This procedure is

followed until all have had a turn. This type of relay is useful when the
activity area is restricted because of lack of space.

Relay Formations

There are a number of relay formations which can serve certain purposes. All of these have certain advantages and disadvantages. The teacher
will need to determine the relay formation which will be most suitable
under given conditions. Four different relay formations will be discussed
here. They are (1) straight formation, (2) shuttle formation, (3) circle
formation, and (4) spoke formation.

1. In the *straight* formation the teams are arranged in files as in the
following diagram.

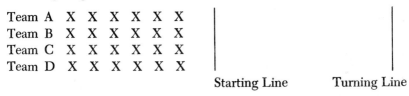

Team A X X X X X X
Team B X X X X X X
Team C X X X X X X
Team D X X X X X X

                 Starting Line   Turning Line

The distance from the starting line to the turning line can vary as desired.
The occasion sometimes arises when the group is not divisible by the desired number of teams, causing an unequal number of participants on one
or more teams. When this condition prevails teams can be equalized by
having one participant run more than once. This will prevent elimination
of a player in order to make the teams equal. This applies to any relay regardless of the formation.

2. The *shuttle* formation differs from the line formation in that each
relay team is divided into two parts. Each part of the team is arranged in
a file opposite the other part with the traveling area between the parts
as shown in the following diagram.

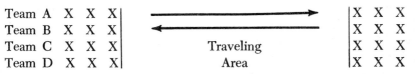

Team A X X X   X X X
Team B X X X   X X X
Team C X X X   Traveling   X X X
Team D X X X   Area   X X X

In this formation each person travels to the opposite file and "touches
off" his teammate who travels back. That is, the participants shuttle back
and forth. At the end of the relay the participants are at the opposite end
of the area from which they started. This formation may be more difficult
to control because the teams are spread over a larger area than in the
straight formation. However, theoretically twice as many relays can be

conducted in the same amount of time because each participant travels only half the distance as he would in the straight formation.

3. In the *circle* formation the teams are arranged in circles and the participants travel around the circle and back to their original place. This procedure continues until all have had a turn. In this formation it is more difficult for participants to tell how well their team is progressing in a race in relation to the other teams. This is not the case in either the straight or shuttle formations. The circle formation can be satisfactorily used to pass an object around the circle to see which team finishes first. An example of this is the game Ball Pass (page 122).

4. In the *spoke* formation the teams are aligned in the manner of the spokes of a wheel as in the following diagram.

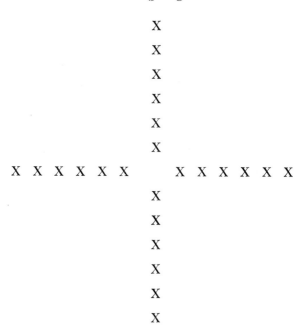

As in the case of any relay formation, as many teams (spokes) can be formed as desired. The first person and last person on each team can be designated as standing at the "hub end" or the "spoke end" of the file. To start the relay the participants at the spoke ends travel around the circle (imaginary wheel) to the right. This person "touches off" the next player at the spoke end and takes his own place at the hub end. A distinct advantage of the spoke formation is that it can be used when space is limited to the extent that there is no area available for traveling to a point and returning. Rather than going to a given distance and back, each person does his traveling around the circle.

Progression in Games

Essentially, progression in games is concerned with getting the activities in a progressive sequence in terms of degree of difficulty of performance. This is to say that in the same manner as other learning sequences, for example, mathematics (addition–subtraction–multiplication–division), game activities should progress from the simple to the more complex.

There are a variety of different ways in which progression in game activities can be effected, and four such possibilities are considered here. These are (1) progression of games on the basis of organization and function, (2) progression of games with the same common element, (3) progression of games of the same type, and (4) progression within the same game (modification). Perhaps at one time or another all of these ways of progression should be utilized depending, of course, on circumstances and needs.

Progression Based on Organization and Function

When games are placed in a progressive sequence with regard to organization and function, the main concern is with complexities of formation and what the children are required to do in the game. The following list with examples suggests such a progressive sequence that might be considered for use with primary level children:

1. *Informal or scattered formation without materials.* Example: Squirrels in Trees (page 126).
2. *Informal or scattered formation with materials.* Example: Leader Ball (page 124))
3. *Single base formation.* Example: Midnight (page 125).
4. *Double base formation.* Example: Red Light (page 125)
5. *Double base formation with identified groups without materials.* Example: Crows and Cranes (page 123)
6. *Double base formation with identified groups with materials.* Example: Steal the Bacon (page 126)

Progresssion of Games with the Same Common Element

Some games contain certain common elements, and such games can be placed in a progressive sequence in terms of complexity and difficulty of performance. The example of such progression given here utilizes the three games of Call Ball, Ball Stand, and Ball Toss and Run, in which the common element is *retrieval of an object* which is most important to successful performance in these games.

In the game of *Call Ball*, six or more children form a circle. One child stands in the center of the circle holding a rubber ball. He tosses the ball into the air and at the same time calls out the name of one of the children. The child whose name is called attempts to catch (retrieve) the ball either on first bounce or on the fly, depending upon the ability level of the children. If the player whose name is called catches the ball, he changes places with the child in the center and the game continues in this manner. When the ball is not caught by the child whose name is called, the thrower remains in the center of the circle and tosses the ball up again. It should be noted that in this game emphasis is only on the retrieval of the object.

Ball Stand has the same common element as *Call Ball*, that of retrieving an object. However, the game continues with a purpose beyond just catching the ball. The game starts in the same manner as Call Ball. However, when a child's name is called, all other players scatter and stop only when the child whose name was called retrieves the ball and calls out, "Stand!" At this signal all children stand still and the player who retrieved the ball throws the ball at one of the children trying to hit him. Some sort of scoring plan can be devised whereby a child hit has a point scored against him. The game continues in this manner for a specified period of time.

The game of *Ball Toss and Run* is still more complex than Ball Stand. The child whose name is called must retrieve the ball on the fly. As in Ball Stand, all other children scatter. If the child whose name was called retrieves the ball successfully he throws the ball into the air again calling another child's name. This continues until a child is not successful in retrieving the ball on the fly. When this occurs this child calls out "Stop!" and the procedure is then the same as in Ball Stand. The main difference in Ball Toss and Run and Ball Stand is that in the former the game can continue as long as the ball is retrieved and thus the children need to make a judgment on how far to scatter when the ball is tossed into the air.

Progression of Games of the Same Type

In games in which the basic objective is essentially the same and yet which have so many variations may be considered as a specific *type* game. Dodge ball, mentioned previously, is a case in point. Since there are so many versions of dodge ball, these can be considered as games of the dodge-ball type. The illustration of this aspect of progression which follows utilizes the games of Roll Dodge, Circle Dodge, and Chain Dodge, all of which are played in circle formation.

Since there are various ways of organizing dodge-ball type games, a comment about organization seems appropriate at this point. The kind of organization preferred by the present author involves dividing the large group into about four smaller groups. Each small group becomes the "dodgers" for a specified period of time while the other three groups are throwers. Each succeeding small group takes its place as dodgers. Each time a person in the group is hit with the ball, it counts a point against his group, and the group with the lowest score, after all four groups have been dodgers, is the winner.

The game of *Roll Dodge* has a circle of throwers with a group of dodgers in the circle. Emphasis is placed *only* upon dodging. The throwers *roll* the ball back and forth across the surface area as rapidly as they can while the dodgers try to dodge the ball. Children should be encouraged to use the underarm throwing pattern, as in bowling, and to release the ball quickly. The previously mentioned method of scoring can be used.

In Circle Dodge the organization and scoring method is the same as for Roll Dodge. However, the emphasis is placed both upon dodging and attempting to strike a dodger. The ball is thrown rather than rolled, and the children can use either the underarm or sidearm throwing pattern.

In *Chain Dodge* the dodgers make a *chain* by forming a file. Each player gets a firm hold around the waist of the player in front of him. The only person eligible to be hit in the chain is the person at the end of the chain. Any type of throwing pattern can be used. The throwers must move the ball rapidly to each other in various parts of the circle in order to make a hit, and the chain must move in such a way as to protect the person on the end of the chain. If the last person is hit, the game stops temporarily and he goes to the front of the chain, with the previous next-to-last player becoming the player on the end of the chain. The same scoring method prevails.

Progression within the Same Game (Modification)

The purpose and process of game modification was discussed in Chapter 4. A specific example here should suffice to illustrate game modification as an aspect of progression.

The game of Call Ball can be used for this purpose. The degree of difficulty in retrieving the ball can be decreased or increased by the number of times the ball bounces. For example, it is easier to retrieve the ball if it is allowed to bounce twice than if the child is required to catch it on the fly. In addition, if the teacher is the one to put the ball into play, the degree of difficulty in retrieval can be effected by how high or low the ball is thrown into the air. Another way to increase or decrease difficulty is to make the circle of children larger or smaller as desired. The imaginative teacher could have several difficult combinations of these modifications and thus effect progression of the game within itself.

General Teaching Procedures*

By and large it seems advisable that games be presented in terms of the whole activity. Thus the child should gain an insight into the requirements necessary for successful performance in the game. As a result he should develop an appreciation of the skills involved in playing the game to the best of his ability. In games of low organization that have a few simple rules and involve little strategy, this procedure may be carried out with little or no difficulty. As games become more complex, however, part-whole relationships need to be made meaningful to pupils. This means that teachers should take into account the important factor of like elements appearing in various games. For example, running is an element common to many different kinds of games. As games become more complex, more elements may be added or methods of performing the various elements may become more complex. In presenting games to children at the various age levels, it becomes necessary that the teacher understand that a single presentation may be a part related to other parts within a whole. This implies that teachers must analyze game activities for the purpose of providing games that reflect the growth and development of the child in relation to the gradated complexity of the games. The following additional guides are recommended to the teacher as a help in the successful presentation of game activities to children:

1. Be sure all necessary equipment is readily accessible. It may be a good idea to conceal equipment until proper time for use. A ball can sometimes become an attention-distracting factor.

2. A game may be related to something that children already know about. If it resembles another game they have played, this should be indicated. Aspects of the game can be related to another subject-matter area,

---

*It is expected that the reader will take into account the principles of learning and the various phases of a physical education teaching-learning situation presented in Chapter 5 (auditory input-visual input-participation-evaluation). This applies to the teaching of games as well as the teaching of rhythmic activities and self-testing activities in the two subsequent chapters.

thus providing an outstanding opportunity for the cognitive aspect of physical education.

3. Determine the best formation for arrangement of the children when the game is being explained or demonstrated. In some cases it may be best to have the children in the regular game formation when presenting it. This may be advantageous if the formation is compact or if there is a small number of children.

4. Use diagrams and visual aids when necessary. This procedure may be useful when the teacher is explaining a game in the classroom before going on to the outdoor activity area. Court dimensions and the like can be diagramed on the blackboard, providing a good opportunity for integration of other areas such as mathematics and drawing to scale.

5. Start the game as soon as is feasibly possible. The game should not be stopped too often to make corrections; however, spot evaluation may take place as seems necessary.

6 Strive for maximum activity for all children by utilizing such procedures as two circles instead of one for a large group in a circle game. Avoid game procedures which tend to eliminate players.

7. Be alert to all safety hazards involved in the game. For example, in a game where children run for a goal, the goal line should be a reasonably safe distance from the wall rather than the wall itself used as the goal.

Games for Primary Level

In general, games played in small groups are enjoyed most by children at the primary level (Kindergarten through Grade 3). These games ordinarily involve a few simple rules and in some cases elementary strategy. Games that involve chasing and fleeing, tag, and one small group against another, as well as those involving fundamental skills, are best suited to children at the lower elementary levels. In addition, children at this age level enjoy the game with an element of surprise, such as those that involve running for a goal at a given signal.

Descriptions of several representative games suitable for use at the primary level are presented here. In reading the directions for playing the games, the reader should think about ways in which they might be modified to meet the needs of a particular group as well as ways to provide for individual differences of children within the group. It should be recalled that detailed information regarding this was presented in Chapter 4.

The games presented here are in alphabetical order by name. However, the reader should experiment with placing the games in sequential progression using the information previously presented in this chapter for that purpose.

Animal Chase

The children choose the names of four different animals. The group is then divided into four small groups with each group given one of the chosen animal names. All of the children then stand in line at one end of the activity area. A Hunter is selected and he stands in the center of the activity area. The Hunter starts by calling out an animal name. When he calls out the name of one of the animal groups, all in that group try to run to the opposite end to a goal line. The Hunter tries to tag as many as he can. Any who are tagged are put into the animal cage which is a part of the activity area previously designated for this purpose. After all animal names have been called, the number in the cage are counted. The animal group with the least number caught can be declared the winner. The game can continue with a new Hunter and the same animal names or new animal names chosen, if desired.

Ball Pass

The players are divided into two or more groups and each group forms a circle. The idea is to pass the ball around the circle to see who can get it around first. The teacher gives the directions for the ball to be passed or tossed from one player to another. For example, the teacher may say, "Pass the ball to the right, toss the ball over two players," etc. The game may be varied by using more than one ball of different sizes and weights. For instance, a basketball, volleyball, and tennis ball might be used.

Circle Chase

The players form a single circle and count off by fours. Each pupil will then have a number between 1 and 4. The leader calls out a number (1, 2, 3, or 4). The players with the number called take a step back and at a signal they all run counterclockwise once around the circle. Each runner attempts to tag the runner ahead. When tagged, the player steps out of the path of the runner behind him. When all runners are back to their original places, the tagged players go to the center of the circle. The game continues until all players, except one, are caught or a specified time limit is reached.

Crows and Cranes

The class is divided equally into two groups, the Crows and the Cranes, who stand facing each other on two parallel lines three to five feet apart. A goal line is drawn 20 to 30 feet behind each group. The teacher or leader calls out the name of one of the groups—Crows *or* Cranes. Members of the group whose name is called run and try to reach their goal line before they are tagged by any member of the other group. All of those tagged lose a point to the other group. The groups return to their original places and the same procedure is followed.

Double Circle

The players are arranged in a double circle. The outside circle has one more player than the inside circle. The players in both circles skip around to their right (each circle goes in the opposite direction) until a signal is given to stop. Each player then tries to find a partner from the other circle. The player left without a partner is said to be "in the doghouse." Play is continued as long as desired.

Fire Engine

The class is divided into four groups. Each group is designated as Fire Station No. 1, 2, 3, and 4. All of the groups go to a line at the end of the activity area. Another line is designated at the far end of the activity area. A Fire Chief is selected and he stands in the middle of the area at the side where there is a line across the middle. The Chief calls out "Fire!" giving the number of the station to run. At this signal all children having the number of that station run to the line at the far end and turn and run back to the middle line. The child finishing first becomes the new Fire Chief. The game can be varied to keep all children alert by allowing the Chief to call out more than one station at a time or to call out "All Stations."

Fox and Geese

All of the children with the exception of one stand in a column with their hands at the waist of the child in front of them. The extra child is "it" and is designated as the fox. The children in the column are the geese. To start the game the fox stands in front of the column, facing the first child. At a signal, the fox attempts to tag the last child in the file. The file tries to maneuver to protect the last child. The fox should be changed frequently so that all children have an opportunity to be "it." After the children learn the game, a number of columns can be formed so as to have more foxes.

Hill Dill

Two parallel goal lines are established approximately 60 feet apart. One person is selected to be "it" and stands midway between the two goal lines. The rest of the class is divided into two equal groups, with one group standing on one goal line and the other on the other goal line. "It" tries to tag as many as he can while they are exchanging goals. All of those tagged become helpers and the game continues in this manner until all but one have been tagged. This person is "it" for the next game.

Hunting the Fox

The players are divided into groups of ten, with two players chosen from each group to be foxes. The rest of the players stand behind a starting line until the foxes cross a line a given distance away. As soon as the foxes cross this line, the other players (hunters) chase them, but the hunters must follow the same path as the foxes. If a hunter catches a fox before the fox gets back to the original starting line, the hunter becomes a fox for the next game.

Leader Ball

Children are divided into groups of six or eight. One child is selected to be the Leader and he stands facing the line of his group. The Leader throws the ball to each member of his group who in turn returns it to him. When a player misses, he goes to the foot of the line. If the Leader misses, he goes to the foot of the line and the player at the head of the line replaces the Leader. Leaders can be changed if no one misses over a period of time. The game can be varied by using different kinds of throwing patterns and increasing or decreasing the distance between the Leader and his group.

Lions and Tigers

The class is divided into two equal groups. One group is called the Lions and the other the Tigers. Each group stands on a goal line at opposite ends of the playing area. Both groups face in the same direction. To start the game the Lions walk up behind the Tigers as quietly as possible. The Tigers listen for the Lions and when it is determined from the sound that they are near, one person who has been previously designated calls out, "The Lions are coming!" The Tigers turn and give chase and try to tag as many of the Lions as they can before the Lions reach their own goal line. When a child is tagged it counts a point for the opposite side. The above procedure is reversed and the game continues for as long as desired.

Midnight

One child is selected as the chaser and he goes to a designated line a given distance away with his back toward the rest of the group. The other players line up on a starting line and approach the chaser. As they approach, they ask him what time it is. He can give any time he wishes, such as eight o'clock, eleven o'clock, and the like. If he says, "Midnight," the players run back toward the starting line and he attempts to tag as many as possible. All of thise caught become chasers as the game continues. When all but one have been caught, that person becomes the chaser for the next time the game is played.

Poison

The players form a circle and join hands. A circle is drawn on the floor or playground inside the circle of players and about 12 to 18 inches in front of the feet of the circle of players. With hands joined, they pull and tug each other, trying to make one or more persons step into the drawn circle. Anyone who steps into the circle is said to be "poisoned." As soon as a person is poisoned, someone calls out "Poison" and the one who is poisoned becomes "it" and gives chase to the others. The other players run to various places previously designated as "safety," such as wood, stone, metal, or the like. All of the players who are tagged are poisoned and become chasers. When those not tagged have reached safety, the leader calls out, "Change" and they must run to another place of safety. Those poisoned attempt to tag as many as possible. The game can continue until all but one have been poisoned.

Red Light

In this game one child is selected to be a policeman. The other children stand on a line called the "curbing." The policeman stands with his back to the players about 20 to 30 feet away on a line which represents the curb on the other side of the street. The policeman counts "One, two, three, four, five" (or more) and turns around quickly and says either, "Red Light," or "Green Light." (He may also hold up the color instead of saying the words.) As soon as the other players hear the policeman counting, they may leave the curb and keep walking until he says, "Red Light." Then they must stand very still. If the policeman sees any of the players move, he sends them back to the curb to start over. Children who were not seen to move when the policeman called "Red Light" remain in place. The game continues and the first player to reach the curb where the policeman is standing wins the game.

Shadow Tag

The players are dispersed over the playing area, with one person designated as "it." If "it" can step on or get into the shadow of another player, that player becomes "it." A player may keep from being tagged by getting into the shade or by moving in such a way that "it" finds it difficult to step on his shadow.

Squirrels in Trees

With the exception of one player, the children are arranged in groups of three. Two of the players in each group of three face each other and hold hands, forming a "hollow tree." The third player is a squirrel and stands between the other two in the hollow tree. The extra player, who is also a squirrel, stands near the center of the playing area. The extra player calls out "Change!" On this signal all squirrels attempt to get into a different hollow tree, and the extra squirrel also tries to find a tree. There will always be one squirrel left who does not have a tree. After playing for a time, the players are alternated so that all have an opportunity to be a squirrel.

Steal the Bacon

Two lines of children eight or ten in number stand facing each other about 15 feet apart. An object (the bacon) is placed in the middle of the space between the two lines. The members of each team are numbered so that each child on the team has a different number. The teacher calls out a number and the two children with that number run out and try to grab the object and return it to their own line. If a player does so, his team scores two points, and if he is tagged by his opponent in the process the opposing team scores one point. If desired the teacher can call out more than one number at a time. The game continues for a specified period of time and the team with the most points is the winner.

Games for the Upper Elementary Level

Children at the upper elementary level (Grades 4-6) retain an interest in some of the games they played at the primary level, and some of them can be extended and made more difficult to meet the needs and interests of these older children. In addition, games may now be introduced which call for greater bodily control, finer coordination of hands, eyes, and feet, more strength, and the utilization of some of the basic skills acquired in previous grades.

It has been found that children in the upper elementary grades and sometimes as low as third grade can engage satisfactorily in various types of team games, such as Basketball, Soccer, Softball, Flag Football, and Volleyball. These games as played at the high school or college level are ordinarily too highly organized and complex for the majority of upper elementary school children. It is therefore necessary to modify these activities to meet the needs and interests of this age level. By way of illustration let us consider the game of Basketball as played at the high school or college level. Players at this level use the regulation size basketball of 29½ inches in circumference and the goal is at a height of ten feet. For upper elementary school children the game could be modified by using a smaller ball and lowering the goal. At this level more simple strategies also would be used in playing the game. Teachers can use their own ingenuity along with the help of children in modifying the highly organized games to adjust them for suitability for specific groups of upper elementary school children.

One approach to the introduction of the more highly organized team games is the use of *preparatory games*. These contain many of the same skills used in the advanced games. These games are within the capacity of children at this age level and provide them an opportunity to learn many of the basic skills and some of the rules of the more advanced games.

It seems appropriate at this point to comment on participation of boys and girls in the highly organized team games. It should be recalled that mention was made in Chapter 4 regarding the segregation of boys and girls for certain physical education activities. Generally speaking, it is best to have boys participate with boys, and girls with girls, in most of the highly organized games. That is, in all of the highly organized games discussed here all participation should be on a sex segregation basis. This does not necessarily apply to some of the preparatory games for the highly organized team games. In some of the preparatory games boys and girls can participate satisfactorily together. The individual teacher should be the judge of this and the reader can utilize the information in Chapter 4 to serve as criteria in making such a judgment.

At one time it was the usual recommendation that girls not participate at all in Flag Football. However, in recent years more and more girls have demonstrated an interest in this activity; that is, on a segregated basis. Those physical educators who have experimented with girls participating in Flag Football have ordinarily found that it can be a suitable activity for girls under proper guidance.

The remainder of this chapter will be concerned with certain types of highly organized team games which can be made suitable for use for children at the upper elementary level. The games to be considered are Basketball, Soccer, Softball, Flag Football, and Volleyball. In each case certain specific *skills*° for the game will be taken into account along with some representative preparatory games which give children an opportunity to practice these skills and develop strategies under less complex circumstances than are ordinarily called for in the game itself. In addition, where applicable, certain suggestions for modification of the highly organized team game will be made to adjust it more to the needs and interests of children of upper elementary level.

Basketball

The game of Basketball, truly American in origin, was invented by Dr. James Naismith of Springfield, Massachusetts in 1891. Dr. Naismith was said to have derived the idea for the game when he was a member of a psychology class. The instructor of the class had suggested as an assignment in inventiveness a game that could be played on a limited indoor area with a limited number of players. Dr. Naismith invented the game of basketball to meet the conditions of the assignment as well as an activity to fill in the time during the winter between the end of football season in the fall and the start of baseball in the spring.

The first game was played with bottomless peach baskets and there were nine players on each team. In the early days the number of players on a team depended upon the space available, but eventually a five-player standard was adopted for men and six players for women. The game caught on rapidly and after it was introduced to Europe by American soldiers in World War I, it soon became a very popular international sport.

°Specific skills refer to those skills that are pertinent to a particular game. Numerous other general skills, i.e., skills of propulsion and skills of retrieval were discussed in Chapter 4. It might be well for the reader to review these in connection with the highly organized games presented in this chapter.

Modern-day basketball is played on a minimum-sized court 42 feet by 74 feet to a maximum size of 50 feet by 90 feet. The basketball goals (hoops) at either end of the court are ten feet high with each team having its own goal. The purpose of the game is to score more points than the opponents by throwing the ball through the hoop. A goal counts 2 points and a free throw caused by certain infractions of the rules counts one point. The game can be modified to meet the needs of children by lowering the goals, using a smaller ball, decreasing the size of the playing area, as well as the modification of certain rules. (Information on the official rules of all of the games discussed here is available from the American Association for Health, Physical Education, and Recreation, 1201 Sixteenth Street, N.W. Washington, D. C. 20036. Any of the official rules can be adjusted by the teacher to meet the needs of a particular group of children.)

Specific Basketball Skills

As mentioned previously the purpose of the game of basketball is to score by putting the ball through the goal. However, in order to do this the ball must be advanced toward the goal. This can be done by a single player dribbling (bouncing) the ball or a combination of players passing (throwing) the ball to each other. The basic aspects of these skills were discussed in Chapter 6 as was the skill of *pivoting* which is important in the game of basketball. The specific skills considered here are *shooting* at the goal and *guarding* an opponent.

Shooting

Shooting may be done with one or both hands. In the *one-hand-push-shot* for the right-handed shooter the right foot is slightly ahead of the left with knees slightly bent. The left hand positions the ball to the right hand and a pushing motion is made with the right hand. The eyes are kept on the rim of the goal. Another one hand shot is the *lay-up*. The right-handed shooter takes off from the left foot and jumps as high as he can toward the goal. He "lays" the ball on the backboard so that it will go into the goal. (For the left-handed shooter the above procedures are reversed.)

The *two-hand-chest-shot* is probably best for beginners because the ball may be easier to control for some children. The ball is held in both hands about chest high. The ball is tipped back on the fingers and pushed toward the goal as the shooter attempts to maintain a proper arch of the flight of the ball. Either foot can be in advance of the other or the feet can be together. In the *two-hand-free-throw-shot* the ball is held between the legs and tossed at the goal with an underhand motion.

Guarding

In basketball a player is not allowed to put his hands on an opponent. However, he can block a shot or pass, and this is done by guarding. In guarding, the player stands in a position with feet comfortably apart and parallel, or with one foot a little in advance of the other. He moves from side to side with the skill of sliding. It may be recalled that emphasis was put on the skill of sliding in Chapter 6 as an important skill to help children become proficient in moving over the surface area in a lateral plane. He positions his hands and arms in such a way to attempt to block the ball if it is passed to an opponent or thrown at the goal.

Preparatory Games for Basketball

The preparatory games for basketball suggested here are representative of the numerous possibilities for such games. Imaginative teachers with the assistance of children can devise many others. The games suggested here involve one or more of the following skills: passing, catching, guarding, dribbling, and shooting.

Bear in the Circle

Two circles with eight to twelve players each are formed with each circle comprising a team. A member of the opposing team (the bear) stands in the center of each circle. The players in the circle pass the ball around and the Bear tries to touch it. If he does so he scores a point for his team. Bears are changed frequently so that every player gets to be the Bear (Guard).

Keep Away

Several teams of six to eight players each are selected. Play starts with one of the teams having possession of the ball. This team passes the ball around to its own players and all other teams try to intercept the ball. When this occurs the team intercepting is given possession of the ball. All of the rules of basketball prevail and the object of the game is to see which team can keep the ball for the longest period of time.

Tag Ball

Several teams of six to eight players each are selected. One player on each of the teams is designated as "it." The purpose of the game is to tag a person on a team, who is "it," with the ball. When this is accomplished the tagging team scores a point. All of the rules of basketball prevail and the ball can be advanced to "it" by passing or dribbling. All players who are "it" should be designated in some way, perhaps with an armband, so that the others can tell easily the players who are "it."

Half-Court Basketball

All of the rules of basketball prevail in this game and the only difference from the regular game is that only one-half of the court is used. Both teams use the same goal. When a goal is made or a ball is intercepted by the opposing team, the other team must start again with the ball at a designated distance behind the free-throw line near the center of the court.

Soccer

Soccer is a game which is played principally with the feet. The game was originally called "Association Football," the rules for which were developed in 1863 by the *London Football Association.* Later the term "Association" was abbreviated to "Assoc" which eventually became "Soccer," as the game is currently referred to in modern times. The game of Soccer is an international sport and perhaps has its greatest popularity in certain South American countries.

The game is played on a field with maximum dimensions of 130 yards by 100 yards and minimum dimensions of 100 yards by 50 yards. At each end of the area and in the center there is a goal consisting of two posts eight yards apart with a crossbar on the posts eight feet from the ground. The game is played with a round heavy ball 27 to 28 inches in circumference. The purpose of the game is to score more goals than the opponent. A goal is scored when a player propels the ball with his feet or head through the goal and under the crossbar. The official number of players on a team is eleven and they may advance the ball by kicking it or propelling it with the head (heading). There is limited use of the hands but the hands can be used by the goalkeeper. Also when the ball goes out of bounds it can be put into play with the hands.

The game can be modified for upper elementary school children by using a smaller playing area, using a lighter more resilient ball, and permitting more use of the hands.

Specific Soccer Skills

It was mentioned previously that Soccer is a game that is played principally with the feet. Thus, it is recommended that the reader review the basic kicking skills discussed in Chapter 6. The specific skills to be discussed here are soccer dribbling, heading, and trapping.

Soccer dribbling involves one player moving the ball with his feet while on the run. The player tries to keep the ball a short distance ahead of him as he runs along. He contacts the ball with either the inside or outside of the foot, and the foot that makes contact with the ball is the dribbling foot.

Heading means that the ball is propelled by the head. This skill can be used when the ball comes to the player on the fly. As the ball approaches, the player balances his weight equally on the balls of his feet with the knees bent. The player "heads" the ball in the direction he wants it to go by using a butting motion with the head. For elementary school children heading should be done with a lighter rubber ball rather than the ordinary heavy soccer ball.

Since the use of the hands are restricted in the game of Soccer the ball is stopped by *trapping*. The ball can be trapped by the sole of the foot, with the inside of the foot, or with the body. In trapping with the sole of the foot the player puts his foot on top of the ball when it comes to him. In traping with the inside of the foot, the foot gives with the impact of the ball to slow it up. Body trapping is used when the ball is too high to be trapped by the feet. The ball may be trapped against the thighs, chest, or shoulders depending on the height of the flight of the ball. The body gives with the force of the ball so that it will not bounce away and thus allowing the player to keep the ball near him.

Preparatory Games for Soccer

The preparatory games for Soccer suggested here involve one or more of the following skills: kicking, dribbling, trapping, and heading.

Circle Soccer

A circle is formed with any number of players. The players kick a ball around in the circle as rapidly as possible. The object of the game is to keep the ball from going out of the circle. If it goes out it counts a point against player on either side of the ball where it went out of the circle. The ball should not be kicked above the waist and an attempt should be made to keep it on the ground. The game can be made more interesting by putting two balls into play.

Hit Pin Soccer

Two teams of six to eight players each form lines about 15 feet apart. Several objects such as bowling pins are placed at a midpoint between the two teams. The players on each team kick a ball back and forth trying to knock over the objects. A point is scored when an object is knocked over. The team with the highest score at the end of a designated time is the winner.

Leader Ball Soccer Relay

The formation for this game is the same as for Leader Ball described on page 124. Rather than the ball being thrown back and forth to the leader, the ball is moved back and forth with a designated soccer skill.

Square Soccer

Four teams of ten to twelve players each form a square with each team as a side of the square. All players of each team are numbered consecutively. The ball is dropped in the center of the square and a number is called. All four of the players with this number run to the center and try to get the ball through any side of the square. The players at the side of the square are goalkeepers and can use their hands to stop the ball. As soon as a score is made another number is called and the game continues.

Softball

Softball is a form of baseball but differs in the following ways.

1. The game can be played indoors as well as outdoors and teams are composed of women as well as men.
2. A ball larger and softer is used rather than the hard baseball.
3. The official distance between bases in softball is 55 feet while in baseball this distance is 90 feet.
4. The pitching distance is 43 feet for men and 35 feet for women, while the pitching distance for baseball is 60½ feet.
5. Pitching in softball is done with the underarm throwing pattern while the overarm throwing pattern is permitted in all other aspects of the game.

Softball was started in the early 1900's by American professional baseball players because they wanted to keep in practice during the off-season. Thus, they used the game of Softball, then called *Indoor Baseball*, to practice during the winter months.

During the late 1920's the game became popular in Canada and players from that country began to play the game outdoors on playgrounds and other activity areas. As a result the game became known as "Playground

Ball" for a time. Softball began to generate a great deal of interest in the United States around 1930 and is now played by thousands of men and women throughout the country.

Some degree of criticism has been leveled at the game of softball as a part of the regular physical education program at the elementary school level. This is based on the idea that an inordinate amount of space is needed to play the game, in addition to the lack of activity provided by the game. However, this should not preclude children learning and practicing the skills of softball even though they do not participate in the game during physical education class time.

Specific Softball Skills

Softball involves the various skills of propulsion and retrieval discussed in Chapter 6. Two more or less specific skills discussed here are *batting* and *base running*.

Batting involves striking as a skill of propulsion in that it is concerned with propelling the ball with the bat. The description that follows is for a right-handed batter and just the opposite should prevail for the left-handed batter.

The batter stands at home plate with his left shoulder facing the pitcher. The feet are in a stride position with knees slightly bent and a slight bend forward at the waist. The bat is gripped at a point comfortable to the batter. The elbows are out with the left forearm nearly parallel with the ground. The bat should be brought back as far as the left arm can reach across the chest. As the ball comes in, the batter attempts to make contact with it, with the bat parallel to the ground.

Base-running is difficult because it requires turning at nearly a right angle to the left at the base. The runner should attempt to touch the bases on the inside corner with his foot. He needs to adjust his speed so as not to run too far out of the baseline after touching a base. When stopping at a base the runner should bend at the knees and lower his body weight to keep from overrunning the base.

Preparatory Games for Softball

The following preparatory games for Softball involve one or more of the following skills: baserunning, throwing, catching, batting, and pitching.

Base Running Relay

The spoke relay formation is used with each spoke end being at one of the four bases. At the signal to start, each runner completes the circuit

of all bases, comes back to original spoke, and touches off the next runner
The team finishing first is the winner.

Hand Bat Ball

In this game the rules of softball are used. The batter bats the ball with
his hand or fist and a large rubber playground ball is used.

Bases on Balls

This game is played on a softball diamond with the baseline distance
adjusted to meet the needs of the particular group. Each team can consist
of from ten to twelve players. One team is in the field while the other is at
bat. The batter tries to hit the ball into the field as in the game of Hand
Bat Ball using the same procedure. The player in the field who retrieves
the ball runs in and places it on home base. The batter runs the bases after
he hits the ball and gets a point for every base he touched before the fielder
touches home base with the ball. There are no outs in this game and every
player gets a chance at bat. When all players on a team have had a chance
at bat, the teams change places with the fielders becoming the batters. As
many innings as desired can be played.

Hit Pin Baseball

This game is played somewhat like softball except that objects such
as bowling pins are used rather than bases. The pitcher throws the ball
in easily so that the batter can hit it. When the batter hits the ball he starts
around the bases. The fielder who retrieves the ball throws it to first base.
The first baseman knocks the object over with the ball and throws the ball
to second base. This continues in this manner until the ball has gone
around to all the bases and the objects have been knocked down. The batter stops when the object (base) he is heading for is knocked down. The
batter scores one point for his team for every base he reaches before the
object has been knocked down. As in the case of Bases on Balls there are
no outs and every member of the team gets to bat in each inning.

Flag Football

Flag Football is derived from Touch Football which was, in turn, derived from the game of American Football. The game of Touch Football
evolved as an informal substitute for the highly organized game of football because of interested persons who did not have the opportunity to

participate in regular football. For this reason it is difficult to identify an exact date when it was first inaugurated. The essential difference between Football and Touch Football is that in the latter body contact in the form of tackling is prohibited. A person is stopped by being touched rather than tackled. Because touching sometimes resulted in a form of pushing, predisposing a player to injury, the game of Flag Football was introduced. This is the same as Touch Football except that a cloth (flag) is tucked in at the back part of the waist of the player. The player is stopped when an opponent pulls the flag loose from his waist.

There are many different sets of rules for Flag Football and it is suggested that teachers plan with children in establishing rules most suitable for a particular group. Ordinarily a team is comprised of nine players, four in the backfield and five in the line.

Specific Skills for Flag Football

Most of the basic skills previously discussed can be adapted to Flag Football as played by children of upper elementary school age. Two specific skills discussed at this point are blocking an opponent and centering the ball.

In *blocking* an opponent the feet should be a comfortable distance apart with the knees bent and the body inclined slightly forward. The hands or clenched fists are placed against the chest with the elbows pointed out to the sides. The player (blocker) should be ready to move in any direction. It should be remembered that the blocker cannot leave his feet or use his hands on his opponent.

In *centering* the ball the player crouches over it with the feet spread and one foot slightly in advance of the other. Little if any weight is placed on the ball. The centering movement involves throwing the ball back between the legs with the arms extended backward. If right-handed, the right hand actually passes the ball back and the left hand guides it.

Preparatory Games for Flag Football

The following preparatory games for Flag Football include such skills as passing, catching, centering, and kicking.

Football Keep Away

This game is played the same way as the game of Keep Away described on page 130. A football is used to help the players develop the skill of handling the oval-shaped ball.

Leader Ball Centering Relay

This relay is conducted the same as Leader Ball Soccer Relay except that the players in turn *center* the ball to the leader and he *passes* it back.

Football Kickball

In this game the regular rules of softball apply. The ball is kicked instead of batted, that is, the kicker stands at home plate and kicks the ball from his hands (punt) and runs to base if the ball goes into fair territory within the base lines. All other rules of softball prevail.

Volleyball

Like basketball, the game of Volleyball is American in origin, having been originated by William Morgan at the Y.M.C.A. in Holyoke, Massachusetts, in 1895. The game has become tremendously popular in recent years with women as well as men.

The game is played on a court 60 feet in length and 30 feet in width. A net is placed over the middle of the court at a height of eight feet for men and seven feet for women. There are six persons on a team with three in the front line and three in the back line. The purpose of the game is to hit (volley) the ball over the net and the opponents try to keep it from striking the surface area in the playing area of the court.

The game can be modified for upper elementary school children in such ways as lowering the net, using a slower ball such as a beachball, having more players on a team, and allowing the ball to bounce rather than hitting it on the fly.

Specific Volleyball Skills

The principal specific skills of Volleyball discussed here are serving, volleying, and spiking.

Serving is done with an underarm pattern. The server stands facing the net with weight equally distributed on both feet. For a right-handed server the left foot is slightly forward. The right arm swings back and the weight is shifted to the rear foot and as the serve is made, the weight shifts to the forward foot. The ball is struck with the heel of the hand or the fist.

In *volleying* the ball the player distributes the weight equally on both feet and strikes the ball from the fingertips with both hands in an upward pushing motion.

Spiking is a means of driving the ball across the net to make it difficult for the opponent to volley it back. The player goes up with the ball and hits it downward with a forceful motion.

Preparatory Games for Volleyball

The following preparatory games for Volleyball involve practice in getting the ball over the net, volleying, and serving.

Net Ball

Net Ball is played the same as volleyball except that the ball is thrown back and forth across the net rather than having the players volley it back and forth. The idea is to accustom the players to get the ball over the net.

Leader Volleyball Relay

The same provisions of the previously discussed Leader Ball Relays prevail except that the players serve the ball to the leader and he in turn serves it back.

Keep It Up

Several teams of from six to eight players form into circles with each circle comprising a team. At a signal the members of each team volley the ball and try to keep it from touching the surface area as they volley it to each other. The object of the game is to see which team can keep it up for the longest period of time.

Games have always played an important part in the lives of children.

Chapter 8

Rhythmic
Activities

Those human movement experiences that *require* some sort of rhythmical accompaniment may be placed in the broad category of rhythmic activities. As in the case of descriptions of other terms throughout this text, this description of rhythmic activities is arbitrary and used for purposes of discussion here. The author is aware that some authorities consider the meaning of the term "dance" to be a broader one than the term "rhythmic activities." However, the point of view is that there are certain human movement experiences that require some form of rhythmical accompaniment that do not necessarily have the same objectives as those ordinarily associated with dance.

The term "rhythm" is derived from the Greek word *rhythmos*, which means "measured motion." One of the most desirable media for child expression through movement is found in rhythmic activities. One need look only to the functions of the human body to see the importance of rhythm in the life of the elementary school child. The heart beats in rhythm, the digestive processes function in rhythm, breathing is done in rhythm; in fact, almost anything in which human beings are involved is done in a more or less rhythmic pattern.

It would be difficult to name a sports activity that does not involve rhythm. For example, we read in the sports pages that the "shortstop scooped up the ball and threw to first with precise rhythmic motion." Rhythmic activities, as such, should occupy an important place in a well-balanced program of physical education at all levels of the elementary school.

The purpose of this chapter is to help the reader find answers to such questions as:

1. What is the current status of rhythmic activities in the elementary school?
2. What are some suitable ways to classify rhythmic activities?
3. What are some of the advantages and disadvantages of various forms of accompaniment for rhythmic activities?
4. What kinds of rhythmic activities are suitable for use with elementary school children?
5. What are some of the valid procedures that might be used in the teaching of rhythmic activities?

Status of Rhythmic Activities in Elementary Schools

It is extremely difficult to identify a precise time when rhythmic activities were introduced into the elementary schools of America. Perhaps one of the early attempts in this direction came around the turn of the century when John Dewey was director of the University of Chicago Laboratory School. At this time Dewey introduced folk dancing into the program, which could possibly be the first time such an activity took place in the schools on a more or less formalized basis. Up until that time rhythmic activities, if used at all, undoubtedly took place on a sporadic and spasmodic basis. For example, there were instances when certain types of singing games were a part of the "opening exercises" of some elementary schools.

During the decade preceding World War I, some aspects of nationality dances found their way into the school program. This ordinarily occurred in those large cities where certain ethnic backgrounds were predominant in a given neighborhood.

The period between the two World Wars saw rhythmic activities introduced into more schools and this was probably due to the fact that more emphasis was beginning to be placed on the social aspect of physical education. By the late 1920's some elementary schools were allotting as much as 25 percent of the physical education time to rhythmic activities.

In modern times rhythmic activities in elementary schools are characterized by diversity. This is to say that this aspect of physical education encompasses a wide variety of activities and there appears to be little standardization from one school to another. Perhaps one of the reasons for this is the variation in teacher preparation as well as the reluctance on the part of some elementary school physical education teachers to teach these kinds of activities.

It is interesting to note that with the introduction of the *axials* in the form of the "twist" as a new kind of dancing in the early 1960s by the young adult population, many children of upper elementary school age likewise became interested in this approach to dancing. As a result some children began to rebel against some of the traditional forms of dancing. This feeling has subsided somewhat in recent years and children are again developing an interest in folk and square dancing under the guidance of skillful elementary school physical education teachers and classroom teachers.

Classification of Rhythmic Activities

Classification of physical education activities into certain broad categories is a difficult matter. This is partly due to inconsistencies in the use of terminology to describe certain activities. Thus, any attempt at classification tends to become pretty much an arbitrary matter and is likely to be based upon the experience and personal feelings of the particular person doing the classifying.

When attempts are made to classify activities within a broad category, it should be kept in mind that a certain amount of overlapping is unavoidable and that in some instances activities may fit equally well into more than one category. For example, singing games might be classified as either game activities or rhythmic activities. It is also important for teachers to know that activities within a category may vary with regard to similarity in scope. In other words, some of the activities may be broad enough to utilize others in the same category. For instance, one may wish to classify game activities as "indoor games" and "outdoor games." If this were the case, these classifications would be very broad in scope and would encompass practically any type of game. Another important consideration is that in some cases different names may be given to the same activity, which is concerned with the inconsistencies of terminology mentioned previously. For example, "creative rhythms" and "free-response rhythms" might be considered one and the same.

The examination of literature by the author referred to in the previous chapter regarding games and their classification also included rhythmic activities. This information which yielded the following classifications should give the reader an idea of the various possibilities as far as classification of rhythmic activities is concerned:

1. Activity songs and poems
2. American dances
3. American Indian dances
4. Choral reading
5. Clog dancing
6. Couple dances
7. Creative dances
8. Creative rhythms
9. Customs dances
10. Dramatization

11. Folk dances	22. Nursery rhymes
12. Free-response rhythms	23. Play-party games
13. Fundamental rhythms	24. Rhythm bands
14. Greeting and meeting dances	25. Round dances
15. Gymnastic dancing	26. Singing games
16. Imitative rhythms	27. Skill dances
17. International dances	28. Social dancing
18. Interpretative rhythms	29. Square dances
19. Mimetic rhythms	30. Story rhythms
20. Mixers	31. Tap dancing
21. Modern dance	32. Trade dances

One approach to the classification of rhythmic activities centers around the kinds of *rhythmic experiences* that one might wish children to have. It is recommended here that these experiences consist of (1) unstructured experiences, (2) semistructured experiences, and (3) structured experiences. It should be understood that in this particular way of grouping rhythmic experiences a certain amount of overlapping will occur as far as the degree of structuring is concerned. That is, although an experience is classified as an unstructured one, there could possibly be some small degree of structuring in certain kinds of situations. With this idea in mind the following descriptions of these three types of rhythmic experiences are submitted.

Unstructured experiences include those in which there is an original or creative response and in which there has been little, if any, previous explanation or discussion in the form of specific directions. The *semistructured* experiences include those in which certain movements or interpretations are suggested by the teacher, a child, or a group of children. *Structured* experiences involve the more difficult rhythmic patterns associated with the various types of dances. A well-balanced program of elementary school rhythmic activities should provide opportunities for these various types of rhythmic experiences. An arbitrary classification of rhythmic activities designed to provide such experiences for children gives consideration to (1) fundamental rhythms, (2) creative rhythms, (3) singing games, and (4) dances. (Representative examples of these classifications of rhythmic activities along with suggested teaching procedures are presented in ensuing sections of this chapter.)

At the primary level, *fundamental rhythmic activities* found in the locomotor movements of walking, running, jumping, hopping, leaping, skipping, galloping, and sliding, and the nonlocomotor or axial movements, such as twisting, turning, and stretching, form the basis for all types of rhythmic patterns. Once the children have developed skill in the fundamental rhythms, they are ready to engage in some of the more complex dance patterns. For example, the combination of walking and hopping to musical accompaniment is the basic movement in the dance known as the *schottische*. In a like manner, galloping is related to the basic pattern used in the *polka*.

Children at the primary level should be given numerous opportunities to engage in *creative rhythms*. This kind of rhythmic activity helps them to express themselves in just the way the accompaniment "makes them feel" and gives vent to expression so necessary in the life of the child.

The *singing game* is a rhythmic activity suitable for primary age children. In this type of activity children can sing their own accompaniment for the various activity patterns that they use in performing the singing game.

Various kinds of *dances* may be included as a part of the program of rhythmic activities for the primary level. Ordinarily, these have simple movement patterns which the child learns before progressing to some of the more complex patterns.

At the upper elementary level children can engage in rhythmic activities that are more advanced than those at the primary level. Creative rhythms should be continued and children should have the opportunity to create more advanced movement patterns.

Dance patterns involved in the various kinds of folk dances may be somewhat more complex, provided children have had a thorough background in fundamental rhythms and less complicated folk dances at the primary level. Primary level dances can be individual activities and many of them involve dancing with a partner. At the upper elementary level, "couple dances" which require closer coordination of movement by partners may be introduced.

Some of the forms of American square dancing are ordinarily introduced at the upper elementary level although many teachers have had successful experience with square dancing at the lower grade levels.

Accompaniment for Rhythmic Activities

There are many different forms of accompaniment that are suitable for use with rhythmic activities. All of these can be useful when employed under the right conditions. At the same time all of them have certain disadvantages. In the final analysis it will be up to the teacher to select the form of accompaniment that will best meet the needs in a particular situation.

Five forms of accompaniment for rhythmic activities are presented here along with what might be considered as advantages and disadvantages of each.

1. *Clapping* as a form of accompaniment can be useful in helping children gain a better understanding of tempo. There is also something to be said for the child actually becoming a part of the accompaniment on a physical basis since it gives him a feeling that he is more involved. This is particularly important in the early stages when rhythmic activities are being introduced. Clapping can be done with the hands or by slapping various parts of the body such as the thighs or knees. A major disadvantage of clapping as a form of accompaniment is that it is virtually impossible to obtain a melody through this procedure.

2. Various kinds of percussion instruments may be used as accompaniment, the most prominent being the *drum*. The drum is an instrument which is easy to learn to play and the person furnishing the accompaniment can change the tempo as he wishes. Actually some kinds of dances such as some of the Indian dances require the use of a drum as accompaniment. Likewise, as in the case of clapping, the use of a drum makes it difficult to have a melody with the accompaniment.

3. *Singing* as a form of accompaniment is ordinarily required in singing games and in square dances where singing calls are used. All children can become involved as in the case of clapping. One of the disadvantages of singing as a form of accompaniment is that the singing voices may become weaker as the child participates in the activity. For example, if singing games require a great deal of skipping, it is difficult for the child to do both tasks of singing and skipping for a very long period of time.

4. At one time the *piano* was a very popular form of accompaniment for rhythmic activities. The chief disadvantage of the piano is that it is a difficult instrument to learn to play and all teachers have not included it as a part of their professional preparation. Another disadvantage is that even though one is an accomplished pianist, the player must obviously be at the piano and thus is away from the activity. The piano has an advantage in that a melody can be obtained with it.

5. Perhaps the most popular form of accompaniment at the present time is *recordings*. Sources of this form of accompaniment are so plentiful at the present time that almost any kind of accompaniment is available. One distinct disadvantage of recordings concerns those that furnish instructions intended for children. Sometimes these instructions are confusing and too difficult for younger children to understand. The teacher should evaluate such instruction and determine if the above is the case. If it is found that the instructions are too difficult for a particular group of

children, the teacher can use just the musical accompaniment. The major advantage of recordings is that they are professionally prepared. However, teachers might well consider using a tape recorder to record their own music or singing voices of children as a form of accompaniment.

The following is a list of representative sources of recorded accompaniment for rhythmic activities:

1. Bee Cross Media, Inc., Department JH, 36 Dogwood Glen, Rochester, New York 14625.
2. Bowmar Records, Department J-569, 622 Rodier Drive, Glendale, California 91201.
3. Childhood Rhythms, Forest Park Station, Springfield, Massachusetts 01108.
4. Children's Music Center, Inc., 5373 West Pico Boulevard, Los Angeles, California 90019.
5. Dance Record Center, 1161 Broad Street, Newark, New Jersey. 07114.
6. David McKay, Inc., 750 Third Avenue, New York, New York 10017.
7. Educational Activities, Inc., Box 362, Freeport, New York.
8. Educational Recordings of America, Inc., Box 6062, Bridgeport, Connecticut 06606.
9. Folkcraft Records, 1159 Broad Street, Newark, New Jersey 07114.
10. Freda Miller Records, Department J, Box 383, Northport, Long Island, New York.
11. Imperial Records, 6425 Hollywood Boulevard, Hollywood, California.
12. Kimbo Educational, Box 246, Deal, New Jersey.
13. RCA Victor Education Department J, 155 East 24th Street, New York, New York.
14. Record Center, 2581 Piedmont Road, N. E., Atlanta, Georgia 30324.
15. Russell Records, Box 3318, Ventura, California 91403.

All of the preceding forms of accompaniment can be considered for use with the rhythmic activities that are presented in subsequent sections of the chapter.

Fundamental Rhythms

As mentioned previously fundamental rhythms are basic to other more complex rhythmic patterns. Almost any form of accompaniment can be used for the fundamental locomotor movements of walking, running, jumping, leaping, hopping, skipping, galloping, and sliding. The same can be said for the axial or nonlocomotor movements such as bending, twisting, and stretching.

An important factor in fundamental rhythms is that of *cadence*. Theoretically, this refers to the number of steps or paces taken over a period of time or accompaniment tempo. If one were to have children perform the fundamental movement of walking to the accompaniment of a drum, this could be done at the tempo of four beats to a *measure* in 4-4 time. This is shown in the following score with *quarter* notes. The quarter note is referred to as a *walk* note.

Accompaniment for running is twice as fast and is depicted with *eighth* notes (*run* notes as in the following score).

♪ ♪ ♪ ♪ ♪ ♪ ♪ ♪

Many different sequences of walking and running can be used by various beats as follows:

walk, walk, run   ♩ ♩ ♪

walk, walk, run, run, run,   ♩ ♩ ♪ ♪ ♪

run, run, walk, run, run, walk   ♪ ♪ ♩ ♪ ♪ ♩

walk, walk, run, run, run, run,   ♩ ♩ ♪ ♪ ♪ ♪

A walk and run note can be used together for the uneven fundamental rhythms of skipping, galloping, and sliding. The following score depicts the use of this for skipping (step-hop).

♩ ♪ ♩ ♪ ♩ ♪ ♩ ♪

In addition to drum accompaniment suggested above and controlled by the teacher, many records provide musical accompaniment for the performance of the various fundamental rhythms. The information presented here is merely suggestive, and the creative teacher, along with the collaboration of the children, can develop many exciting aspects of fundamental rhythms.

Suggested Teaching Procedures for Fundamental Rhythms

The following teaching procedures are submitted as suggestive points of departure that the teacher may take in providing learning experiences for children through fundamental rhythms:

1. Play accompaniment so that children can listen to it.
2. Have the children describe the accompaniment in terms of what it sounded like to them.

3. Ask what they might do to the accompaniment, such as walk, run, skip, etc.
4. Let them clap to get the tempo of the accompaniment.
5. Let them try the fundamental rhythmic activity.
6. Select some children who were performing the activity well, play the accompaniment again, and have the other children observe them.
7. Have the children evaluate good features of the performers. ("What did you like about the way they did it?")
8. Have all of the children do the activity again, analyzing their own performance.

Creative Rhythms

A paradoxical phenomenon as far as the broad category of rhythmic activities is concerned is the widespread lack of use of creative rhythms over the years. This is borne out by the various surveys made by the author which invariably indicate that creative rhythmic experiences for children are provided on a minimal basis. However, the fact that this condition is being ameliorated to some extent, at least in some places, was reported in Chapter 4. It was mentioned there that the trend in curriculum development concerned with intellectual needs of children will provide the opportunity for children to participate in creative experiences rather than always having to conform.

It is indeed an unfortunate circumstance that more widespread use of creative rhythms has not prevailed because of the importance of creativity in the life of the child. Creative experience involves *self*-expression. It is concerned with the need to experiment, to express original ideas, to think, to react. Creativity and childhood enjoy a congruous relationship, in that children are naturally creative. They imagine. They pretend. They are uninhibited. They are not only original but actually ingenious in their thoughts and actions. Indeed, creativity is a characteristic inherent in the lives of practically all children. It may range from some children who create as a natural form of expression without adult stimulation to others who may need varying degrees of teacher guidance and encouragement.

Such forms of creative expression as art, music, and writing are considered the traditional approaches to creative expression. However, the very essence of creative expression is *movement*. Movement as a form of creativity utilizes the body as the instrument of expression. For the young child the most natural form of creative expression is movement. Because of their nature, children have an inclination for movement and they use this medium as the basic form of creative expression. Movement is the child's universal language, a most important form of communication and a most meaningful way of learning.

There are various ways to subclassify creative rhythms; as in the case of classification of other physical education activities, it becomes an arbitrary matter. The two subclassifications suggested here are designated as *dramatization* and *individual interpretation*. The essential difference between the two is in the degree of structuring of the activities. Dramatization centers around some sort of story, plan, or idea which can provide various kinds of clues for children, while individual interpretation has little if any structuring and involves children moving in the way the accompaniment makes them feel. That is, the ideas for movement are supposed to originate with the children.

Dramatization

Dramatization can involve (1) a story or idea that the children already know about or something with which they are familiar; (2) a story made up by the teacher; or (3) a story started by the teacher and added to by the children.

In using a familiar story such as "Jack and the Beanstalk," the children can act out the story to drum accompaniment provided by the teacher.

Two examples of dramatization of something that the children are likely to know about are "Flower Garden" and "Snowman." In Flower Garden the children curl up on the floor, each representing a flower seed. To suitable accompaniment the children use axial movements (rising, stretching, turning) to "grow" as a flower. They finally rise to a standing position with arms above the head.

In Snowman the children stand in informal order about the area as snowmen. To a suitable musical or percussion accompaniment (designated as the bright shining sun) they do a variety of movements that depict the snowmen melting as a result of the hot sun.

An example of a story made up by the teacher is shown in the following simulated teaching procedure in which a *parade* theme is used.

Teacher: Boys and girls how many of you know what a parade is?
(Children)
Teacher: Good. How many of you have seen a parade?
(Children)
Teacher: That's fine; most of you have seen a parade. What kinds of parades are there?
(Children)
Teacher: On what days do we have parades?
(Children)

Teacher: You have given several examples, and now I would like to tell you a story about a Fourth of July parade. This is a story about children watching a parade. In the parade was a group of soldiers. They marched along to the sound of music and the beat of a drum. Would someone like to show us how they marched?

(One child demonstrates to the drum accompaniment provided by the teacher. The children then evaluate the good things the "marching soldier" did.)

Teacher: George, because you did such a good job, you can be the head soldier and everyone will march along behind you.

(The teacher accompanies the marching soldiers on the drum for a period of time and then they return to their original places.)

Teacher: The children enjoyed watching the soldiers so much and tried to keep pace with them. How could they do this? (The teacher sounds several "run notes" and a child mentions that the children would have to run to keep up.)

Teacher: That's right, Jack, can you show us how?

(The child runs to the accompaniment, good points are evaluated, and then all children run for a short period of time and then return to their places.)

Teacher: Now, boys and girls, something very interesting happened. (The teacher sounds several slow loud beats on the drum.)

Teacher: What do you think that could have been?

(Children give several suggestions such as a cannon, base drum, etc. If none of the children suggest that it was a giant taking big steps, the teacher continues.)

Teacher: Boys and girls, it was a giant taking great big giant steps.

(The teacher goes through the same procedure as with the marching soldiers and running children, and the children move around the surface area with big giant steps to the drum accompaniment and back to their original places. The teacher can continue on with suggestions from the children or end the story at this point.)

All of the ideas for dramatization given above are suggestive points of departure to be taken. The imaginative teacher along with the children can develop many such ideas along these lines.

Individual Interpretation

As mentioned before, in individual interpretation, ideas for movement originate with the children. Although some children might be influenced by others, the movements that each child makes to the accompaniment are likely to be unique and different from other members of the group.

Individual interpretation might be perceived in the following manner. The accompaniment is received through the auditory sense. It is "syphoned" through the human organism and nervous system and the child reacts with a movement which expresses the way the accompaniment makes him feel.

One of the important aspects of individual interpretation lies in the selection of the proper kind of accompaniment. This is to say that accompaniment should be sensitive enough to depict different kinds of moods for the physical expressions of one's feelings.*

Suggested Teaching Procedure for Creative Rhythms

The following teaching procedures are submitted as suggestive points of departure that a teacher may take in providing learning experiences for children through creative rhythms. In following these suggestions the reader should take into account the various degrees of structuring to be considered in *dramatization* and *individual interpretation*:

1. The teacher must recognize that in creative rhythms each child's interpretation of the accompaniment will vary. For this reason the teacher's comments to the child should be characterized by praise and encouragement.

2. Although creative rhythms are essentially individual in nature, the teacher should perhaps introduce this type of rhythm to groups of children. This helps to avoid embarrassment of children and tends to build up their self-confidence.

3. The group may be dispersed informally about the activity area. Formal arrangement is not always conducive to creativity.

4. The children listen to the accompaniment for the purpose of becoming accustomed to its tempo and mood. In the case of a dramatization, the teacher might introduce the activity with a rhythm or a story.

5. The children should be given an opportunity to discuss the accompaniment in terms of "what it says" or "how it makes us feel."

6. The children can give their creative interpretations to the accompaniment.

7. Some children may be selected to show their interpretations to the rest of the class. This procedure provides a medium for evaluation.

---

*A particularly good source of accompaniment for individual interpretation is Album #4, parts V and VI of #10 (Freda Miller) of the previously listed sources of recorded accompaniment on page 147.

Singing Games

Singing games are actually dances with relatively simple patterns that children perform to their own singing accompaniment, or, as in the case of recorded accompaniment, when the singing is furnished by others. There are various ways to classify singing games and one source suggests the following classification.[1]

1. Those which enact simple stories or imitate the actions of everyday life.
2. Those which are based on familiar nursery rhymes of folktales.
3. Those which involve choosing partners.
4. Those in which children follow the leader in improvising rhythmic actions.

Several representative examples of singing games follow. These are recommended generally for the levels from Kindergarten through Grade Two. It will be noticed that musical scores are not included. There are two major reasons for this. First, the traditional melody for the words of most of the singing games will already be known by many readers; and second, teachers should be encouraged to develop their own melodies. This can be done in many instances in collaboration with the children. To provide musical scores would be meaningless for those who do not read music. In addition, while it can be helpful in the teaching of singing games for the teacher to be able to read music, it is not absolutely essential.

A-Hunting We Will Go

Verse

1. A-hunting we will go.
2. A-hunting we will go.
3. We'll find a fox and put him in a box.
4. But then we'll let him go.

Action

Either four or six children stand in, two lines, partners facing each other. The two partners nearest the front of the room should be designated as the head couple. The head couple joins hands and slides four steps down away from the front of the room between the two lines while singing the first line of the verse. The other children clap and sing the accompaniment. On the second line of the verse the head couple slides four steps back to their original position. The head couple then drops hands and the head girl skips around to the right and to the end of her line. The head boy does

---

[1]Richard Kraus, A *Pocket Guide of Folk and Square Dances and Singing Games for the Elementary School* (Englewood Cliffs, New Jersey: Prentice-Hall, Inc., 1966).

the same thing to his left. This is done while singing the last two lines of the verse. They both meet at the other end of the line. The new head couple follows this procedure and then all succeeding couples become head couples until everyone has had an opportunity to be the head couple. After each couple has had an opportunity to be the head couple, the children all join hands and circle clockwise while singing the entire verse.

Cobbler, Cobbler

Verse 1
1. Cobbler, Cobbler
2. Mend my shoe.
3. Have it done by
4. Half-past two.

Verse 2
5. Sew it up
6. Sew it down.
7. Now see with whom
8. The shoe is found.

Action

The children form a large single circle with one child in the center. The child in the center holds a shoe, or an object representing a shoe. During the singing of Verse 1, the child in the center passes the shoe to another in the circle. The shoe is then passed behind the backs of the children during the singing of Verse 2. On the word "found," the child who has the shoe becomes "it" and goes to the center of the circle. This continues for as long as desired.

Did You Ever See a Lassie?

Verse
1. Did you ever see a lassie, a lassie, a lassie?
2. Did you ever see a lassie go this way and that?
3. Go this way and that way, go this way and that way.
4. Did you ever see a lassie go this way and that?

Action

The children form a circle and one child is chosen to be the leader and stands in the center. On Line 3 of the Verse the leader goes through some sort of motion and the children in the circle follow. This continues with different children going to the center of the circle. When a boy is the leader, "laddie" is substituted for "lassie."

Diddle Diddle Dumpling

Verse

1. Diddle Diddle Dumpling, my son John,
2. Went to bed with one shoe on.
3. Yes, one shoe off, and one shoe on,
4. Diddle Diddle Dumpling, my son John.

Action

The children can be in any formation. On the first line they can either clap hands, knees, or thighs, or they can do the sailor hop. (The sailor hop is done by standing with the feet together and then placing first one heel and then the other in front of the other with a short hop.) On the second line they can pretend to sleep, such as placing head on hands. On the third line they hop on one foot and then on the other to indicate they have a shoe off. On the fourth line they repeat the action of the first line.

Hickory Dickory Dock

Verse

1. Hickory Dickory Dock.
2. The mouse ran up the clock.
3. The clock struck one!
4. Watch the mouse run!
5. Hickory Dickory Dock.

Action

The children form a double circle with partners facing. On Line 1 the hands are in front of the body to form pendulums and the arms are swung left and right. On Line 2 partners change places with six short running steps. On Line 3 they clap hands over head. On Line 4 they go back to their original place with six short running steps. On Line 5 they swing the arms as in Line 1.

Jolly is the Miller

Verse

1. Jolly is the miller who lives by the mill.
2. The wheel goes round with a right good will.
3. One hand in the hopper and the other in the sack.
4. The right skips forward and the left skips back.

Action

The children form a double circle facing counterclockwise with inside hands joined. An extra player takes a place near the center of the circle. On

Lines 1, 2, and 3 the children move in a circle by walking or skipping, stopping on the word "sack." On Line 4 partners drop hands. The children on the outside move backward one step to get a new partner. The procedure continues.

London Bridge

Verse

1. London Bridge is falling down, falling down, falling down.
2. London Bridge is falling down, my fair lady.

Action

Two children stand facing each other, hands clasped and arms extended over head to form an arch or bridge. The other players form a line holding hands. These players walk under the bridge. On the words "my fair lady," the two who have formed the bridge (bridge tenders) let their arms drop, catching the child who happens to be passing under at that time. The bridge tenders then ask him to choose something that each of the tenders represents, such as gold or silver. The player caught stands behind the bridge tender who represents gold or silver as the case may be. The game proceeds until all have been caught and the side with the most players wins. There should not be too many children in the line so that there will not be a long wait for the children caught.

Looby Loo

Verse

1. Here we dance Looby Loo, here we dance Looby Light,
2. Here we dance Looby Loo, on a Saturday night.
3. I put my right hand in, I take my right hand out,
4. I give my right hand shake, shake, shake, and turn myself about.
   (turn around in place)
I put my left hand in, etc.
I put my right foot in, etc.
I put my left foot in, etc.

Action

The children form a single circle with hands joined. On Lines 1 and 2 the children walk three steps into the circle and three steps back, and repeat. As the rest of the verses are sung, the children do the actions indicated by the words. For example, with "I put my right hand in" they lean forward and extend the right hand and point it to the center. At the end of each verse the children repeat the first verse again, taking three steps in and three steps out. The procedure can be continued with other parts of the body as desired, ending with "I put my whole self in," etc. (Take a short jump in and then back.)

Rabbit in the Hollow

Verse
1. Rabbit in the hollow sits and sleeps,
2. Hunter in the forest nearer creeps.
3. Little rabbit, have a care,
4. Deep within your hollow there.
5. Quickly to the forest,
6. You must run, run, run.

Action

The children form a circle with hands joined. One child, taking the part of the rabbit, crouches inside the circle while another child, taking the part of the hunter, stands outside the circle. A space nearby is designated as the rabbit's home, to which he may run and in which he is safe. On Lines 1 and 2 the children in the circle walk clockwise. On Lines 3 and 4 the children in the circle stand still and the rabbit tries to get away from the hunter by breaking through the circle and attempting to reach home without being tagged. If the rabbit is tagged he chooses another child to be the rabbit. The hunter chooses another hunter.

Suggested Teaching Procedures for Singing Games

The following teaching procedures are submitted as suggestive points of departure that the teacher may take in providing learning experiences for children through singing games.

1. The teacher can sing the entire song.
2. The teacher may wish to have the children discuss the song in terms of what it says.
3. The song can then be sung by phrases, with the teacher singing a phrase and then the children repeating the phrase.
4. The phrases can then be put together with the children singing the whole song.
5. The movement pattern that goes with the song can then be introduced using appropriate visual input, and the song and activity can be combined.
6. In cases where the singing game is long and has several verses, each verse and the activity that goes with the verse can be learned. All verses can then be combined into the whole singing game.

7. Depending upon the movement involved, singing games can be vigorous activities for children. Because voices tend to tire when activity is
engaged in while singing, it may be a wise practice not to have too
many singing games in succession. In other words, it might be well to
combine singing games and other activities during the physical education period.

Dances

In the literature review on rhythmic activities reported earlier in the
chapter, there were 32 different classifications of these activities. The fact
that over half of these were classified as dance activities gives one an idea
of the numerous possibilities available for classifying dances. However, as
in the case of other physical education activities, classification of dances
becomes an individual matter.

Two broad classifications dealt with here are *folk* dances and *square*
dances. It should be understood that a certain amount of overlapping is
unavoidable as far as these broad classifications are concerned. This is to
say that while each of the broad classifications has some degree of unique-
ness, at the same time both are characterized by certain similarities.

Folk dances, sometimes referred to as *ethnic* or *nationality* dances,
were defined many years ago as the traditional dances of a given country
which have evolved nationally and spontaneously in conjunction with the
everyday activities and experiences of the people who developed them.[2]
The dance patterns are performed in group formation and range from
simple to rather complex forms. For the most part folk dances used in
American elementary schools have been derived from Great Britain and
Europe, although some have their origin in our own country.

Square dancing appears to be uniquely American in origin. It is sometimes referred to as American *country* dancing or *Western* dancing. The
square dance gets its name from the starting position of the dancers which
is that of a quadrille or square. Square dancing is done to musical accompaniment with a *caller* who gives cues as to what the dance patterns are.

Progression of Dances

As in the case of other physical education activities, developing a progressive sequence of dances in order of degree of difficulty of performance
is not an easy matter. One satisfactory way of providing for progression in
dances is to do so in terms of *organization* and *function*. Teachers can
analyze dances with reference to degree of difficulty of performance with

---

[2]Anne Schley Duggan et al., *The Teaching of Folk Dance* (New York: A. S. Barnes
& Company, 1948).

these two factors in mind. *Organization* is concerned with the degree of complexity of the formation from which the dance is executed, and *function* is concerned with the degree of difficulty of the dance patterns.

A simple form of organization would be one in which the children are in a single circle without partners, while a more complex form of organization would involve a double circle and performing with a partner. As far as function is concerned a simple dance pattern would be one in which only one or possibly two different basic locomotor movements are performed. Dance patterns become more complex as more basic locomotor movements are used in various combinations. In the examples of dances that follow, the reader can experiment with placing them in sequential order of progression by using the above information for this purpose. It should be understood that the dances which follow are merely representative of an extremely large number of possibilities. It is suggested that the reader send for the most recent catalogs of the record accompaniment sources on page 147. Many of these sources contain explicit directions for conducting many kinds of dances.

Folk Dances

Children's Polka—German
(#13°—45-6179,2042; #9—1187; #15—750

In the starting position for this dance the children form a single circle. Partners turn and face each other. They join hands and extend the arms shoulder height.

Accompaniment Action

Measures	1- 2	Partners take two slides toward the center of the circle, and stamp feet three times in place—right, left, right.
Measures	3- 4	Partners take two slides back to original position and stamp feet three times.
Measures	5- 8	Repeat the action in Measures 1-4
Measures	9-10	Clap hands against own thighs, clap own hands, and clap partner's hands three times.
Measures	11-12	Repeat the action in Measures 9-10.
Measure	13	Extend the right foot to the side with the toe down. Hold the right elbow in the left hand and shake the right forefinger at partner three times.
Measure	14	Same as Measure 13 except that the position is reversed with left foot and left hand.
Measures	15-16	Each person turns around with four fast running steps and then stamps feet three times—right, left, right.

°The numbers refer to the list of record accompaniment sources on page 147.

Chimes of Dunkirk—English
(#9—1188; #13—45-6176, 17327)

The starting position is a double circle with the girls making up the outside circle and boys the inside circle.

Accompaniment *Action*

Measures 1-2   Stamp feet three times—right, left, right.
Measures 3-4   Each person claps his own hands three times with the arms extended over the head.
Measures 5-8   Partners join hands and skip around each other in place.
Measures 9-16   Partners hold inside hands and skip around the circle to either the right or left.

Csebogar—Hungarian
(#13—45—6182)

The starting position is a single circle of partners with the girls on the right of their partners. All join hands.

Accompaniment *Action*

Measures 1-4   With two slides to a measure the circle takes eight slides to the left.
Measures 5-8   Repeat of Measures 1-4 but going to the right, or back to original position.
Measures 9-12   Four walking steps to the center and four walking steps back (when the circle reaches the center raise arms over head and shout, Hey!)
Measures 13-16   Do the Hungarian Turn with partner. (Partners place right hands at each other's waists raising left hands high over head and skip around partner twice.)
Measures 17-20   Partners face each other and take hands extending arms shoulder high, taking four slow slides to the center with one slide to each measure.
Measures 21-24   Take four slow slides back to place.
Measures 25-26   Take two slow slides to center.
Measures 27-28   Take two slow slides back to place.
Measures 29-32   Hungarian Turn as in Measures 13-16.

Dance of Greeting—Danish
(#9—1187; #13—45-6183; #15—726)

The starting position is a single circle of partners with the girl to the right of the boy.

Accompaniment Action

Measure 1   Each person claps own hands twice and then turns and bows
                 to partner.
Measure 2   All facing center of circle clap own hands twice and then
                 turn and bow to neighbor.
Measure 3   Stamp right foot and then left foot.
Measure 4   Turn all the way around in place with short running steps.
Measures 5-8   Join hands in single circle and skip to the right.

Pop Goes the Weasel—American
(#13–45-6180)

In the starting position for this dance the children form groups of three.
These small groups of three are then arranged into a large circle.

Each group of three walks around counterclockwise to the musical accompaniment until the strain "Pop Goes the Weasel" is heard. At this time
one child is "popped" under the joined hands of the other two and sent
to the next couple in the large circle. Progression of those popped is counterclockwise. Before starting the dance it must be decided which person in
each group will be popped through, and the sequence in which the other
two will be popped through.

Example of a folk dance teaching procedure using Pop Goes the Weasel

The following illustration concerns a procedure which integrates a folk
dance with the study of fractions at the fourth-grade level. In this particular instance the classroom teacher has become aware of a difficulty in
getting boys and girls to choose partners with each other in some of the
activities that they have been playing. Because of this she feels that possibly a dance activity could help them to overcome the problem. She feels
also that it may be necessary to provide a certain amount of motivation for
dancing, particularly for the boys. (In this case there is no physical education teacher and it is the responsibility of the classroom teacher to provide physical education learning experiences. This particular group of
children has had no experience with dance activities.)

TEACHER: Boys and girls when reading about some sports events in
            the paper the other day, I came across some sentences that
            I thought would be of interest to you. In a story about a
            football game, one sentence said, "The halfback *danced*
            down the field." In another report on a championship box-
            ing match, there was a sentence that said, "The boxer
            danced away from the punch." As I thought about this, it
            occurred to me that dancing might be a good way to de-
            velop some of the skills needed to play well in sports and

games. Have any of you ever heard of how rhythm and dancing could help to make better players?

PUPIL: Gee, I never thought of it that way before.

PUPIL: Me, either.

TEACHER: Please form a large circle with a boy and a girl in every other place. (*Pupils form the circle*) Today we are going to learn a dance called, "Pop Goes the Weasel." Probably many of you have heard the tune before. Let me see the hands of those who have. (*Some pupils indicate that they are familiar with the tune.*) Do you remember the other day, when we were studying fractions what we said the bottom number told us?

PUPIL: I think it was how many parts something is divided into.

TEACHER: Yes, that's right, and now we are going to divide our large circle into groups of three. Starting here we will form small circles with three persons in each small circle with hands joined. (*Teacher demonstrates with first group of three to her left.*)

Now each group is a circle made up of three persons. If something is divided into three parts, what do we call the name of each part?

PUPIL: One-third?

TEACHER: Yes, that's right. Can someone tell me how many thirds make a whole?

PUPIL: Three.

PUPIL: (*Aside to another pupil*) Oh! I see now what she meant the other day.

TEACHER: All right. Now let's have each person in the small circles take the name of either First-Third, Second-Third, or Last-Third. Just take a minute to decide within your own circle who will take each part. (*Teacher demonstrates with one of the small circles.*) Let me see the hands of all First-Thirds, the Second-Thirds, the Last-Thirds. Now here is something that is very important. The magic word in this dance is "Pop." That is, if the words to the tune were to be sung. We will move to the right in our own circles. When we come to the part of the music where the word "Pop" would be sung, the person in each circle with the name First-Third will pop under the arms of the other two persons in his circle and become a part of the circle to his right. The people in the small circles will immediately begin to walk again, and this time on the word "Pop" the person named Second-Third will leave his circle. The next time the person named Last-Third leaves. Who do you think will pop the next time?

PUPIL: Would we start all over again with First-Third?

TEACHER: Yes, that's right, and we will continue that way until the record has finished playing. I am going to play a part of the record for you. This time I want you to listen to the music, and when you hear the part where you pop into the next circle raise your hand so that we can make sure that you will know when to pop. That's fine. Everyone seems to know when to pop. Listen for the chord to start (*Pupils participate in the dance, and after the record is played through, the teacher evaluates the activity with them.*)

TEACHER: What were some of the things you noticed that you thought were good about our first attempt at this dance?

PUPIL: We all seemed to go in the right direction and didn't get mixed up.

PUPIL: We kept time pretty well.

TEACHER: What are some of the things you liked about it?

PUPIL: I like always being in a different circle.

PUPIL: Well, it made me catch on to fractions better.

PUPIL: Me too. We ought to do arithmetic that way all the time.

TEACHER: You think it was easier to learn fractions that way?

PUPIL: I'll say and it was lots more fun.

TEACHER: What are some of the ways we might improve it if we tried it another time?

PUPIL: We ought to all try to pop at the same time.

PUPIL: Maybe we shouldn't try to go around the circle so fast.

TEACHER: Yes, those are good suggestions. Personally, I think it was rather well done for our first attempt.

Square Dances

The following diagram represents the starting position for square dances. The boy is on the left and the girl is on the right.

X X
(Third Couple)

(Fourth Couple)
X X
X

(Second Couple)
X
X

X X
(First or Head Couple)

There are three general calls for square dancing. These are (1) the *prompt* call, (2) the *patter* call, and (3) the *singing* call. The prompt call involves simple and precise commands. This type of call is not done to a melody or rhyme. Commands are given and the caller waits until the steps are executed and then gives the next call. This call may be used in preparation to do patter calling since it is easier than patter calling. Patter calling is done by chanting or in a singsong fashion and generally in rhyme. The amount of time for each patter call is the same as the number of beats necesssary to do a particular step or pattern that is called. The singing call is essentially the same as the patter call except that it is done to the melody of a particular song.

With practice, children as well as the teacher can become reasonably proficient at calling. It is perhaps best for the beginner to use the singing call because the caller need not count the number of beats which is necessary in prompt and patter calling.

The following are representative of some of the square dances utilizing singing calls that have been used with success at the elementary school level. Although for the most part square dancing is ordinarily done at the upper elementary level, it is possible to do it at a lower level depending upon the skill of the teacher and the complexity of the dance patterns.

Pig in the Parlor

This dance involves a singing call which is sung to the tune of "For He's a Jolly Good Fellow."

Call
1. There is a pig in the parlor
2. There is a pig in the parlor,
3. There is a pig in the parlor,

4. And he is fat and round.
5. Your right hand to your partner.
6. Your left hand to your neighbor.
7. Back again to your partner,
8. And swing her round and round.

Action

On Lines 1-4 all members of the square join hands and circle around to the right returning to their original positions. On Line 5 partners do an *allemande right*. This is done by grasping right hands and completing a circle by walking all the way around the partner and back to original position. On Line 6 an *allemande left* is performed. This is just the opposite of the allemande right with the boy taking the left hand of the girl on his left (his corner or neighbor). On Lines 7-8 an elbow swing is performed with the partner. This is done by interlocking elbows and skipping around in a circle one or more times. (If there is an extra person, he or she can stand in the center of the square and try to get a partner just before the elbow swing. The person whose partner is "stolen" then becomes the pig.)

Red River Valley

(#11-1096)

The singing call for this dance is sung to the tune of "Red River Valley."

Call

1. Now you all join hands in the valley.
2. And you circle to the left and to the right.
3. And now you swing that girl in the valley.
4. Now you swing with your Red River girl.
5. First couple lead to the valley.
6. And you circle to the left and to the right.
7. And now you swing the girl in the valley.
8. Now you swing with that Red River girl.
9. Now all of you go in to the center.
10. And all of you come right back out again.
11. Now you skip with your partner around the circle,
12. Until you get back home once again.

Action

On Lines 1-2 everyone joins hands and walks four steps to the right and then reversing this procedure with four steps to the left. On Line 3 boys swing the girl on their left. On Line 4 all boys swing their own partner. On Lines 5-6 the First Couple moves to the Second Couple. Both couples join hands and walk in a circle four steps to the right and then reverse with four steps to the left. On Line 7 the boys in Couples One and Two swing opposite girls. On Line 8 boys swing own partner.

(This is what is known as a *Visiting Couple Dance* and after the First Couple has visited the Second Couple they go on and visit the Third and Fourth Couples. In doing this the dance patterns in Lines 5-8 are repeated. The Second, Third, and Fourth Couples visit around the square in the same manner as the First Couple. They each do this in turn and the dance patterns in Lines 5-8 are repeated each time.)

On Line 9 all join hands and walk four steps in to the center of the circle raising hands as they go. On Line 10 four steps are taken back and hands are lowered. On Lines 11-12 all partners join inside hands and skip around the circle and back to their original place.

Oh Johnny
(#9-1037)

The singing call for this dance is sung to the tune of "Oh Johnny."

Call

1. Now you all join hands and you circle the ring.
2. When you get back home you give your partner a swing.
3. Swing your neighbor girl right behind you.
4. Now swing your own so that she won't be alone.
5. It's allemande left with your neighbor girl.
6. Now back and swing your own.
7. Skip all around with your own partner bound.
8. Singing Oh Johnny, Oh Johny, Oh.

Action

On Line 1 all join hands and circle to the right and back to original position. On Line 2 boys swing their partners. On Line 3 boys swing the girl on their left. On Line 4 boys swing partners again. On Line 5 boys do an allemande left with the girls on the left by taking hands and walking all the way around each other. On Line 6 boys swing own partners. On Lines 7-8 holding inside hands partners skip around the circle and back to their orginal places.

Suggested Teaching Procedures for Dances

The following teaching procedures are submitted as suggestive points of departure that the teacher may take in providing learning experiences for children through dances.

1. The name of the dance should be given. If the teacher knows where the dance got its name, and if this seems important to the learning situation, the teacher can give this information to the children.
2. If the teacher feels that it is important to the learning situation, the background of the dance can be given with respect to the culture of the

people who previously danced it, when they danced it, and for what purpose.

3. The introductory discussion of the dance (auditory input) should not be so intense and involved that it detracts from actual participation in the dance. It should be remembered that the greatest appreciation is likely to come from engaging in the dance.

4. Have the children listen to the accompaniment to become acquainted with the tempo and mood. Give them an opportunity to discuss the accompaniment.

5. Introduce the various movement patterns using appropriate auditory and visual input. Give the children an opportunity to practice the patterns.

6. Teach one part of the dance at a time, adding each part after the preceding part is learned. This procedure will depend to some extent upon the length and complexity of the dance. If it is short the children may be able to learn the entire dance. (Teaching by counting or phrasing, or a combination of the two, should be optional with the individual teacher.)

7. All of the parts and accompaniment should be put together into the whole dance.

Chapter 9

Self-Testing
Activities

Those physical education activities based upon the child's desire to test his ability in such a way that he attempts to better his performance may be placed in the broad category of self-testing activities. Such activities as stunts and tumbling, exercises with or without apparatus, and individual skill proficiency such as throwing for accuracy and/or distance, and jumping for height or distance, can be classified in this broad category.

With regard to stunts and tumbling it should be mentioned that these activities are closely related and alike. Stunts are concerned predominantly with certain kinds of imitations and the performance of a variety of kinds of feats that utilize such abilities as balance, coordination, flexibility, agility, and strength. Tumbling involves various kinds of body rolls and body springs that encourage the development of these same abilities.

At the primary level children should be given the opportunity to participate in self-testing activities commensurate with their ability. For example, stunts which involve imitations of animals are of great interest to boys and girls at this age level. Tumbling activities which involve some of the simple rolls are suitable. Simple apparatus activities involving use of such equipment as ladders, bars, and balance beams can be utilized and are very popular.

Self-testing activities at the upper elementary level should be somewhat more advanced provided the child has had previous experience and teaching in them at the primary level. Tumbling activities that involve more advanced rolls and various kinds of body springs may be successfully introduced. In a like manner more difficult kinds of balance stands may be used in the stunt program.

Pupils at the upper elementary level may continue to take part in apparatus activities, using much the same equipment that was used for the primary level, but moving to more advanced skills.

It will be the function of this chapter to familiarize the reader with several representative examples of self-testing activities suitable for use with elementary school children. An attempt will be made to suggest answers to such questions as:

1. Why are self-testing activities important in the curriculum?
2. What are satisfactory ways to organize self-testing activities?
3. What are some suitable learning experiences in such self-testing activities as stunts and tumbling, ball handling, balance beam, and rope jumping?
4. How can performance be evaluated in certain self-testing activities?

Some Values of Self-Testing Activities

One of the major values ordinarily attributed to self-testing activities is their specific contribution to such elements of physical fitness as strength, agility, coordination, and flexibility. Zealous proponents of self-testing activities stoutly maintain that contributions to these various factors are more likely to accrue through self-testing activities than may be the case through games and rhythmic activities. The reason for this lies in the fact that successful performance of certain of the self-testing activities requires the involvement of the various elements of physical fitness.

It has also been suggested by many teachers that some of these kinds of activities help to build courage, confidence, and poise in children, although this is difficult to evaluate objectively.

An important value of self-testing activities, but one that is often overlooked, is the contribution that might be made to *tactile perception*. This is particularly true in the case of stunts and tumbling activities. In this regard it has been suggested by Smith[1] that through such tumbling activities as the log roll, forward roll, and backward roll, the child is given the opportunity to explore the environment *tactilely* with the various body segments.

Stunts and Tumbling

An appreciable amount of the content for this section of the chapter has been adapted from the following source: James H. Humphrey and

---

[1] Hope M. Smith, "Implications for Movement Education Experiences Drawn from Perceptual-Motor Research," *Journal of Health, Physical Education, and Recreation,* April 1970.

George F. Kramer, *Stunts and Tumbling for Elementary School Children,*
LP 5060, Kimbo Educational, Deal, New Jersey, 1969. (By permission.)

This material was developed by the present author and one of his as-
sociates after a considerable amount of experimentation with elementary
school children. The original material is designed to be used as a *self-teach-
ing* device and consists of one long play record, 50 frames of film strip, and
a teacher's manual. The illustrations in the text are facsimilies of the pictures on the filmstrip of the original materials. Testimonial from those
teachers who have used the original material attest to its value as a teaching aid. Thus, it is highly recommended that the reader explore these original materials.

Class Organization

One of the most important aspects of the teaching-learning situation in
stunts and tumbling is that which is concerned with the way the class is
organized for activity. The suggestions that follow are intended to serve as
organization guidelines for the teacher.

Safety Precautions

One of the reasons why stunts and tumbling have been neglected in
some instances in the elementary school physical education program is the
fact that many teachers associate this type of activity with accidents and
resulting injuries. However, if proper precautions are taken, safety hazards
can be reduced to a minimum. The following list indicates some of these
precautions that the teacher might consider:
1. Activities should be analyzed for all possible safety hazards; that is,
   the teacher should try to anticipate any accident that might occur.
2. The teacher should become acquainted with what constitutes good
   form in the performance of an activity.
3. In discussing an activity, the discussion should be characterized by a
   positive approach. For example, if the teacher says, "If you do it in
   'such and such' a way you will break your neck," a child may immediately become aware of a danger that actually may be nonexistent.
4. A suitable soft landing surface such as matting should be provided for
   activities requiring it.
5. Sufficient space should be provided for performance.
6. Short practice periods help prevent fatigue and thus injuries that
   might occur as a result of fatigue.
7. The teacher should learn to recognize fear symptoms in children.
   When it is noticed that a child may fear a certain activity the teacher
   should attempt to instill confidence and proceed in accordance with the
   best interests of the child.

8. Activities should be introduced in order of difficulty, progressing from simple to more complex. (The stunt and tumbling activities included in this chapter are presented in sequential order in terms of degree of difficulty of performance.)

Grade Placement of Activities

The teacher will need to determine those activities most suitable for use at a particular age or grade level. The ability range of children, even at the same age, will vary. It is possible that some children at the fourth grade, or even lower, may be able to perform proficiently all of the activities presented here. On the other hand, it may be difficult for some sixth-grade children to do some of the very simple stunts. As the activities are analyzed for such difficulty factors as balance, strength, flexibility, and coordination, the teacher should be able to determine fairly acccurately those activities most suitable for use with children in a particular group. Generally speaking, the materials on traits and characteristics of children appearing in the Appendix should be helpful in grade placing activities.

Suggestions for Organizing the Class for Activity

It appears to be a good practice to have the class arranged so that all or at least a majority of the children can be seen at all times. Several general patterns may be utilized, depending upon the desire of the teacher and the number of mats available. Many of the stunts do not require mats; however, the teacher should be the judge as to whether or not mats are needed for a particular activity. In practically all cases some sort of matting is required for tumbling activities.

Following are some suggested forms of organization:

(Legend   T—teacher   p—pupils)

"U" Pattern

T

p   p

p   p

p   p

p   p

p p p p p p p p p p

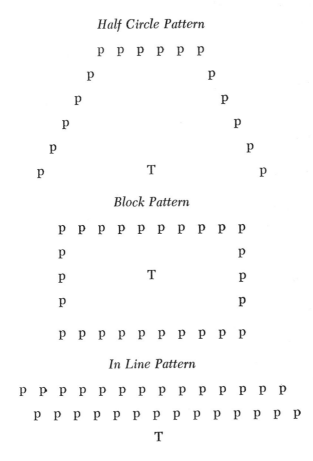

Half Circle Pattern

p   p   p   p   p   p

p   p

p   p

p   p

p   p

p   T   p

Block Pattern

p   p   p   p   p   p   p   p   p   p

p   p

p   T   p

p   p

p   p   p   p   p   p   p   p   p   p

In Line Pattern

p p p p p p p p p p p p p p

p p p p p p p p p p p p p p

T

Whichever pattern is selected, the teacher might well consider the following:

1. All matting should be arranged with great care to provide adequate protection for children. The arrangement of the mats should offer the greatest opportunity for as many pupils as possible to perform at one time. Care should be taken to arrange the mats and place pupils in such a way that they will not execute the skills in the path of each other.

2. Although many elementary schools are not equipped to have pupils change into some type of physical education apparel, it is highly recommended that some arrangement in this regard be made for participation in stunts and tumbling. Besides the obvious reason for what is appropriate for mixed classes of boys and girls, a change in clothes will add to a pupil's

ability to move with greater ease, to move with greater safety, and to move without fear of damaging street clothing. Attire that is loosely fitted, such as shorts or slacks, is appropriate.

3. It appears to be a good practice to have pupils seated during the auditory-and visual-input phases of the lesson. Moreover, pupils should be placed in such a way that all will be able to see and hear in a comfortable manner as far as these input phases are concerned.

General Teaching Procedures

The following list suggests some procedures that teachers might use in teaching stunts and tumbling.

1. Activities should be selected which correspond with the needs and interests of the group. As mentioned previously, for example, primary level children enjoy stunts that involve imitations of animals. In teaching this type of stunt the teacher should give the children an opportunity to suggest their own ideas of the various animal imitations.
2. Tell the children the name of the activity and ask what it suggests to them.
3. The activity should be described by an explanation (auditory input) of the *whole* activity.
4. Demonstrate or have one or more children demonstrate the entire activity, (visual input).
5. The demonstrator should then go through the activity position by position, showing the step-by-step procedure involved in its performance.
6. The whole activity should be performed again.
7. The children should be given the opportunity to practice the activity with the teacher and other children observing performance.
8. Select one or more children who perform the activity fairly well and have the other children evaluate the good elements of their performance. ("What did you like about the way Johnny did that stunt?")
9. Have all the children perform the activity again in groups, evaluating their own performance as well as that of others.

(The activities that follow consist of eight stunts and ten tumbling activities. These should be considered as representative examples. Numerous other possibilities are available from various sources.)

Puppy Dog Run

FIGURE 9.1

Stunt Activities

Description

The pupil places his hands, palms flat and fingers forward, on the surface area in front of his feet. The hands should be under his shoulders for support. The pupil bends his legs slightly to allow his back to come parallel with the surface area. He then moves forward, using both arms and both legs to imitate a running dog. Occasionally the pupil should bring both legs forward at the same time to imitate a dog running at a faster gait.

Teaching Suggestions
1. Suggest that the pupils observe a running dog.
2. Be sure to have the pupils moving in one direction.

Evaluation
1. Does the pupil move in a coordinated fashion?
2. Does the pupil use the arms and legs for support as opposed to the use of just the legs?

Elephant Walk

FIGURE 9.2

Description

From an erect standing position, the pupil bends forward at the waist until his back is parallel with the floor. His arms are straight and held beneath his shoulders. His legs remain straight throughout the walk. As the pupil steps slowly, he swings his arms from side to side. The swaying motion will resemble an elephant swinging its trunk as it walks.

Teaching Suggestions

1. Some pupils may have difficulty in bending while keeping their legs straight. In these cases the teacher can give additional flexibility activities such as bending at the waist while holding the knees straight.
2. Be sure to have the children watch where they are going while moving about.

Evaluation

1. Does the pupil keep his legs straight while walking?
2. Does the pupil walk with a heavy swaying gait?
3. Does the pupil keep his back nearly parallel with the floor?

Seal Crawl

FIGURE 9.3

Description

The seal crawl is an activity in which the pupil supports himself on his hands with his body extended back. The pupil squats and places his hands shoulder width apart, palms flat and fingers pointed forward. He extends his legs in back of himself until his body is straight. (Note: The back is not "sway-back"; but straight.) The pupil points his toes so that a part of his weight will be on the top of his foot. The pupil is now ready to move forward on his hands, dragging his feet.

Teaching Suggestions
1. Have the pupils keep their heads high and their arms slightly in back of their shoulders as they do the seal crawl.
2. Have the pupils shift their weight slightly from side to side to assist in moving their arms.

Evaluation
1. Does the pupil move from side to side as he moves forward?
2. Does the pupil keep his back straight?
3. Does the pupil keep his arms straight?

Coffee Grinder

FIGURE 9.4

Description

    For the coffee grinder the pupil assumes the same position as for the seal crawl—that is, in an extended prone position with both arms supporting the body weight. From this position the pupil supports his straight body on one hand and arm and places the other arm directly over his shoulder. The pupil now has his side toward the surface area and one hand and arm are supporting his weight. With his body remaining straight, the pupil walks slowly around his supporting arm.

Teaching Suggestions
1. Have the supporting hand slightly toward the feet so that the weight can be controlled without falling.
2. Have the pupil change to the other hand and arm and repeat the activity.

Evaluation
1. Does the pupil retain a straight body position throughout the activity?
2. Does the pupil keep his arms straight?
3. Does the pupil circle completely around in coordinated movements?
4. Can the pupil switch position to the other hand and arm?

Thread the Needle

FIGURE 9.5

Description

At a standing position the pupil clasps his hands in front to form a circle with his arms. He then steps through his arms with one foot and then the other. He returns to his original position by stepping out of his arms.

Teaching Suggestions

1. Have the pupil step through while bending forward more than is necessary when he first starts to learn the stunt.
2. If the pupil keeps losing his balance, have him practice standing on one leg without clasping his hands.

Evaluation

1. Does the pupil accomplish the activity without losing his balance?
2. Can the pupil "lead" with either leg?
3. Does the pupil keep his hands clasped throughout the activity?

Squat Thrust

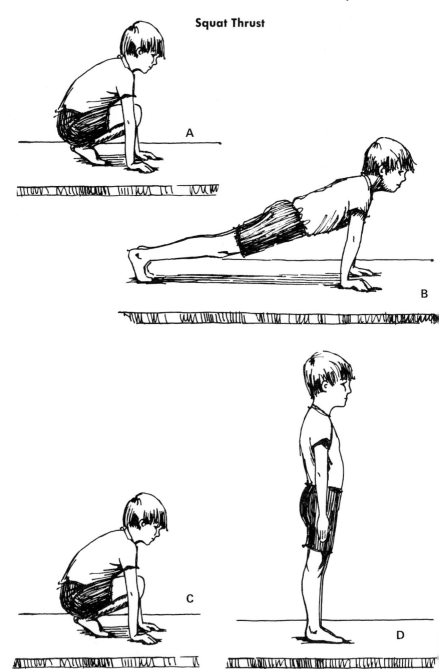

FIGURE 9.6

Description

   From a standing position the pupil assumes a squatting stance, placing his hands on the mat to the outside of his legs with the palms flat and the fingers forward. This is count #1. Switching the weight to the hands and arms, the pupil then extends his legs sharply to the rear until his body is straight. The weight of the body is now on the hands and the balls of the feet. This is count #2. On count #3 the pupil returns to the squatting position, and on count #4 the pupil returns to the erect standing position.

Teaching Suggestions

1. The pupil should be directed through the activity slowly at first, correcting each position.
2. Have the pupil lift vigorously at the hips when moving from count #1 to count #2, and from count #2 to count #3.

Evaluation

1. Does the pupil extend until his body is in a straight line?
2. Does the pupil return to an erect standing position before starting the next squat thrust?

Chinese Get Up

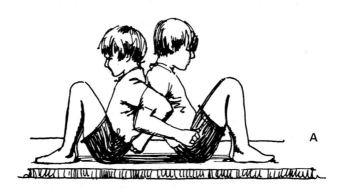

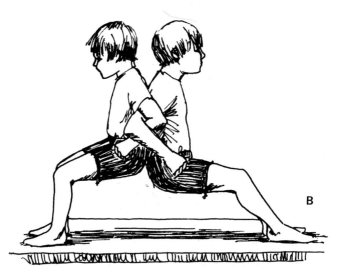

FIGURE 9.7

Description

The Chinese Get Up is an activity that involves two pupils. These two pupils sit with their backs to each other and with their feet close to their buttocks. They lock their arms at their elbows and keep them bent close to their sides. The two pupils then lean back against each other and straighten their legs until they both are in a standing position. They need to use walking steps to get to the standing position.

Teaching Suggestions

1. The pupils should keep the elbows at their sides and should not draw them too far forward.
2. Be sure the pupils keep their backs straight and their heads close to each other.

Evaluation

1. Do the pupils make a coordinated effort so that both are lifting into a standing position?
2. Do they keep their elbows locked?

Churn the Butter

A

B

C

FIGURE 9.8

Description
    Churn the Butter involves two pupils. These two pupils turn back-to back and lock elbows by bending the arms to an approximate ninety-degree angle. The elbows are held in back of each performer and the forearms are held against the ribs. This position is like the finish of the Chinese Get Up. Pupil #1 then picks up pupil #2 from the surface area by bending forward with a slow controlled movement. Pupil #2 will momentarily have his feet in the air. Pupil #1 releases the lifting force by straightening to an erect standing position, and pupil #2 then lifts pupil #1 in the same manner. This action is repeated and can be done in a circular motion by allowing the lifted pupil to come back to the mat slightly to the side.

Teaching Suggestions
1. Have the pupils keep their backs and shoulders straight in order to form a flat surface.
2. Do not allow the pupils to bend forward more than to a position where the uper body is parallel to the mat.
3. Have the pupil who is bending forward hold his head up as opposed to flexing the neck.
4. Pair the pupils by size for this activity.
5. Have the pupil who is lifting place his feet shoulder-width apart and parallel to each other.

Evaluation
1. Do the pupils keep their backs flat and shoulders square?
2. Does the movement seem controlled and coordinated?

Stunts and tumbling contribute to physical development.

Tumbling Activities

Log Roll

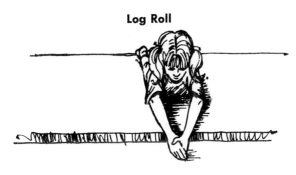

FIGURE 9.9

Description

An introduction to tumbling is easily started with the Log Roll. The pupil assumes an extended prone position with his stomach facing toward the mat. The extended body position along the vertical axis is accomplished by placing the arms over the head along the mat until they are straight. The legs are also extended with the feet together and the toes pointed. The pupil then uses his head, shoulders, and hips to turn 360 degrees along the mat. The pupil should learn to roll in both directions and in a straight line down the mat.

Teaching Suggestions

1. If necessary, assist the pupil by lifting at the hip area.
2. The pupils should be on the mat so that their heads are toward the teacher.
3. If good form is practiced (toes pointed, legs straight, hands together) this will help the pupil to extend his body.
4. Have the pupils roll at different speeds and in both directions.

Evaluation

1. Does the pupil keep his body extended and straight as he rolls?
2. Does the pupil roll smoothly and with an even pace?
3. Does the pupil keep his toes pointed?
4. Does the pupil keep his hands together?
5. Does the pupil keep his head between his arms?

Side Roll

A

B

C

D

FIGURE 9.10

Description

As in the Log Roll, the pupil retains a close contact with the mat, moving in a sideward motion along the mat. The pupil assumes the starting position by kneeling to the mat and placing his forehead on the mat as near his knees as possible. He then grasps his shins with his hands and pulls his feet from the mat. The objective is for the pupil to start the roll to either side, roll to the back, to the other side, and back to the knees and forehead position. The pupil should concentrate on rolling in a straight pattern along the mat.

Teaching Suggestions

1. Have the pupil kneel in the center of the mat with his head toward the teacher.
2. All pupils should be facing the same way (when more than one is performing).
3. All pupils should roll in the same direction, either to the right or left.
4. The pupil should keep his head off the mat after leaving the starting position.
5. The pupil may be assisted by lifting at the shoulders and hips.

Evaluation

1. Does the pupil assume the correct starting position?
2. Does the pupil maintain a tuck position throughout the roll?
3. Does the pupil roll in a straight line when doing two or three consecutive rolls?
4. Does the pupil point his toes?
5. Does the pupil roll smoothly and evenly?

Egg Roll

A

B

C

D

FIGURE 9.11

Description

In the Egg Roll the pupil should roll from a sitting position, to his side, to his back, to his other side, and back to the sitting position. The start is a sitting position on the mat with the knees close to the chest and the heels close to the buttocks. The pupil reaches inside of his knees with his hands and grasps the outside of his shins. The pupil is now ready to move to his side, in either direction, continuing to his back, to his other side, and back to the sitting position.

Teaching Suggestions

1. Make sure the pupil leads directly to his side at the start with more matting in back of him than in front.
2. Have the pupil keep his momentum throughout the activity.
3. Assist the pupil who cannot do the activity by grasping his shoulders.
4. Have the pupil stay in a tightly tucked position.
5. Have the pupil learn the activity by going in both directions.

Evaluation

1. Does the pupil maintain a tucked position?
2. Does the pupil maintain the hold on the shins?
3. Does the pupil roll in the proper sequence?
4. Does the pupil continue smoothly through the roll?
5. Does the pupil end in the proper position?

Forward Roll

A

B

C

D

FIGURE 9.12

Description
    The hands are placed on the mat, palms flat and fingers forward, shoulder-width apart, as the pupil assumes a squatting position. The knees are between the arms, and the neck is flexed to allow the head to be tucked tightly. The chin should be close to the chest. The initial movement is given to the body by an extension of the ankle joint so that force is exerted at the balls of the feet. This forward motion moves over the arms and hands as the head is lowered and the buttocks raised. The arms are closely bent in order to allow the head to move under the hips without touching the mat. The nape of the neck will come in contact with the mat first and then the momentum will be transferred to the back, continuing to the buttocks and the feet, respectively. The body should retain the tight tuck position throughout the skill and the pupil should not allow the hands to touch the mat after the original placement at the starting position.

Teaching Suggestions
1. If the pupil continually rolls over his shoulder, have him move his legs to the outside of his elbows. Place the hands a little more than shoulder-width apart.
2. Watch to see that the weight is on the arms.
3. Have the pupil keep the chin tightly tucked.
4. If the pupil is having difficulty, have him spread his feet as far apart as possible to do the roll.
5. Have the pupil roll from a tuck sitting position to the shoulders.
6. Assist the pupil who needs help by lifting at the nape of the neck and at the shin of the leg.

Evaluation
1. Does the pupil have his palms flat, shoulder-width apart, and knees on the inside of the arms?
2. Does the nape of the neck touch the mat first?
3. Does the pupil roll smoothly over the back and buttocks?
4. Does the pupil roll to his feet without pushing on the mat with his hands?
5. Throughout the first part of the activity, does the pupil support himself on his arms?

Backward Roll

FIGURE 9.13

Description

The Backward Roll, when executed, moves the body from a tightly tucked position on the feet backward 360 degrees while maintaining constant contact with the mat. The pupil assumes the starting position by squatting on the feet, which are approximately shoulder-width apart. Place the hands, palms up, slightly above the shoulders and keep the bent elbows in front of the chest. The thumbs are pointed toward the ears and the fingers are pointed backward. The head is tightly tucked so that the pupil's chin touches his chest. Momentum is created by a loss of the equating balance backward (push with the balls of the feet). The tuck position is maintained as the buttocks, back, hands, and feet, respectively, come in contact with the mat. Remember to have pupils straighten the arms at the point where the shoulders and hands touch the mat and their buttocks are over the hands. This action will allow the pressure of body weight to be taken from the neck region. The pupil will end on his feet in the same squatting position as in the beginning.

Teaching Suggestions

1. Remember to have pupils on the front part of the mat to allow space to roll backward.
2. If necessary, lift under the pupil by grasping each side of his hips.
3. Make sure pupils maintain tuck position throughout the activity and bring their pointed toes together as they roll.
4. Sometimes pupils will assume too much of a squat. Have them raise to a position of sitting on their heels.
5. If a pupil is having difficulty doing the activity, have him assume a position on his back and place his hands on the mat as if he is doing the roll. Then have him spread his legs apart and reach over his head with his legs until his toes touch the mat. Pick up under his hips. This will give him the "feel" of the activity.

Evaluation

1. Does the pupil assume the correct starting position including placing the hands in proper position?
2. Does the pupil lead with his buttocks and keep his body rounded?
3. Does the pupil place his hands on the mat with the palms down and thumbs toward his head?
4. Does the pupil straighten the arms in order to support his body weight as it comes over his neck region?

Fish Flop

A

B

C

FIGURE 9.14

Description

The Fish Flop is executed from the same starting position as a backward roll except for minor changes in the positions of the heads and arms. After a pupil has assumed a squatting position with his feet shoulder-width apart, one arm is extended to the side. The other arm is bent ready to guide the body as it comes in contact with the mat, and the neck is flexed so that the head is tilted to the opposite side from the extended arm. When the buttocks contact the mat, the backward momentum is partially directed upward by casting the legs above the head and shoulders. The extended arm and shoulder act as a supporting surface with neither losing contact with the mat. When the cast carries the body to an inverted extended position over the shoulder, an extreme hyperextension occurs and then the pupil should be able to roll to his chest, stomach, and thighs. The Fish Flop ends on the stomach and thighs.

Teaching Suggestions

1. Have the pupil assume the starting position with plenty of matting in back of him, and in a position that he will not tumble into another pupil.
2. Assist the pupil by lifting at the ankles until his body is extended over his shoulder.
3. Slight pressure at the midsection when the pupil is being lifted over his shoulder will assist in an hyperextended position.
4. To assist the feeling of rolling down the chest, stomach, and thighs, have the pupil lie face down on the mat and arch his back. He should be able to rock from chest to thighs.

Evaluation

1. Does the pupil start with his head tilted away from the direction of his extended arm?
2. Does the pupil cast his legs directly over the shoulder?
3. Does the pupil assume a complete hyperextended position over the shoulder?
4. Does the pupil roll from the chest, stomach, and thighs?
5. Does the pupil execute the skill smoothly and in a straight line in back of him?

Backward Extension Roll

FIGURE 9.15

Description

The Backward Extension Roll simulates the backward roll except at the point the shoulders and hands come in contact with the mat when a full body extension occurs. The pupil assumes the starting position by squatting on the feet, which are approximately shoulder-width apart. Place the hands, palms up, slightly above the shoulders and keep the bent elbows in front of the chest. The thumbs are pointed toward the ears and the fingers are pointed backward. The head is tightly tucked so that the pupil's chin touches his chest. Momentum is created by a loss of the squatting balance backward (push with the balls of the feet). The tightly tucked position is maintained until the buttocks come in contact with the mat. When the buttocks contact the mat, the feet are cast upward and the roll continues down the back to the shoulders and the hands. As the hands touch the mat, the body position has reached complete extension and the arms are straightened so that a handstand position is reached. This split-second handstand position is held just long enough to allow the hips to flex which brings the feet to the mat and the torso over the feet. The knees are bent slightly as this standing position is reached.

Teaching Suggestions

1. Be sure the pupils can do the backward roll first.
2. If a pupil is having difficulty, have him assume a position on the mat on his back and have him cast his legs upward. At this point he should not try to do the complete activity.
3. When spotting the pupil on the ankles by pulling upward, be very quick to slip an arm under the waist so that the pupil will be able to bend over it on landing.
4. Have the pupil maintain a tuck position with his head until the arms have started to straighten and then have him look at his fingers,
5. A verbal timing for the cast could be given to the pupil as his buttocks contact the mat.

Evaluation

1. Does the pupil assume the correct squatting starting position.
2. Does the pupil cast straight over his hands with his legs?
3. Does the pupil straighten his arms completely at the handstand position?
4. Does the pupil extend to a slightly arched handstand position?
5. Does the pupil snap (flex at the waist) to his feet in a controlled fashion indicating a smooth execution all through the activity?

Cartwheel

FIGURE 9.16

Description

The Cartwheel resembles a wheel without the rim as the pupil bends laterally to use his arms and legs as spokes. Standing, with ample matting in front, the pupil steps forward with either foot. As the leading foot touches the mat, the leg is bent and the lead hand is placed on the mat directly in front of the lead foot. Remember that the lead hand is located on the same side as the leading leg. With a thrust upward and forward from the trailing leg and the bent leading leg, the pupil places the other hand on the mat approximately shoulder-width from the first. The pupil will have twisted his body so that, at this point, a handstand position has been reached. The pupil then bends laterally, places the first foot coming over his head on the mat and then the other foot; thus, he ends in a standing sideward position.

Teaching Suggestions

1. Remember to emphasize that the Cartwheel is a lifting activity, where the pelvis is actually lifted over the hands.
2. Emphasize to the pupil that the activity is accomplished in a straight line. Sometimes a piece of tape or a chalk line will assist.
3. Have the pupil hold an eye contact with the mat until he is ready to come to the standing position at the end of the activity.
4. An assist by the teacher (cross the arms and grasp the waist from in back of the pupil) will sometimes help to orient the pupil.
5. Remind the pupil that the body is to be straight throughout the activity. An additional forward momentum may help.

Evaluation

1. Has the pupil placed his hands directly in front of the lead leg?
2. Has the pupil lifted his pelvis over his hands?
3. Has the pupil reached a handstand position with body in alignment?
4. Has the pupil bent laterally and not frontward as he places his feet on the mat?
5. Does the pupil accomplish the activity in a smooth 1, 2, 3, and 4 count? (Each count corresponds to the timing of the hands and the feet.)

Round Off

FIGURE 9.17

Description

The Round Off is similar to the Cartwheel; however, the approach is slightly different. The activity is executed with more force, and a one-quarter twist occurs at the handstand position. Therefore, have the pupil approach the point of execution with a slight run and use a "step-hop-step" movement to gather momentum. After taking the final step with a bent leg, place the hand located on the same side of the body as the leading foot on the mat. Quickly follow with an extension with the bent leg and a casting of the trailing leg until the body is extended into a handstand position over the hands. (Note: As the leg action occurs, the other hand is placed on the mat.) At this point snap the legs together, twist vigorously a one-quarter turn and come to a landing position facing the opposite direction. Finish the landing position by bending the legs and bringing the arms from the mat.

Teaching Suggestions

1. Practice the "hurdle" (step-hop-step) before trying the whole activity.
2. Be sure that the pupil lifts into the activity as opposed to dropping to the hands.
3. Have the pupil maintain eye contact with the mat throughout the activity.
4. A line drawn or taped on the mat may assist the pupil in keeping the Round Off in the proper position, directly in front of the approach.

Evaluation

1. Does the pupil use a "step-hop-step" approach?
2. Does the pupil extend his leading leg in order to lift his body into the activity?
3. Does the pupil bring his buttocks and legs directly over his hands?
4. Does the pupil bring his feet together and execute the activity smoothly?
5. Does the pupil land in balance with his hands off the mat?

Front Limber

A

B

C

FIGURE 9.18

Description

A kick to a handstand position starts the Front Limber. In the hand-stand position the body should have a slight arch with the hands, shoulders, and ankles in line above each other. At this point the shoulders are extended and kept above the hands. A hyperextension occurs at the "small of the back" and a loss of balance should allow the feet to come to the mat. As the feet touch the mat they are placed parallel with each other and shoulder-width apart. The feet should also be placed as close to the hands as possible, enabling the hip region to move over them with ease. As the pelvis moves over the feet, the weight acts as a counterweight allowing the torso to be lifted, and the pupil will end in a balanced standing position.

Teaching Suggestions

1. Have matting in front, to the sides, and in back of the pupil.
2. Be sure the pupil keeps the shoulders over the hands throughout the activity
3. When spotting, have the spotter lift at the top of the buttocks, and not in the small of the back. The spotter should lift up and over the feet.
4. Have the pupils work on flexibility of the back region.
5. Be very careful if you have the pupil bend over a fixed object, such as another person or a rolled mat.
6. Two spotters can very easily be utilized for this activity, one on each side of the pupil.

Evaluation

1. Does the pupil get to a handstand position before proceeding with the activity?
2. Does the pupil hyperextend with his shoulders remaining above the hands?
3. Does the pupil arch enough to accomplish the activity?
4. Does the pupil move the pelvic area over his feet in order to assume a standing position?
5. Does the pupil execute the activity with control (not a lunge for momentum)?

Ball Handling

Activities with inflated balls include tapping (ordinarily referred to as bouncing),* throwing, or rolling to a partner or target, and catching. Most of the balls used for the purposes indicated here are not inflated to pound pressure. On the other hand, some specifications indicate inflating the ball to diameter length. Thus, a six-inch ball would be inflated to six inches in diameter, and an eight-inch ball would be inflated to eight inches in diameter, and so on. These kinds of balls sometimes come in sets ranging from a five-inch ball to a thirteen-inch ball. Although these are the specifications, the teacher can make the ball "faster" (more resilient) by inflating it more, or "slower" (less resilient) by inflating it less. Obviously, a slower ball should be easier to handle. In addition to the various sizes of balls, they sometimes come in a variety of colors. Preschool children are not as likely to be concerned with color as they are with size. At this level the size of the ball should be such that it is easy for a child to visualize it. At kindergarten level color begins to play a part and by grades one and two *both* color and size are important.

Some years ago naturalistic observations by the present author of five-year-old identical twin girls—left on their own to select a size and color of ball—yielded some interesting results. Each twin was placed alone with an observer in a separate room and given liberty to select a ball with which to play. The sizes of the balls were five, six, eight, ten, and thirteen inches (measured through the diameter as previously mentioned). Each size of ball came in colors of green, red, blue, orange, and yellow. Each of the twins was observed to do essentially the same thing. First, they selected the smallest ball. After playing with this ball for a time (most of the activity involved tapping), there was a direct change to the largest ball. And finally, they settled on the midpoint eight-inch ball.

It was theorized that the small ball was selected first, perhaps because little children tend to like little things, such as little tables and chairs and little dishes. Upon having difficulty in manipulating the five-inch ball, the move was then made to the large ball probably because it had "more room on it" and could be more easily handled. After a reasonable degree of success, such as with bouncing, the final selection was the eight-inch ball.

The final color decided upon by each twin was yellow. This was counter to most color preference studies which tend to show that blue is the most popular color and yellow the least popular.

---

*Actually the ball bounces and the child causes it to bounce by tapping. Thus, theoretically the term "tapping" should be used. However, the term bounce will be used throughout this discussion as the term is colloquial.

It seems obvious that the size of a ball in relation to the size of the hand is an important factor in the development of ball bouncing. In studying ball bouncing as long ago as the late thirties, it was found that children at approximately 27 months of age, using one hand, were able to bounce a small ball of 9½ inches in circumference for a distance of one to three feet. At the age of 40 months the distance increased to four to five feet, and it was not until 46 months of age that the children were able to bounce a larger ball of 16¼ inch circumference over an equal distance using the two-hand tap. The larger ball presented certain problems of control and sufficient strength to the young child, for it was not until about 71 months of age, (45 months after bouncing a ball for a distance of one to three feet) that children, using one hand, were able to bounce the large ball a distance of one to three feet.[2]

Activities

The following ball handling activities are representative of the numerous possibilities that might be used with young children. The activities are intended to be in a progressive sequence with respect to degree of difficulty of performance. The imaginative teacher should be able to develop many other activities of this nature, and children should be encouraged to create some activities on their own.

Stationary Bounce

Using both hands, bounce the ball to the surface area and catch it while standing in place. This can be repeated any number of times.

Walking Bounce

Using both hands, bounce the ball to the surface area and catch it while walking.

Partner Bounce

Using both hands, bounce the ball to a partner who returns it. The distance between the partner can be increased as desired.

Bounce Around

Children form a circle and using both hands bounce the ball around the circle with each child retrieving it and bouncing it to the next. The circle can be made up of any number of children; however, not more than five is recommended so that children will get the greatest number of turns.

[2]B. L. Wellman, "Motor Achievements of Preschool Children," *Childhood Education* 13 (1937): 311-316.

Rhythm Bounce

Using both hands, bounce and catch the ball to some sort of rhythmical accompaniment.

Stationary Tap

Tap the ball with one hand while standing in place. Either hand can be used depending upon the individual child, and the tapping can be repeated any number of times.

Walking Tap

Tap the ball while walking along. This can be done any number of times. (Bouncing the ball in this fashion while walking or running is called *dribbling*, as in the game of basketball.)

Throw and Catch

Throw the ball into the air and catch it. The height of the throw can be increased as desired.

Target Roll

Roll the ball at a target. The distance of the roll and the size of the target can be adjusted for the individual child.

Bounce-Clap-Catch

Bounce the ball to the surface area and clap the hands before catching it.

Bounce-Turn-Catch

Bounce the ball and turn around and catch it before it bounces a second time. At the outset of this activity it may be well to throw the ball into the air and then turn around to catch it on the bounce. In this procedure the child has more time to turn around before the ball bounces.

Leg-Over Bounce

Bounce the ball, swing the leg over it, and catch it. This can be done with either leg, and then legs can be alternated.

Leg-Over Tap

This is the same as the Leg-Over Bounce except that the child causes the ball to bounce by continuous tapping.

Wall Target Throw

Throw the ball at a wall target, catching it when it returns. The distance can be increased and the size of the target decreased as desired.

Balance Beam

Generally speaking, there are two classifications of balance beams—
the *high* balance beam and the low balance beam.

The high balance beam, although adjustable, is ordinarily placed at a
height of four feet from the surface area., The width of the high balance
beam is four inches. The high balance beam is considered to be the official
beam for higher level gymnastic competition.

The low balance beam is ordinarily eight to ten inches above the surface area and the width of the beam is two inches. When a four-inch width
is used at this height it is generally referred to as a *walking board*. This
greater width is often desirable when young children are beginning to
learn balance beam activities. All of our discussions here and the activities
that will follow are concerned *only* with the *low* balance beam.

The vital importance of balance in the acquisition of skills and ultimate
success in most physical education activities should not be underestimated.
There are two types of balance, i.e., *static* balance and *dynamic* balance.
Static balance is concerned with balance while remaining in a stationary
position, while dynamic balance involves the ability of the individual to
maintain a position of balance during body movement. We are predominantly concerned here with dynamic balance.

Research in the area of dynamic balance is somewhat sketchy; as a
result, few, if any, conclusions can be made with reference to balance as a
phase of child development.

General Teaching Procedures

Two important factors need to be considered as general procedures
employed in the teaching of balance beam activities. These are (1) mounting and (2) spotting.

Mounting

In a very large majority of cases the lack of success in balance beam
activities is due to the fact that the child mounts the beam incorrectly. The
usual procedure is for the child to stand in front of the beam, instead of
in the correct mounting position of standing *astride* the beam. When a
child stands in front of the beam he must shift his weight forward rather
than sideward, and thus mounts the beam in an "off-balance" position. In
standing astride the beam the child places his foot on the beam and then
shifts his weight sideward before releasing the opposite foot from the surface area. With this procedure it is much easier to maintain balance while
mounting the beam.

Spotting

In spotting or assisting the child, there is a tendency for most teachers to do this from the side rather than from the front or the rear. When the teacher walks along at the side of the child holding his hand, there appears to be a psychological tendency for the child to lean in that direction whether he needs assistance or not. This can cause him to lose his balance. For this reason, if the child needs assistance, it appears best to walk behind him with the teacher's hands on the child's waist, or in front of him with the teacher holding the child's hands. The same situation holds true if the balance beam is placed close to a wall for the purpose of the child using the wall for support. The psychological tendency seems to prevail and the child tends to lean toward the wall. Moreover, the child can inadvertently push away from the wall, causing the balance beam to slide and exposing the child to injury.

Activities

The following low balance beam activities are representative of many possibilities suitable for use with elementary school children. The activities are intended to be in a progressive sequence with respect to degree of difficulty of performance. As in the case of other self-testing activities, the creative teacher should be able to develop numerous other balance beam activities, and the children should be encouraged to create some activities on their own.

Front Walk

Walk forward on the beam using any length of step.

Back Walk

Walk backward on the beam using any length of step.

Front and Back Walk

Walk to the center of the beam using any length of step; turn and continue walking backward using any length of step to the end of the beam.

Forward Front Foot Walk

Walk forward on the beam with either foot always in front of the other. The lead foot moves forward and the trailing foot comes up to the lead foot but not beyond.

Backward Foot Back Walk

Walk backward on the beam with either foot always in the lead.

Front Walk Retrieve Object

Place an object such as a chalkboard eraser or a book in the center of the beam. Walk forward, stoop down and pick up the object and continue walking to the end of the beam before dismounting.

Front Walk Kneel

Walk forward to the center of the beam, kneel down until one knee touches the beam, rise to an upright position and continue walking to the end of the beam.

Front Walk Object Balance

Place an object on the head. Mount the beam and walk the length of the beam while balancing the object on the head.

Back Walk Object Balance

Place an object on the head. Mount the beam and walk backward the length of the beam while balancing the object on the head.

Front Walk Retrieve and Balance Object

Place an object in the center of the beam. Walk forward to the center of the beam, stoop down and pick up the object, place it on the head, and continue walking to the end of the beam while balancing the object.

Front Walk Over

Have two children hold a piece of string or rope stretched across the center of the beam at about a height of 12 to 15 inches. Walk forward on the beam, step over the string and continue walking to the end of the beam.

Back Walk Over

The same procedure is used as for the Front Walk Over, except that the child walks backward on the beam.

Front Walk Under

Have two children hold a piece of string or rope stretched across the center of the beam at a height of from three to four feet. Walk forward on the beam, stoop down and go under the string, and then continue walking to the end of the beam.

Back Walk Under

The same procedure is used as for the Front Walk Under, except that the child walks backward on the beam.

Front Walk Kneel with Leg Extension

Walk forward to the center of the beam, and kneel down until one knee touches the beam. From this position extend the opposite leg forward until leg is straight and the heel of the extended leg is touching the beam. Return to the upright position on the beam and continue walking to the end of the beam.

Back Walk Kneel with Leg Extension

The same procedure is used as for the Front Walk Kneel with Leg Extension, except that the child walks backward on the beam.

Rope Jumping

In general, there are two kinds of rope jumping. One is long rope jumping where two children turn a rope while another jumps. The second is individual rope jumping where the child turns the rope himself as he jumps. The discussions and activities presented here will be concerned only with *individual* rope jumping.

There are many important values that teachers attribute to rope jumping. Not only does it contribute to the all-around physical fitness of the child, but in addition it tends to help the child develop and improve his rhythmic ability and coordination. This, of course, is an important factor in the successful performance of most physical education activities.

Our culture has tended to identify rope jumping as an activity exclusively for girls, particularly in the early age years of the child. The fallacy of this is seen with the extensive use of rope jumping by skilled and mature athletes as a body conditioner and an activity to improve timing and rhythm. Nevertheless, preschool experience in rope skipping is limited almost entirely to little girls. Thus, upon entering school, girls appear to be ahead of boys in this activity. However, it has been our observation that with skillful teaching boys will tend to improve much more rapidly than girls at rope jumping. This may be due to the fact that before entering school girls have likely learned to jump rope by watching others. Thus, without the benefit of skillful teaching it is sometimes necessary for girls to "relearn" rope-jumping skills.

Some General Teaching Procedures

The following list of suggested teaching procedures is intended to serve as a guide for the teacher when providing rope-jumping experiences for children.

1. There are certain mechanical factors that should be taken into account. These center around composition and/or texture of the rope and

rope length. At the present time there are many types of materials used for jumping ropes. Among others these include plastic or plastic links, sash cord, nylon cord, or plain rope. Many teachers prefer to make their ropes by cutting up lengths of clothesline. It becomes more or less a matter of individual preference with regard to the type of rope used. Regardless of the kind of material used, most teachers consider it essential that there are handles on the rope. Without handles, it is easy for the rope to become tangled while turning it.

Rope length is important because if the rope is too long it will strike the floor in front and make it difficult to turn. Conversely, if the rope is too short the child has to "hunch up" in order for the rope to clear his body on the turn. One satisfactory determinant of rope length is to have the child stand on the middle of the rope and pull each end taut to the sides of the body. The ends should come somewhere around waist height.

2.   Children can experiment with the proper way to jump rope without the use of the rope. This can be accomplished by having the child push off lightly from the balls of the feet and jump up and down in this manner several times. This will help him to develop rhythm and to keep him from bending his knees when he attempts to jump the rope.

3.   The child can take the ends of the rope in his hands with the center of the rope on the surface area directly in front of him. He can practice jumping over the rope as it remains in this position. The purpose of this is to have him see that he has to jump just a short height to clear the rope when he turns it.

4.   In turning the rope, the first turn is the only one where a full arm swing is necessary. The reason for this is that sufficient momentum is needed to get the rope all the way around the first time. Succeeding turns of the rope should be done with a wrist motion only. To emphasize this, the child can press his elbows to his body as he turns the rope.

5.   Teachers sometimes find it helpful to the child to furnish him with some sort of rhythmical accompaniment such as a drum beat. The teacher should take care to sound the accompaniment at the proper time.

6.   If the child is having difficulty getting the proper rhythm, it is sometimes helpful to have him turn two separate lengths of rope while he jumps. In this way he gets practice in turning the rope without actually jumping the rope.

7.   When the child first learns to jump, he should be taught to do so without an extra "rhythmic bounce." If the habit of the extra rhythmic bounce is formed, the child may have difficulty in performing some of the more complex rope-jumping activities. For example, in jumping for speed he does not have the time to take the extra bounce.

Activities

The following individual rope-jumping activities are representative of many possibilities suitable for use with elementary school children. The activities are intended to be in a progressive sequence with regard to degree of difficulty of performance.

Two Foot Jump

Turn the rope and jump with both feet together. This can be done any number of times and with varying rates of speed.

Right Foot Jump

In reality this is a hop since the takeoff and landing are on the same foot. This can be done any number of times and with varying rates of speed.

Left Foot Jump

Same as above except with left foot.

Alternate Foot Jump

The left and right feet are used alternately as the rope is turned. The child runs in place while turning the rope and lifting each foot over it.

Forward Alternate Foot Jump

Same as above except that the child runs forward as he lifts each foot over the rope.

Spread Jump

The feet are placed apart at a distance desired by the child and he jumps in this manner as he turns the rope. The distance of the spread of the feet can be increased as the child desires.

Stride Jump

The child stands in stride with one foot slightly ahead of the other and jumps the rope in this manner. The length of the stride can be increased as the child desires.

Figure Eight

The child swings the rope first to the right of his body and then to the left and then jumps over the rope as he turns it. The sequence is swing right—swing left—turn and jump. This can be continued any number of times and with varying rates of speed.

Cross Rope Jump

As the rope is turned it is crossed in front of the body making a loop. The child jumps through this loop. The rope should be crossed close to the body and the arms crossed at about the level of the wrists. The child may need to "bunch up" a little in order to get through the loop.

Double Swing Jump

In this jump the child turns the rope twice while he is off the surface area. The rope needs to be turned very quickly and the child should elevate himself a little higher from the surface area in order not to come down before he makes two turns of the rope.

Part Two

Cognitive
Physical
Education

Chapter 10

The Nature
of Cognitive
Physical Education

It will perhaps be recalled that cognitive physical education was one of the branches of physical education identified in Chapter 1. The present chapter will elaborate more on this branch and the following three chapters will go into detail regarding skill and concept development through physical education in the specific subject areas of reading, mathematics, and science.

The primary function of this chapter will be to help the reader to deal more effectively with such questions as:

1. What is the underlying theory of cognitive education?
2. How is this approach to learning concerned with the short attention span?
3. How is motivation a factor in the physical education learning medium?
4. How is competition as it is related to motivation involved in this type of learning?
5. How is this approach concerned with proprioception?
6. In what way does reinforcement theory apply to the physical education learning medium?

The Theory of Cognitive Physical Education

The important role of play in cognition and learning has been recognized for centuries. In fact the idea of the playing of games as a desirable learning medium has been traced to the ancient Egyptians. Through the ages some of the most profound thinkers in history have expounded positively in terms of the value of pleasurable physical activity as a way of learning. Perhaps one of the earliest pronouncements in this regard was Plato's suggestion that . . . in teaching children; train them by a kind of game and you will be able to see more clearly the natural bent of each.

The physical education learning medium is concerned with how children can develop skills and concepts in other school subject areas while actively engaged in certain kinds of physical education activities. Although all children differ in one or more characteristics, the fact remains that they are more *alike* than they are different. The one common likeness of all children is that they all *move*. Cognitive physical education is based essentially on the theory that children will learn better when what we might call *academic learning* takes place through pleasurable physical activity. The procedure of learning through physical education involves the selection of a physical education activity which is taught to the children and used as a learning activity for the development of a skill or concept in a specific subject area. An attempt is made to arrange an active learning situation so that a fundamental intellectual skill or concept is being practiced in the course of participating in the physical education activity. Activities are selected on the basis of the degree of inherence of a skill or concept in a given school subject area, as well as the appropriate physical ability and social level of a given group of children.

Essentially, there are two general types of such activities. One type is useful for developing a specific concept, where the learner "acts out" the concept and thus is able to visualize as well as to get the "feel" of the concept. Concepts become a part of the child's physical reality as the child participates in the activity where the concept is inherent. An example of such an activity follows.

The concept to be developed is the science concept *electricity travels along a pathway and needs a complete circuit over which to travel.* A physical education activity in which this concept is inherent is *Straddle Ball Roll.*

The children stand one behind the other in relay files with from 6 to 10 children in each file. All are in stride position with feet far enough apart so that a ball can be rolled between the legs of the players. The first person in each file holds a rubber playground ball. At a signal, the person at the front of each file starts the activity by attempting to roll the ball between the legs of all the players on his team. The team which gets the ball to the last member of its file first in the manner described scores a point. The last player goes to the head of his file and this procedure is continued with a point scored each time for the team that gets the ball back to the last player first. After every player has had an opportunity to roll the ball back, the team which has scored the most points is declared the winner.

In applying this activity to develop the concept, the first player at the head of each file becomes the electric switch which opens and shuts the circuit. The ball is the electric current. As the ball rolls between the children's legs it moves right through if all of the legs are properly lined up. When a leg is not in the proper stride, the path of the ball is impeded and the ball rolls out. The game has to be stopped until the ball is recovered and the correction made in the position of the leg. The circuit has to be repaired (the child's leg) before the flow of electricity (the roll of the ball) can be resumed.

The second type of activity helps to develop skills by using these skills in highly interesting and stimulating situations. Repetitive drill for the development of skills related to specific concepts can be utilized. An example of this type of activity follows.

This activity is an adaptation of the game *Steal the Bacon* and is used to drill on *initial consonants*. Children are put into two groups of seven each. The members of both teams are given the letters *b, c, d, h, m, n,* and *p,* or any other initial consonants with which they have been having difficulty. The teams face each other about ten feet apart as in the following diagram.

b		p
c		n
d		m
h	beanbag	h
m	(bacon)	d
n		c
p		b

The teacher calls out a word such as *ball,* and the two children having the letter *b* run out to grab the beanbag. If a player gets the beanbag back to his line, he scores two points for his team. If his opponent tags him before he gets back, the other team scores one point. The game ends when each letter has been called. The scores are totalled and the game is repeated with the children being identified with different letters.

A very important precautionary measure with regard to cognitive physical education was mentioned in Chapter 1, and it bears repeating here. That is, this approach should be considered as only *one* aspect of physical education and not the major purpose of it. We should consider physical education as a subject in its own right, that is, *curricular physical education* which comprised Part One of the book. Consequently, the use of physical education as a learning medium in other subject areas should not ordinarily occur during the regular time allotted to physical education.

On the contrary, this approach should be considered a learning activity in the same way that other kinds of learning activities are used in a given subject area. This means that, for the most part, this procedure should be used during the time allotted to the particular subject area in question. Moreover the classroom teacher would ordinarily do the teaching when this approach is used. The function of the physical education teacher would be to work closely with the classroom teacher and furnish him or her with suitable physical education activities to use in the development of concepts. This is to say that the classroom teacher is familiar with the skills and concepts to be developed, and similarly the physical education teacher should know those activities that could be used to develop the skills and concepts.

Factors Influencing Learning Through Cognitive Physical Education

During the early school years, and at ages six to eight particularly, it is possible that learning is limited frequently by a relatively short attention span rather than only by intellectual capabilities. Moreover, some children who do not appear to think or learn well in abstract terms can more readily grasp concepts when given an opportunity to use them in an applied manner. In view of the fact that the child is a creature of movement and also that he is likely to deal better in concrete rather than abstract terms, it would seem to follow naturally that the physical education learning medium is well suited to him.

The above statement should not be interpreted to mean that the author is suggesting that learning through movement-oriented experiences (motor learning) and passive learning experiences (verbal learning) are two different kinds of learning. The position is taken here that *learning is learning,* even though in the physical education approach the motor component may be operating at a higher level than in most of the traditional types of learning activities.

The theory of learning accepted here is that learning takes place in terms of reorganization of the systems of perception into a functional and integrated whole because of the result of certain stimuli. This implies that problem solving is the way of human learning and that learning takes place through problem solving. In a physical education learning situation that is well planned, a great deal of consideration should be given to the inherent possibilities for learning in terms of problem solving. In fact, in most physical education lessons, opportunities abound for near-ideal teaching-learning situations because of the many problems to be solved. Using games as an example the following sample questions asked by children indicate that there is a great opportunity for reflective thinking, use of judgment, and problem solving in this type of experience.

1. Why didn't I get to touch the ball more often?
2. How can we make it a better game?
3. Would two circles be better than one?
4. What were some of the things you liked about the game?
5. How can I learn to throw the ball better?

Another very important factor to consider with respect to the physical education learning medium is that a considerable part of the learnings of young children is motor in character, with the child devoting a good proportion of his attention to skills of a locomotor nature. Furthermore, learnings of a motor nature tend to usurp a large amount of the young child's time and energy and are often closely associated with other learnings. In addition, it is recognized by experienced classroom teachers at the primary grade levels that the child's motor mechanism is active to the extent that it is almost an impossibility for him to remain for a very long period of time in a quiet state regardless of the passiveness of the learning situation.

To demand prolonged sedentary states of children is actually, in a sense, in defiance of a basic physiological principle. This is concerned directly with the child's basic metabolism. The term "metabolism" is concerned with physical and chemical changes in the body which involve producing and consuming energy. The rate at which these physical and chemical processes are carried on when the individual is in a state of rest represents his *basal metabolism*. Thus, the basal metabolic rate is indicative of the speed at which body fuel is changed to energy, as well as how fast this energy is used.

Basal metabolic rate can be measured in terms of calories per meter of body surface, with a calorie representing a unit measure of heat energy in food. It has been found that on the average, basal metabolism rises from birth to about two or three years of age, at which time it starts to decline until between the ages of twenty to twenty-four. Also, the rate is higher for boys than for girls. With the highest metabolic rate and therefore the greatest amount of energy occurring during the early school years, deep consideration might well be given to learning activities through which this energy can be utilized. Moreover, it has been observed that there is an increased attention span of primary-age children during play. When a task such as a physical education experience is meaningful to a child, he can spend longer periods engaged in it than is likely to be the case in some of the more traditional types of learning activities.

The comments made thus far have alluded to some of the general aspects of the value of the physical education learning medium. The ensuing discussions will focus more specifically upon what we call certain *inherent facilitative factors* in the physical education learning medium which are highly compatible with child learning. These factors are *motivation, proprioception,* and *reinforcement,* all of which are somewhat interdependent and interrelated.

Motivation

In consideration of motivation as an inherent facilitative factor of learning through the physical education medium, we would like to think of the term as it is described in the *Dictionary of Education,* that is, "the practical art of applying incentives and arousing interest for the purpose of causing a pupil to perform in a desired way."[1]

We should also take into account *extrinsic and intrinsic* motivation. Extrinsic motivation is described as "the application of incentives that are external to a given activity to make work palatable and to facilitate performance," while intrinsic motivation is the "determination of behavior that is resident within an activity and that sustains it, as with autonomous acts and interests."[2]

Extrinsic motivation has been and continues to be used as a means of spurring individuals to achievement. This most often takes the form of various kinds of reward incentives. The main objection to this type of motivation is that it tends to focus the learner's attention upon the reward rather than the learning task and the total learning situation.

In general, the child is motivated when he discovers what seems to him to be a suitable reason for engaging in a certain activity. The most valid reason, of course, is that he sees a purpose for the activity and derives enjoyment from it. The child must feel that what he is doing is important and purposeful. When this occurs and the child gets the impression that he is being successful in a group situation, the motivation is intrinsic, since it comes about naturally as a result of the child's interest in the activity. It is the premise here that the physical education medium contains this "built-in" ingredient so necessary to desirable and worthwhile learning.

The ensuing discussions of this section of the chapter will be concerned with three aspects of motivation that are considered to be inherent in the physical education learning medium. These are (1) motivation in relation

---

[1]Carter V. Good, *Dictionary of Education,* 2d ed. (New York: McGraw-Hill, Inc., 1959), p. 354.
  [2]Ibid.

to *interest*, (2) motivation in relation to *knowledge of results*, and (3) motivation in relation to *competition*.

Motivation in Relation to Interest

It is important to have an understanding of the meaning of interest as well as an appreciation of how interests function as an adjunct to learning. As far as the meaning of the term is concerned, the following description given sometime ago by Lee and Lee expresses in a relatively simple manner what is meant by the terms *interest* and *interests*: "Interest is a state of being, a way of reacting to a certain situation. Interests are those fields or areas to which a child reacts with interest consistently over an extended period of time."[3]

A good condition for learning is a situation in which a child agrees with and acts upon the learnings which he considers of most value to him. This means that the child accepts as most valuable those things that are of greatest interest to him. To the very large majority of children their active play experiences are of the greatest personal value to them.

Under most circumstances a very high interest level is concomitant with physical education situations simply because of the expectation of pleasure children tend to associate with such activities. The structure of a learning activity is directly related to the length of time the learning act can be tolerated by the learner without loss of interest. Physical education experiences by their very nature are more likely to be so structured rather than many of the traditional learning activities.

Motivation in Relation to Knowledge of Results

Knowledge of results is most commonly referred to as *feedback*. It was suggested by Brown many years ago that feedback is the process of providing the learner with information as to how accurate his reactions were.[4]

Ammons has referred to feedback as knowledge of various kinds which the performer received about his performance.[5]

It has been reported by Bilodeau and Bilodeau that knowledge of results is the strongest, most important variable controlling performance and

[3]J. Murray Lee and Dorris May Lee, *The Child and His Development* (New York: Appleton-Century-Crofts, 1958), p. 382.

[4]J. S. Brown, "A Proposed Program of Research on Psychological Feedback (knowledge of results) in the Performance of Psychomotor Tasks." Research Planning Conference on Perceptual and Motor Skills, AFHRRC Conf. Rept. 1949, U.S. Air Force, San Antonio, Texas, pp. 1-98.

[5]R. B. Ammons, "Effects of Knowledge of Performance: A Survey and Tentative Formulation," *Journal of General Psychology*, LIV (1956): 279-99.

learning, and further that studies have repeatedly shown that there is no improvement without it, progressive improvement with it, and deterioration after its withdrawal.[6] As a matter of fact, there appears to be a sufficient abundance of objective evidence that indicates that learning is usually more effective when one receives some immediate information on how he is progressing. It would appear rather obvious that such knowledge of results is an important adjunct to learning because one would have little idea of which of his responses was correct. Dolinsky makes the analogy that it would be like trying to learn a task while blindfolded.[7]

The physical education learning medium provides almost instantaneous knowledge of results because the child can actually *see* and *feel* himself throw a ball, or tag, or be tagged in a game. He does not become the victim of a poorly constructed paper-and-pencil test, the results of which may have little or no meaning for him.

Motivation in Relation to Competition

Using games as an example to discuss the motivational factor of competition, we refer back to our description of games in Chapter 7. That is, games imply *active interaction of children in cooperative and/or competitive situations.* It is possible to have both cooperation and competition functioning at the same time, as in the case of team games. While one team is competing against the other, there is cooperation within each group. In this framework it could be said that a child is learning to cooperate while competing. It is also possible to have one group competing against another without cooperation within the group, as in the case of games where all children run for a goal line independently and on their own.

As indicated in Chapter 7, the terms *cooperation* and *competition* are antonymous; therefore, the reconciliation of children's competitive needs and cooperative needs is not an easy matter. In a sense, we are confronted with an ambivalent condition, which, if not carefully handled, could place children in a state of conflict.

Modern society not only rewards one kind of behavior (cooperation) but also its direct opposite (competition). Perhaps more often than not our cultural demands sanction these rewards without provision of clear-cut standards with regard to specific conditions under which these forms of behavior might well be practiced. Hence, the child is placed in somewhat of a quandary with reference to when to cooperate and when to compete.

[6]Edward A. Bilodeau and Ina Bilodeau, "Motor Skill Learning," *Annual Review of Psychology,* Palo Alto, California, (1961), pp. 243-270.

[7]Richard Dolinsky, *Human Learning* (Dubuque, Iowa: Wm. C. Brown Company, Publishers, 1966), p. 13.

As far as the competitive aspects of physical education are concerned, they not only appear to be a good medium for learning because of the intrinsic motivation inherent in them but also this medium of learning can provide for competitive needs of children in a pleasurable and enjoyable way.

Proprioception

Earlier in this chapter it was stated that the theory of learning accepted here is that learning takes place in terms of a reorganization of the systems of perception into a functional and integrated whole as a result of certain stimuli. These systems of perception, or sensory processes as they are sometimes referred to, are ordinarily considered to consist of the senses of sight, hearing, touch, smell, and taste. Armington has suggested that "although this point of view is convenient for some purposes, it greatly oversimplifies the ways by which information can be fed into the human organism."[8] He indicates also that a number of sources of sensory input are overlooked, particularly the senses that enable the body to maintain its correct posture. As a matter of fact, the sixty to seventy pounds of muscle which include over six hundred in number that are attached to the skeleton of the average size man could well be his most important sense organ.

Various estimates indicate that the visual sense brings us upwards of three-fourths of our knowledge. Therefore, it could be said with little reservation that man is eye-minded. However, Steinhaus has reported that "a larger portion of the nervous system is devoted to receiving and integrating sensory input originating in the muscles and joint structures than is devoted to the eye and ear combined."[9] In view of this Steinhaus has contended that man is *muscle sense* minded.

Generally speaking, *proprioception* is concerned with muscle sense. The proprioceptors are sensory nerve terminals that give information concerning movements and position of the body. A proprioceptive feedback mechanism is involved which in a sense regulates movement. In view of the fact that children are so movement oriented, it appears a reasonable speculation that proprioceptive feedback from the receptors of muscles, skin, and joints contributes in a facilitative manner when the physical education learning medium is used to develop academic skills and concepts. The combination of the psychological factor of motivation and the physiological factor of proprioception inherent in the physical education learning

[8]John C. Armington, *Physiological Basis of Psychology* (Dubuque, Iowa: Wm. C. Brown Company, Publishers, 1966), p. 16.
[9]Arthur H Steinhaus, "Your Muscles See More Than Your Eyes," *Journal of Health, Physical Education, and Recreation*, September 1966.

medium has caused us to coin the term motorvation to describe this phenomenon.

Reinforcement

In considering the compatibility of the physical education learning medium with reinforcement theory, the meaning of reinforcement needs to be taken into account. An acceptable general description of reinforcement would be that there is an increase in the efficiency of a response to a stimulus brought about by the concurrent action of another stimulus. The basis for contending that the physical education learning medium is consistent with general reinforcement theory is that this medium reinforces attention to the learning task and learning behavior. It keeps children involved in the learning activity, which is perhaps the major area of application for reinforcement procedures. Moreover, there is perhaps little in the way of human behavior that is not reinforced, or at least reinforcible, by feedback of some sort, and the importance of proprioceptive feedback has already been discussed in this particular connection.

In summarizing this discussion, it would appear that the physical education learning generally establishes a more effective situation for learning reinforcement for the following reasons:

1. The greater motivation of the children in the physical education learning situation involves accentuation of those behaviors directly pertinent to their learning activities, making these salient for the purpose of reinforcement.

2. The proprioceptive emphasis in the physical education learning medium involves a greater number of *responses* associated with and conditioned to learning stimuli.

3. The gratifying aspects of the physical education situations provide a generalized situation of *reinforcers*.

Research to Support the Theory of Cognitive Physical Education

Throughout the ages the concept of learning through motor activity has been held in high esteem by many outstanding philosophers and educators. Such pronouncements extend over several centuries from Plato's assertion that "learning takes place best through play and play situations" to a modern twentieth-century statement by L. P. Jacks that "the discovery of the educational possibilities of the play side of life may be counted one of the greatest discoveries of the present day." The favorable comments of such people obviously carry a great deal of weight. However, in an age when so much emphasis is placed upon scientific inquiry and research we cannot and should not rely on the subjective opinion of even some of the most highly regarded thinkers in history. Thus, the need for some supporting evidence.

A good portion of the research in the area of cognitive physical education has been conducted or directed by the present author. The bibliography that follows has been prepared for the reader who is interested in pursuing in detail some of the research that is available in this area. (Among the studies that follow, those that are listed as Master's theses or Doctoral dissertations may be obtained from the University of Maryland through inter-library loan.)

BIBLIOGRAPHY

Reading

BOBBIT, ELEANOR W. "A Comparison of the Use of a Reading Readiness Workbook Approach and the Active Game Learning Medium in the Development of Selected Reading Skills and Concepts." Ph.D dissertation, University of Maryland, College Park, Maryland, 1972.

HUMPHREY, JAMES H. "Comparison of the Use of the Active Game Learning Medium with Traditional Procedures in the Reinforcement of Reading Skills with Fourth Grade Children." *The Journal of Special Education,* (Winter Issue) 1967.

HUMPHREY, JAMES H. "Comparison of the Use of Active Games and Language Workbook Exercises as Learning Media in the Development of Language Understandings with Third Grade Children." *Perceptual and Motor Skills* 21 (1965).

HUMPHREY, JAMES H. "A Pilot Study of the Use of Physical Education as a Learning Medium in the Development of Language Arts Concepts in Third Grade Children." *Research Quarterly,* March 1962.

HUMPHREY, JAMES H., and LINK, RUTH. "An Exploratory Study of Integration of Physical Education and Reading Vocabulary with Selected Third Grade Children." *Proceedings,* Research Section, American Association for Health, Physical Education, and Recreation, Washington, D. C., 1959.

HUMPHREY, JAMES H., and MOORE, VIRGINA D. "Improving Reading Through Physical Education." *Education* (The Reading Issue) May 1960.

Mathematics

CRIST, THOMAS. "A Comparison of the Use of the Active Game Learning Medium with Developmental-Meaningful and Drill Procedures in Developing Concepts for Telling Time at Third Grade Level." Ph.D. dissertation, University of Maryland, College Park, Maryland, 1968. *Research Abstracts,* American Association for Health, Physical Education, and Recreation, Washington. D. C. 1969.

DROTER, ROBERT J. "A Comparison of Active Games and Passive Games Used as Learning Media for the Development of Arithmetic Readiness Skills and

Concepts with Kindergarten Children in an Attempt to Study Gross Motor Activity as a Learning Facilitator." Master's thesis, University of Maryland, College Park, Maryland, 1972.

HUMPHREY, JAMES H. "Use of the Physical Education Learning Medium in the Development of Certain Arithmetical Processes with Second Grade Children." *Research Abstracts,* American Association for Health, Physical Education, and Recreation, Washington, D.C. 1968.

HUMPHREY, JAMES H. "The Mathematics Motor Activity Story." *The Arithmetic Teacher,* January 1967.

HUMPHREY, JAMES H. "An Exploratory Study of Active Games in Learning of Number Concepts by First Grade Boys and Girls." *Perceptual and Motor Skills* 23 (1966).

KRUG, FRANK L. "The Use of Physical Education Activities in the Enrichment of Learning of Certain First Grade Mathematical Concepts." Master thesis, University of Maryland, College Park, Maryland, 1973.

TROUT, EDWIN. "A Comparative Study of Selected Mathematical Concepts Developed Through Physical Education Activities Taught by the Physical Education Teacher and Traditional Techniques Taught by the Classroom Teacher." Master's thesis, University of Maryland, College Park, Maryland, 1969.

WRIGHT, CHARLES. "A Comparison of the Use of Traditional and Motor Activity Learning Media in the Development of Mathematical Concepts in Five and Six Year Old Children with an Attempt to Negate the Motivational Variable." Master's thesis, University of Maryland, College Park, Maryland, 1969.

Science

HUMPHREY, JAMES H. "The Use of Motor Activity in the Development of Science Concepts with Mentally Handicapped Children." *Proceedings,* National Convention of the National Science Teachers Association, Washington, D. C. 1973.

HUMPHREY, JAMES H. "The Use of Motor Activity Learning in the Development of Science Concepts with Slow Learning Fifth Grade Children." *Journal of Research in Science Teaching* vol. 9, No. 3, (1972).

HUMPHREY, JAMES H. "A Comparison of the Use of the Active Game Learning Medium and Traditional Media in the Development of Fifth Grade Science Concepts with Children with Below Normal Intelligence Quotients." *Research Abstracts,* American Association for Health, Physical Education, and Recreation, Washington, D.C. 1970.

HUMPHREY, JAMES H. "Developing Science Concepts with Elementary School Children Through Physical Education." *Proceedings,* Research Section, American Association for Health, Physical Education, and Recreation, Washington D. C., 1960.

ISON, CHARLES. "An Experimental Study of a Comparison of the Use of Physical Education Activities as a Learning Medium with Traditional Teaching Procedures in the Development of Selected Fifth Grade Science Concepts." Master's thesis, University of Maryland, College Park, Maryland, 1961.

PRAGER, IRIS. "The Use of Physical Education Activities in the Reinforcement of Learning of Selected First Grade Science Concepts." Master's thesis, University of Maryland, College Park, Maryland, 1968.

Some Generalizations of the Research Findings

In view of the fact that there are now certain objective data to support a long-held hypothetical postulation, perhaps some generalized assumptions along with reasonable speculations can be set forth with some degree of confidence. Although the data found in the foregoing studies are not extensive enough to carve out a clear-cut profile with regard to learning through the physical education medium, they are suggestive enough to give rise to some interesting generalizations which may be summarized as follows:

1. In general, children tend to learn certain academic skills and concepts better through the physical education medium than through many of the traditional media in such subject areas as reading, mathematics, and science.

2. This approach, while favorable for both boys and girls, appears to be more favorable for boys.

3. The approach appears to be more favorable for children with normal and below normal intelligence.

4. For children with high levels of intelligence, it may be possible to introduce more advanced academic skills and concepts at an earlier age through the physical education learning medium.

Future Prospects of Cognitive Physical Education

Although it is difficult to predict what the future holds for cognitive physical education, we feel pretty well assured that more serious attention is currently being paid to it. Discussions with leading neurophysiologists, learning theorists, child-development specialists and others reveal a positive feeling toward the physical education medium of learning. And there is pretty general agreement that the premise is very sound from all standpoints: philosophical, physiological, and psychological.

It will remain the responsibility for further research to provide more conclusive evidence to support present generalizations and speculations. There is hope, however, based on actual experience with the approach described in Chapters 11, 12, and 13, which follow, to encourage those responsible for facilitating child learning to use this approach and to join in collecting evidence to verify the contribution of cognitive physical education to the educational curriculum.

Chapter 11

How Children
Learn to Read
Through Physical Education

Through reading, the individual receives the thoughts and feelings of others. Thus reading is considered as a receptive phase of language. In this case the word "receptive" might well carry a figurative as well as a purely literal meaning. Indeed, reading has been on the "receiving end" of a great deal of criticism during the past few years. Perhaps more criticism has been directed at it than all of the other elementary school curriculum areas combined. Although it may be difficult to determine precisely why reading has suffered the brunt of attack, one could speculate that it might be due to the fact that, in general, most people consider reading as the real test of learning.

A good bit of the controversy involving reading seems to focus around two general areas. First, there has been criticism of the various methods of teaching reading, and second, there has been some question regarding the validity of the principles upon which these methods are based. Perhaps because of individual differences, any method used in absolute form to the exclusion of all other methods would not meet the needs of all children. For this reason, it seems logical to assume that the procedures or combination of procedures employed should be those which best meet the needs of an individual child or a particular group of children.

It is not the purpose here to extol or criticize any of the past or present methods of teaching reading. On the contrary, the discussions and accompanying illustrations which follow are intended to show how physical education and reading are related to the extent that they can be integrated in the development of common skills and understandings.

The theory that there is a high degree of relationship between participation in physical education activities and reading is not new. For example Fénelon (1651-1715 is reputed to have said "I have seen certain children who have learned to read while playing."[1]

More recently, Beaumont and Franklin have suggested that "their kinesthetic sense—the sense of "feel" they get through their muscles—seems to be highly developed and it helps some children remember words they would take much longer to learn by looking at or sounding out."[2]

Suggestive of the important contribution that physical education activities can make to reading is the following statement made by Vinacke in a discussion on word perception:

> . . . word perception depends upon the interest of the child. Here, of course, is a principle of pedagogy too familiar to require much elaboration; namely, that a child will learn more easily and will remember better if the subject matter is something that he is personally involved in . . . . So with words; children learn and remember words pertaining to their own needs and interests.[3]

Indeed, physical education subject matter "is something that he is personally involved in." Consequently, reading that utilizes the medium of physical education activities as a motivating factor is likely to be very appealing to children. Used in this manner, physical education can make a very fine contribution to the reading ability and interest of some children.

To this end this chapter will attempt to provide some tentative answers to the following questions:

1. How is reading related to the other areas of language arts?
2. What is the theory of motivation as it pertains to physical education reading content?
3. How can children develop reading skills through physical education?
4. What is the underlying theory of learning to read through creative movement, using the AMAV technique?

Relationship of Reading to Other Areas of Language Arts

The language arts program in the elementary school includes the areas of reading, listening, speaking, and writing. All of these areas are concerned with communication. The primary purpose of the language arts in the modern elementary school is to facilitate communication.

[1]George Ellsworth Johnson, *Education by Plays and Games* (Boston: Ginn and Company, 1907), p. 31

[2]Florence Beaumont and Adele Franklin, "Who Says Johnny Can't Read?" *Parents Magazine,* June 1955, p. 42.

[3]W. Edgar Vinacke "Concepts and Attitudes in the Perception of Words," *Education,* May, 1955, p. 571.

Reading and listening are sometimes referred to as the *receptive* phases of language, while speaking and writing are considered as the *expressive* phases. This implies that through reading and listening the individual receives the thoughts and feelings of others, and through speaking and writing the individual has the opportunity to express his own thoughts and feelings.

Although it has been indicated that the language arts program contains reading, listening, speaking, and writing, the reader should not interpret this to mean that these are to be considered as entirely separate entities. On the contrary, they are closely interrelated and each can be considered a component part of the broad area of communication. Such areas of study as spelling, word meanings, word recognition, and the like, are involved in each of the four areas.

The importance of the interrelationship of the various language arts was given strong emphasis by one authority several years ago in the following statement:

> Children must use words in speaking and have them meaningful before they can read them successfully. They can spell better the words which they read with understanding and which they want to use for their own purposes. Their handwriting even improves when they use it in purposeful communication, when someone important to them is going to read it.[4]

The modern elementary school gives a great deal of attention to the interrelationship of the various facets of the language arts. This is reflected in the way in which language experiences are being provided for children in the better-than-average elementary school. In the traditional elementary school it was a common practice to treat such facets of the language arts as reading, writing, and spelling as separate subjects. As a result, they became more or less isolated and unrelated entities, and their full potential as mediums of expression probably never was fully realized. In the modern elementary school, where children have more freedom of expression and, consequently, greater opportunity for self-expression, the approach to teaching language arts is one that relates the various language areas to particular areas of interest. All of the facets of language arts—reading, listening, speaking, and writing—thus are utilized in the solution of problems in all curriculum areas. This procedure is based primarily upon the assumption that skill in communication should be developed in all of the activities engaged in by children.

[4]J. Murray Lee and Dorris May Lee, *The Child and His Curriculum*, 2d ed. (New York: Appleton-Century-Crofts, Inc., 1950), p. 353.

Physical Education Reading Content

Basic facts about the nature of human beings serve educators today as principles of learning. One of these principles, *learning takes place when the child has his own purposeful goals to guide his learning activities,* serves as the basis for physical education reading content material. Generally speaking, there are two ways in which physical education reading content can be developed. These are the *language experience stories* of children and *prepared stories.*

The Language Experience Stories of Children

The language experience approach (LEA) can very effectively involve children developing group or individual stories based on active games they have learned to play. This technique involves the usual procedures of the children first discussing important aspects of their experience in order for their stories to be detailed and accurate enough that other children could read their story and be able to play the game. Such aspect of reading as sufficient detail and accuracy of information plus sequencing of procedures involves many higher-level cognitive aspects of problem solving.

After the discussion the children begin to dictate their story about how to play the game which the teacher records on the board or on large chart paper. It is important that the language patterns of children be recorded intact. The teacher records the words exactly as the children dictate them but spelling the words correctly. The teacher uses guided questioning to help children put in sufficient details and proper sequence in the procedures for playing the game in their story. After the children have dictated their story, they may reread it to be sure it has enough information so that others are able to play the game after reading their story. The children may even play the game again to be sure they have all the necessary steps. The language experience story based on such a physically-oriented activity facilitates the concept that the printed word symbols represent not only their oral language, but also these words (both oral and printed) represent things that they do, see, touch, feel, and think about.

An example of a language experience story with physical education reading content follows:

In a third-grade classroom[5] a particular reading activity was an outgrowth of a social studies unit concerned with the community and people who contribute to a community's welfare. Among the various community helpers studied, the duties of a policeman seemed to be quite fascinating. As an interest-catching device, a large picture of a policeman drawn by the

---

[5]This procedure was employed by Nancy Watkins, New Market, Maryland.

POLICEMAN

Figure 11.1

teacher was displayed in the room. (See Figure 11.1) On one particular afternoon, a second picture of children enjoying a circle game was presented with the caption "We play a game." (See Figure 11.2) The class displayed a great deal of enthusiasm and a chart was quickly written with little teacher guidance. (See Figure 11.3) This particular class consisted largely of a low third-grade group reading on a first-and second-grade instructional reading level. Consequently, the new world load was kept relatively low, and much repetition of these words was encouraged. The children were quite eager to get into the new game, so the first chart (Figure 11.3) was re-read only a few times.

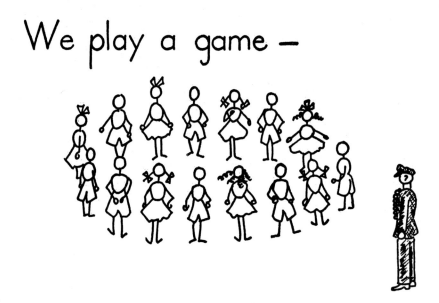

We play a game –

Figure 11.2

The second chart was written after the children had played the new game. (See Figure 11.4) This chart was done by remedial group of children reading on a first-grade level. In a remarkably short time each child in the group was able to read the entire chart quite fluently

Reading in this particular instance was fun and something which each child could do with relatively little difficulty. It was a new experience for several in the group because reading from the basal text was very difficult for them. One child reported that he "read it all for the first time." The teacher observed that this type of activity-experience chart offered in-

Policeman

We are going to learn a new game. It is called "Policeman." All of us will play the game. We will need a policeman. The rest of us will stand in a circle. Someone will be lost. The policeman will say to the teacher, "I am looking for a lost boy. Have you seen him?" "Yes," says the teacher.

Figure 11.3

Then she must describe a child who is in the circle. When the child knows he is being described, he must run. If the policeman catches him before he gets back to his place, he must stand in the center of the circle. If the policeman does not catch him, he gets to be the new policeman.

Figure 11.3 Continued

A New Game

We can play a new game. It is a good game. It is a game we all can play. It is called "Policeman." Don was the policeman. Donald was a lost boy. Sandra was a lost girl. The policeman ran after the lost boy. He ran after the lost girl. Sometimes the

Figure 11.4

policeman got the boy
and girl. Sometimes he
could not get them.
Some of us told about
the lost children. We
told about their hair. We
told about their caps. We
told all we could about
them. We did not tell
their names. We liked the
new game. It was fun to
play.

Figure 11.4 Continued

numerable opportunities for a good developmental-reading lesson. She noticed that the interest appeal was high and the amount of individual success was very gratifying to each child. Three of the slower learners were motivated to read to the extent that they took a greater interest in reading the basal text, and the teacher found that their reading showed decided improvement.

Prepared Stories

An early and perhaps first attempt to prepare physical education reading content as conceived here is the work of Humphrey and Moore.[6] Their original work involved a detailed study of reactions of six-to-eight-year-old children when independent reading material is oriented to active game participation. This experiment was initiated on the premise of relating reading content for children to their natural urge to play.

The original study utilized ten games written with a story setting. From this study additional stories were developed and published as the "Read and Play Series."[7] This series consists of six books in which there are 131 stories.

This carefully developed material in terms of readability, the reading values, and literary merit of the stories utilizes children's natural affinity for active play as the motivation for their reading. This unique reading content calls for active responses to the reading task, the task being one that involves learning to play an active game or to perform physically-oriented stunts or rhythms. Such tasks bring a physical reality to printed word symbols. (Figure 11.5 is an example of one of the stories.)

Physical education reading content stories can be developed by the teacher. This has been done successfully by some teachers who have produced creative stories using games, stunts, and rhythms. Teachers have also involved children in such projects as creative writing experiences. In writing such stories using physical education settings, there are several guidelines that the teacher should keep in mind.

In general, the new word load should be kept relatively low. There should be as much repetition of these words as possible and appropriate. Sentence length and lack of complexity in sentences should be considered in keeping the level of difficulty of material within the independent read-

[6]James H. Humphrey and Virginia D. Moore, "Improving Reading Through Physical Education," *Education* (The Reading Issue), May 1960, p. 559.
[7]James H. Humphrey and Virginia D. Moore, *Read and Play Series.* (Champaign, Illinois: Garrard Publishing Co., 1962). Selected for publication by Frederick Muller, Limited, London, England, 1965. Address: Ludgate House, 110 Fleet Street, London, E. C. 4.

Billy Bear
in the Circle

Once upon a time many bears played
    in the big woods.

The bears stood in a circle.

Billy Bear stood inside the circle.

Billy Bear was "It."

The other bears held paws to make a circle.

Then Billy Bear tried to get out.

He tried to go under to get out.

The other bears tried to keep Billy Bear
    in the circle.

At last Billy Bear got out.

He ran fast.

All the bears ran after Billy Bear.

One of the bears caught Billy Bear.

That bear was "It" for the next game.

Now he was Billy Bear.

Could you play this game
with other children?

Figure 11.5 Billy Bear

From: Set 1, Book 2, *Read and Play Series* by James H. Humphrey and Virginia
D. Moore, Garrard Publishing Company, Champaign, Illinois. Copyright © 1962 by
James H. Humphrey and Virginia D. Moore.

ing levels of children. There are numerous readability formulas that can be utilized.

Consideration must also be given to the reading values and literary merits of the story. Using a character or characters in a story setting helps to develop interest. The game to be used in the story should not be readily identifiable. When children identify a game early in the story there can be resulting minimum attention on the part of the readers to get the necessary details in order to play the game. In developing a game story, therefore, it is important that the nature of the game and procedures of the game unfold gradually.

Teaching Reading Through Creative Movement
(*The AMAV Technique*)

As mentioned in Chapter 4, there are a variety of media for creative expression (art, music, and writing) which are considered the traditional approaches to creative expression. However, the very essence of creative expression is *movement.* Movement, as a form of creativity, utilizes the body as the instrument of expression. For the young child, the most natural form of creative expression is movement. Because of their nature, children have a natural inclination for movement and they use this medium as the basic form of creative expression. Movement is the child's universal language, a most important form of communication and a most meaningful way of learning.

The AMAV Technique of teaching children to read through creative movement was developed by the present author with the assistance of two collaborators in the reading field. This original work consists of four stories on two long play records, or cassettes, a teacher's manual, and sets of eight booklets of the stories, the source of which is: Robert M. Wilson, James H. Humphrey, and Dorothy D. Sullivan, *Teaching Reading Through Creative Movement*, The AMAV Technique, Kimbo Educational, Deal, New Jersey. The AMAV Technique involves a learning sequence of *auditory input* to *movement* to *auditory-visual input* as depicted in the following diagram.

Auditory ⟶ Movement ⟶ Auditory ⎯⎯ Visual

Essentially the AMAV technique is a procedure for working through creative movement to develop comprehension—first in listening, and then in reading. The A⟶M aspect of AMAV is a directed listening-thinking activity. Children first receive the thoughts and feelings expressed in a story through the auditory sense by listening to a recorded story. Following this they engage in movement experiences which are inherent in the story and thereby demonstrate their understanding of and reaction to the story. By engaging in the movement the development of comprehension becomes a part of the child's physical reality.

After the creative movement experience in the directed listening-thinking activity, the children move to the final aspect of the AMAV technique (A-V), a combination of auditory and visual experience, by listening to the story and reading along in the story booklet. In this manner comprehension is brought to the reading experience.

Although the comprehension skills for listening and reading are the same, the sensory input is different. That is, listening is dependent upon the auditory sense and reading is dependent upon the visual sense. The sequence of listening to reading is a natural one. However, bridging the gap to the point of handling the verbal symbols required in reading poses various problems for many children. One of the outstanding features of the AMAV technique is that the movement experience helps to serve as a bridge between listening and reading by providing direct purposeful experience for the child through creative movement after listening to the story.

It is possible for teachers to prepare their own materials to teach children to read through creative movement, using the AMAV technique. Although such a procedure would not likely be so detailed as the original published work and is somewhat of a painstaking task, it can provide an interesting activity for a creative teacher. Preparing such materials can also be creative projects for older children. Remedial readers can help to prepare such stories for younger children.

Developing Reading Skills Through Physical Education

Various case studies have contributed to our knowledge of how children might develop reading skills, and thus improve reading ability, through the physical education medium.[*] Examples of two such cases reported here conclude this chapter.

Case 1: First Grade

Concept: Distinguishing long vowel sounds with the same consonant blend beginning.

---

[*]The interested reader is referred to the following source for detailed information on developing reading skills through active games: James H. Humphrey and Dorothy D. Sullivan, *Teaching Slow Learners Through Active Games* (Springfield, Illinois: Charles C Thomas Publisher, 1970), Chapter Five.

Activity: CROWS AND CRANES. The class is divided equally into two groups, the Crows and the Cranes, who stand facing each other on two parallel lines three to five feet apart. A goal line is drawn 20 to 30 feet behind each group. The teacher or leader calls out the name of one of the groups—Crows or Cranes. Members of the group whose name is called run and try to reach their goal line before they are tagged by any member of the other group. All of those tagged become members of the opposite group. The groups then return to their original places and the same procedure is followed. The group having the greater number of players on its side at the end of the playing period wins the game.

Application: The children and the teacher had discussed sounds of consonants and several consonant blends in reading class. Later vowels were discussed, beginning with long sounds. In making lists of words having long vowel sounds, the children discovered that the bird names "crows" and "cranes" require careful listening to determine which vowel was to be pronounced. Children running in the wrong direction had to leave their own group and become members of the other group.

Evaluation: The children soon learned that each must remember which bird he was supposed to be. He would not know when to run until he heard the name of the bird and compared the sound with his own bird name. It was discovered that words may have the same beginning sound but vowel sounds make different words and make them have different meanings, as in "crows" and "cranes."

CASE 2: FIRST GRADE

Concept: The understanding that each sound has a definite form and that each form has a definite sound (auditory-visual perception).

Activity: STOP, LOOK, AND LISTEN. The children all stand in a line one beside the other. The teacher holds up a letter of the alphabet. At the same time the teacher calls out a word which *does* or *does not* begin with that sound. If the word does not begin with that sound, the children do not run. If the word begins with that sound the children run toward a prearranged goal line to see who can get there first.

Evaluation: Auditory-visual perception is an important part of the readiness and word analysis program in first grade. This game can be used as children get the first sight words in order to secure auditory-visual perception. This game was a good test of how well the children learned the sound of the element, and how well they know the form of the element. Children liked being able to tell whether the sound was the same as the one spoken, and they liked the aspect of suspense as to when the word would be called on which they could run.

Chapter 12

How Children Develop Mathematics Concepts Through Physical Education

The study of arithmetic in the traditional elementary school was based largely upon the idea that learning takes place as a result of repetition. This practice placed major emphasis upon drill in arithmetic facts. These arithmetic facts were most often acquired as isolated entities with little attempt being made to help the pupil gain insight into the relationships among certain basic facts.

A later approach to the study of arithmetic in the elementary school involved situations whereby children could acquire number experiences in a more functional setting. This approach has been described by some authorities[1] as the revolutionary movement known as "meaningful arithmetic." They further assert that the "new" or "modern" mathematics is an extension of this movement. This approach, which has come into being in recent years, is due largely to the work of such groups as the School Mathematics Study Group (SMSG). Among other things it has been demonstrated that subject matter once thought too difficult can be introduced at the elementary level with some degree of success.

The idea of a relationship of number experiences and play is not new. In fact Plato asserted that "by way of play, the teachers mix together (objects) adapting the rules of elementary arithmetic to play." It will be the purpose of this chapter:

1. To indicate some general ways in which children can have mathematics experiences through physical education.
2. To develop the concept of the mathematics motor activity story.
3. To suggest some physical education activities through which children can develop mathematics concepts.

Mathematics Experiences Through Physical Education

The opportunities for such procedures as counting, computing, and measuring abound in situations involving physical education activities. The following illustrative list suggests some general ways in which teachers might relate mathematics experiences with physical education activities.

1. In certain types of games, such as tag games, where a certain number of pupils are caught, the number of pupils caught can be counted. After determining the number caught, pupils can be asked how many were left. The number caught can be added to the number left to check for the correct answer. In this procedure, counting, adding, and subtracting are utilized as number experiences in the game activity.

2. Numbers can be satisfactorily incorporated in the teaching of certain self-testing activities and skills in a variety of ways. For example, counting can be facilitated for younger children when it is done by counting the number of times they bounced a ball. Addition and subtraction can be brought in here also by having them compute the number of times they bounced the ball one time and how many more or fewer times they bounced it another time. This same procedure may be applied to activities such as rope skipping, as indicated by the following examples:

"Let the rope swing forward seven times before you jump over it."
"Joan, after the rope turns five times, you run in and jump nine times."
"Susan jumped four times. How many more times must she jump to make ten?"

3. In any type of activity that requires scoring, for example the number of runs scored in a baseball-type game, there are opportunities for counting, adding, and subtracting. Pupils can compute how many more runs one group scored and how many fewer runs another group scored. Some teachers have found it useful to count a score with a number in which the class needs practice in adding. For example, a score could count five points and the number five would be added whenever a score was made.

4. In games in which players have numbers and they go into action when their number is called, mathematics can be integrated by having the leader who calls the number give a problem which will have as its answer the number of the players who are to go into action. Any of the four processes of addition, subtraction, multiplication, or division, or any combinations of these, may be used.

An example of such a game is Steal the Bacon. It is played with two teams of from 8 to 16 pupils on a team, forming two lines facing each other about 10 to 12 feet apart. A small object such as an eraser, beanbag, or the like is placed in the middle of the space between the two lines. The team members are numbered from opposite directions. The teacher, or a pupil acting as the leader, calls a number and each of the two players with that number runs out and tries to grab the object and return to his line. If the player does so, his team scores 2 points; if he is tagged by the opponent, the other team scores 1 point. The teacher might give a problem in the following manner: "Ready! 10 minus 2 divided by 4 times 3 plus 1, Go! The answer would be 7, and the two players having this number would attempt to retrieve the object.

5. In some activities various kinds of records can be kept by means of which children can experience computations with numbers. For example, in determining team or group standings on a won and lost basis, there is an opportunity for upper elementary pupils to gain insight into decimals and percentages. Team standings can be determined by dividing the number of games won by the number of games played. If a group won 6 games and lost 4 out of a total of 10 games played, 10 would be divided into 6, giving a percentage of .600.

In keeping records of various kinds of activities, practical use can be made of graphs and charts to show pupil progress. Each pupil can graph or chart his progress in any activity that requires the use of numbers. An example of this procedure would be in keeping records of individual pupils in such skills as throwing for accuracy. A graph or chart can be made over a period of several days indicating how well he throws for accuracy at a target.

6. During the organization of classes for certain kinds of physical education activities, various kinds of number experiences can be integrated. The following sample questions are submitted to illustrate this procedure.

"If we divide our class into four teams, what part of the class would each team be?"

"If each has a partner, how many couples will there be in our room?"

"If we need eight or nine couples for a game, how could we divide?"

"One couple is what part of a square-dance set? Two couples? Three couples?"

"We have 32 people present today. What number would we have to divide by to get eight in each group?"

7. Various activities require boundaries and certain dimensions for size of the playing area. Pupils can measure and lay out the necessary boundaries and field dimensions. In studying map making to scale, upper elementary pupils can draw field dimensions for such activities as end ball, kick ball, and softball. The dimensions can be laid out by pupils from their scale drawings.

The following practical example of a teaching procedure is intended to show how mathematics and physical education can be successfully integrated in a combined third-fourth grade teaching-learning situation.

Teacher:	Today we are going to play a game called Triple Change. What do you think the word "triple" means? When we think of "triplets," what number do we think of?
Pupil:	Three
Teacher:	Yes, Frank, how did you know that?
Pupil:	I saw some triplets on television. There were three people who looked alike.
Teacher:	Now, I would like to have three of you be a set of triplets. (Three volunteer.) All right. Will you three stand here by me? Do you remember another word that we used in arithmetic class yesterday that is related to three?
Pupil:	Was it third?
Teacher:	Yes (pointing to each player in the center of the circle), *first, second, third*. Now beginning at your left, let each *third* p t up his right hand. What part of a whole set of triplets is "one"?
Pupil:	One part.
Teacher:	Yes, but what part?
Pupil:	Oh! I see, one third.
Teacher:	Yes, that's it, one third. Who can write one third on the board? (Pupil writes it on the board.) Now how many thirds are there in a whole set?
Pupil:	There are three.
Teacher:	Three thirds is right. (Teacher writes $3/3 = 1$ on the board.) Now let's play the game.
	Form a circle. The set of triplets remains here by me. Those of you in the circle count off in groups of three and remember your number. All right, fine. Now let's have all of the 1's raise their hands, the 2's, the 3's. Very good. Now be sure to remember your number The triplets 1, 2, and 3 in the center will be "callers" and they will take turns in calling their numbers. When a number is called, all who have that number must quickly change places with each other. You may do this by changing with a neighbor or running through the circle. The center players take turns calling. If the first one does not get a place, then the second calls. Should the first succeed in catching one, the player caught will wait his turn in the center until number 2 and number 3 have had a turn at calling before he calls a number. Let's try it once for practice. Fred, call your number.
	(After the demonstration, the game is played for a time, and then the teacher evaluates with the class.)
Teacher:	What were some of our problems?
Pupil:	Some players, mostly the third-graders, did not remember their numbers and ran at the wrong time.
Pupil:	Sometimes it was hard to find a place.
Pupil:	Some kids didn't run when their number was called.

Teacher: Well, now, what do you suppose we could do about some of these things?

(After some discussion, the following decisions were made by the group.)

1. The players in the circle should hold hands, letting only the numbers called go.
2. The players who did not move, or who moved at the wrong time, would have to pay a forfeit.
3. When caught three times, a player would be eliminated. (The purpose of this was to discourage players from being deliberately caught in order to become a caller.)

The Mathematics Motor Activity Story

Another way in which children can derive mathematics experiences through physical education is by use of the "Mathematics Activity Story." This procedure involves essentially the same kind of technique that was described in the previous chapter. A story involving the concept of number and oriented to the performance of a physical education activity is written at the readability level for a specific group of children. The children either may read the story themselves or the teacher may read it to them. Teachers who have experimented with this technique tend to feel that the best results are obtained when the story is read to the children.

The following story was written by the author and used and evaluated by a first-grade teacher with her class of 30 children.[1] The name of the story is "Find a Friend" and it is an adaptation of a game called "Busy Bee." The readability level of the story is 1.5 (fifth month of the first grade). The mathematics concepts and learnings inherent in the story are: *Groups or sets of two; counting by twos; beginning concept of multiplication.*

Find A Friend

In this game each child finds a friend.
Stand beside your friend.
You and your friend make a group of two.
One child is "It."
He does not stand beside a friend.
He calls, "Move!"
All friends find a new friend.
"It" tries to find a friend.
The child who does not find a friend is "It."
Play the game.
Count the number of friends standing together.
Count by two.
Say two, four, six.
Count all the groups this way.

[1]The cooperating teacher in this experiment was Charlotte L. Ruckelhaus, Anne Arundel County, Maryland.

The group of first-grade children with whom this experiment was conducted had no previous experience in counting by twos. Before the activity each child was checked for the ability to count by twos and it was found that none had it. Also, the children had no previous classroom experience with beginning concepts of multiplication.

The story was read to the children and the directions were discussed. The game was demonstrated by the teacher and several children. Five pairs of children were used at one time. As the game was being played the activity was stopped momentarily and the child who was "It" at that moment was asked to count the groups by twos. The participants were then changed, the number participating changed, and the activity was repeated.

In evaluating the experiment it was found that this was a very successful experience from a learning standpoint. Before the activity none of the children were able to count by twos. A check following the activity showed that eighteen of the thirty children who participated in the game were able to count rationally to ten by twos. Seven children were able to count rationally to six and two were able to count to four. Three children showed no understanding of the concept. No attempt was made to check beyond ten because in playing the game the players were limited to numbers under ten.

There appeared to be a significant number of children who had profited from this experience in a very short period of time. The teacher maintained that in a more conventional teaching situation the introduction and development of this concept would have taken a great deal more teaching time and the results probably would have been attained at a much slower rate.

Publication of this experiment[2] resulted in such widespread interest that over twenty stories of this nature were developed and produced as follows: James H. Humphrey, *Teaching Children Mathematics Through Games, Rhythms and Stunts*, Kimbo Educational, Deal, New Jersey, 1968.

This material consists of two long play record albums on which the stories are recorded along with a Teacher's Manual giving detailed instructions on how to use the materials.

Some Physical Education Activities Involving Mathematical Concepts

Concepts of number are inherent in many elementary school physical education activities. In some cases a better understanding of number accrues automatically through participation in certain games, rhythmic ac-

---

[2]James H. Humphrey, "The Mathematics Motor Activity Story," *The Arithmetic Teacher,* January 1967.

tivities, and self-testing activities. When a teacher is aware of a concept inherent in a given activity, however, it is more likely that he or she will be able to develop the concept more systematically.

The variety of physical education activities that follows is representative of some of the possibilities of using certain specific activities to develop mathematics concepts. In the following cases it will be noted that concrete suggestions are given for developing the concepts when presenting the activity. However, these suggestions need not necessarily be followed "to the letter." It remains for teachers to draw upon their own imagination in developing a concept once they recognize it as being inherent in a given activity. It is suggested that the reader take particular note of the *evaluation* in each of the following cases.*

CASE 1: FIRST GRADE

Concept:	Comparison of groups. More or less .
Activity:	LIONS AND TIGERS. A description of this activity is given in Chapter 7.
Application:	The class was working on the one-to-one relationship between groups. This game gave the class another opportunity to use this concept in a real situation. The children understood that each team would try to add to their players. The winner was determined by counting the Lions and Tigers. There were 18 Lions and 12 Tigers. The Lions and Tigers stood in a line face to face to get another demonstration of the one-to-one concept. There were some Lions who did not have a Tiger to face as the Lion line was longer.
Evaluation:	The class was able to see clearly that one group was larger than the other. This group had *more* children in it, the other had *less*. The Lion line was longer than the Tiger line. The class drew the following conclusions: The higher we count, the bigger the number. Therefore, 18 is more than 12; 12 is less than 18; 9 is more than 6; 6 is less than 9. The class made many such group comparisons.

CASE 2: FIRST GRADE

Concept:	Rational counting to 10
Activity:	ROUND UP. All but 10 players of the group take places in a scattered formation on the activity area. The 10 players join hands. These 10 players are called the "Round-Up Crew." The

---

*The interested reader is referred to the following detailed source for developing mathematics concepts through active games: James H. Humphrey and Dorothy D. Sullivan, *Teaching Slow Learners Through Active Games* (Springfield, Illinois: Charles C Thomas Publisher, 1970), Chapter Six.

other players are the "steers." At a signal the Round-Up Crew chases the steers and attempts to surround one or more of them. To capture a steer the two end children of the Round-Up Crew join hands. When 10 steers are captured, they become the Round-Up Crew and the game continues.

Application: As the steers are captured, the children count the number aloud, and when the tenth child is captured, they become the Round-Up Crew and the game continues.

Evaluation: This game enabled the children to apply a number name in sequence to a definite object, in this case a child, and they soon realized that the tenth child meant ten children captured. At times when the children were captured quickly, it was necessary to call time out in order to recount the number of children.

CASE 3: SECOND GRADE

Concept: Meaning of whole, half, and quarter. Understanding about fractional parts.

Activity: AIRPLANE ZOOMING. The child jumps into the air and makes a one-quarter turn to his left. He does this three times until he has made a complete turn. The same procedure is repeated except that he turns to the right. A circle can be drawn with chalk and divided into four parts. The child can stand in the center of the circle and jump from one quarter of the circle to the other.

Application: Each child draws a circle around himself. He then marks an "x" in front of him and directly in back. He marks an "x" at points where his hands reach when extended out at the sides. The child jumps into the air and makes 1/4 turn to his left or right. He does this three times more and has now made a complete turn. All the way around is a whole circle. One jump is 1/4 way around, 2 jumps 1/2 way around, 3 jumps 3/4 way around, and 4 jumps all around, or a whole turn. Some children will follow a command like "half a circle"—but they will jump half around with one turn. This is fine if they have done it once with the quarter turns. They can go on to a complete turn with one jump.

Evaluation: The results of this activity were very gratifying and everyone in the class learned the meaning of whole, half, and quarter. Many of the children suggested dividing the circle into more parts so they could demonstrate thirds and fifths.

CASE 4: SECOND GRADE

Concept: Grouping of numbers

Activity: CLAP FOUR. Children may begin in a circle position or by standing in scattered formation near the teacher. The teacher claps hands a certain number of times and the children get into groups the number of times the hands are clapped.

Application: The concept was developed as the game was being played. The children observed that some of them were not in groups when the teacher clapped a certain number of times. There were 28 children in the class. When the hands were clapped 2 or 4 times all were in groups but when they were clapped 3 or 5 times, someone was left out.

Evaluation: The class learned to get into groups quickly and observe how many groups were made with the whole class. The children were concerned about getting into a group rather than with whom they were.

CASE 5: THIRD GRADE

Concept: Understanding multiples of three.

Activity: PICK UP RACE. Several wooden blocks (three for each player) are scattered over a large playing area. The players, divided into a number of teams, take places behind a starting line and near the circle which has been assigned to their team. On a signal from the leader each player runs into the playing area, picks up one block, returns to the starting line and places it in his team's circle. He goes back after the second block, and then again until he had brought back his third block and placed it in a pile within the circle. Play continues in this manner until all blocks have been picked up and placed in a circle in groups of threes. The team which finishes bringing back the blocks first to the circle is declared the winner.

Application: The class counted out how many threes would be needed for each team. They counted that if there would be 10 on a team they would need 30 blocks. The blocks were placed in groups of threes so the children who were having difficulty could see the groups of threes. The number of players was changed frequently so the groups of three would change. Many of them could see where the multiples of five and two could be learned through this game.

Evaluation: This game proved to be excellent in teaching multiples of threes. One child who could not understand that 4 or 5 groups of 3 would be 12 and 15, etc., soon developed an understanding of the threes. As the number of players on the team were changed, the children counted how many threes would be within the circle when the team finished its play.

CASE 6: THIRD GRADE

Concept: We divide to find how many groups there are in a larger group.

Activity: GET TOGETHER. Players take places around the activity area in a scattered formation. The leader calls any number by which the total number of players is not exactly divisible. All players try to form groups of the number called. Each group joins hands in a circle. The one or ones left out have points scored against them. Low score wins the game.

Application: Numbers called at third grade level usually should be 2, 3, 4, 5, or 10 since these are numbers with which they learn to divide.

Evaluation: This activity was useful for reenforcing the idea of groups or sets and that groups are of like things (in this case children). It gave the children the idea that there may be a *remainder* when dividing into groups.

CASE 7: FOURTH GRADE

Concept: The shortest distance between two points is a straight line.

Activity: THROW AROUND. This game is played on a softball diamond with two teams. One team is at home and the other is in the field. At a signal by the leader a home team member starts to run around the bases. At the same time the catcher of the team in the field throws the ball to the pitcher, who throws it to the first baseman, who throws it to second, who throws it to third, who throws it back to the catcher. If the base runner after touching all bases reaches home before the ball, he scores one point for his team. The team wins which has the larger number of points at the end of an even number of innings. There are no outs and each team has all of its runners up before the teams exchange places. Another way of scoring is to have a point scored for each base successfully touched by the runner before the ball reaches the base. The activity may be used to practice skills of base running and throwing to bases.

Application: After drawing two distinct dots or points denoting two players on the chalkboard, the children were asked the best way to throw the ball from one to the other. As in softball, in mathematics the shortest distance will always be a straight line. If the ball is thrown the shortest distance it is bound to get there in the quickest time.

Evaluation: The children remarked that when the thrower is "wild" the baseman has to leave his position to get the ball so it is a greater distance. Mention was made about double plays (short stop to second base to first base) that there were three points and that it took two straight lines to get the ball to the first baseman.

CASE 8: FIFTH GRADE

Concept: The number above the line in a fraction is the numerator which tells the number of parts of the whole. The number below the line in a fraction is the denominator which tells how many parts make up the whole.

Activity: COUPLE TAG. Players are scattered around the activity area in groups of two. One player is "It." "It" tries to grasp the free hand of one member of a couple and if he succeeds the other member becomes "It" and the game continues.

Application: The teacher developed with the class the idea that, in this game, a group of two equaled one whole. The number of pupils in the class was ascertained to be the numerator of the fraction since it told the number of "parts" with which they were dealing. The number of children in each tag group (in this case two) was ascertained to be the denominator of the fraction since it told how many parts made up the whole. The class recognized the fact that this was an improper fraction and that it would be necessary to divide the denominator into the numerator in order to find how many "wholes" or whole teams there would be and what fractional part of a team would be left over. In successive experiences with this activity, the game was called "Triplet Tag," "Quartet Tag," "Quintet Tag," and "Sextet Tag" as the denominator of the fraction was increased.

Evaluation: This game was effective in helping the children relate the fractional concept and the terms "numerator" and "denominator" to real life situations. As the numerator of the fraction changed with the daily attendance and the denominator changed with the number of children needed to make up each "whole" or tag group, the terms of various fractions became more real and useful to them. They realized that they actually use fractions in their activities without being conscious of it.

CASE 9: SIXTH GRADE

Concept: Adding and subtracting fractions.

Activity: CHAIN DODGE BALL. The group stands in circle formation about two feet apart. Five players in the center are linked together by standing one behind the other and grasping the one in front around the waist. The players in the circle, using a rubber playground ball or a volleyball, attempt to hit the last player in the "Chain." The front player may guard by deflecting the ball with his hands. When the last person is hit by the ball he becomes part of the circle, and the person who threw the ball takes the front position in the chain. The ball may be passed around the circle in order to give a thrower a better chance to hit the end player. If the chain breaks, the five players are replaced by five new ones.

Application: The concept of a whole being made up of several parts is a necessary understanding in teaching fractions. The group of players in the center was considered one whole, since they were not supposed to break apart. Each child was 1/5 of the whole. When the end player was hit, he subtracted himself from the whole, showing that 5/5 minus 1/5 equals 4/5. The new player coming in added himself to the group, showing 1/5 plus 4/5 equals 5/5, or one whole.

Evaluation: This game in which the children themselves acted as the fractions made the mathematical concept more vivid and real. Variations were made in the number of children in the chain, showing that fractions with different denominators (such as four) also may be added to make one whole.

Rhythmic activities can help children with such number experiences as rational counting.

Chapter 13

Science Experiences Through Physical Education
Some Physical Education Activities Involving Science Concepts
Science Concepts in Broad Units of Study

How Children Develop
Science Concepts
Through Physical Education

The science program in the elementary school is characterized by widely divergent practice. In elementary schools where science is a part of the curriculum, its study ranges from the traditional nature study courses to the more modern approach of studying the natural environment in a functional setting.

At the present time, the study of elementary school science seems to be shifting away from a type of curriculum offering that is based merely on satisfying curiosity. On the other hand, the trend appears to be in the direction of providing learning experiences in science that involve the study of problems that are of real concern in the lives of children.

It appears that science currently is in a more or less transitional period as a curriculum offering at the elementary school level. As a consequence, it is an area involving a great deal of experimentation as far as ways of offering it in the curriculum are concerned.

In general, the ways of organizing and providing science learning experiences in the elementary school include (1) science as a separate formalized subject, (2) separate science units, (3) utilizing science opportunities when they occur, and (4) incorporating science experiences in large units of work, as in the social studies. Including science experiences in social studies units appears to be a more or less common practice at the present time. An example of this is shown later in the chapter in the social studies unit "Learning About Our World" in which many science experiences are included.

It is not the purpose here either to extol or criticize any of the existing plans of organization in the elementary school science program. On the contrary, the point of view taken is that the curriculum areas of elementary school science and elementary school physical education are closely related and might be considered mutually dependent. With this general frame of reference in mind, it will be the purpose of the remainder of this chapter to show how elementary school physical education and science can be integrated in such a way as to make a desirable and worthwhile contribution to the total growth and development of the child.

It is the purpose of this chapter to attempt to answer such questions as:

1. What are some of the ways that children can obtain science experiences through physical education?
2. What are some physical education experiences that involve science concepts?
3. How can science concepts be a part of broad units of study?

Science Experiences Through Physical Education

The opportunities for science experiences through physical education are so numerous it should be difficult to visualize a physical education situation that is not related to science in some way. Indeed, the possibilities for a better understanding of science and the application of science principles in physical education activities are almost unlimited.

If children are to be provided with learning experiences in science that involve the study of problems that are of real concern in their lives, teachers might well be on the alert for those things of interest to pupils in the daily school situation. With this idea in mind, the following generalized list is submitted to give the reader an idea of some of the possible ways in which opportunities for science experiences might be utilized through physical education.

1. The physical principle of *equilibrium* or state of balance is one that is involved in many physical education activities. This is particularly true of stunt activities in which balance is so important to proficient performance.

2. *Motion* is the basis for almost all physical education activities. Consequently there is opportunity to relate the laws of motion in an elementary way to physical education movement experiences.

3. Children may perhaps understand better the application of *force* when it is thought of in terms of hitting a ball with a bat or in tussling with an opponent in a combative stunt.

4. *Friction* may be better understood by the use of a rubber-soled gym shoe on the hard-surfaced playing area.

5. Throwing or batting a ball against the wind shows how air friction reduces the speed of flying objects.

6. Accompaniment for rhythmic activities, such as the tom-tom, piano, and records, helps children learn that *sounds* differ from one another in pitch, volume, and quality.

7. The fact that the *force of gravitation* tends to pull heavier-than air objects earthward may be better understood when the child finds that he must aim above a target.

8. Ball bouncing presents a desirable opportunity for a better understanding of *air pressure*.

9. *Weather* might well be better understood on those days when it is too inclement to go out on the playground. In this same connection, weather and climate can be considered with regard to the various sport seasons, i.e., baseball in spring and summer and games that are suited to winter play or cold climates.

The following practical examples of teaching procedures are intended to show how science and physical education can be successfully integrated in given teaching-learning situations. The first procedure shows how the study of kinds of birds, their nesting habits, and their protective nature toward the young might be accomplished with a group of second-grade children through the game Bird Catcher.

Teacher:	Boys and girls, can you tell me the names of some birds that you often see around your home and around school?
Pupil:	Robins.
Pupil:	I saw a bluejay the other day. (As various names of birds are given, the teacher writes them on the board or on a chart as the children say them.)
Teacher:	Yes, that's very good. You have seen many different kinds of birds. Now we have talked about the way some of these birds lay their eggs, and how the mother bird sits on them for two weeks. And then the little birds hatch just as our chicken did. What does the mother robin do for her little ones when they are hatched?
Pupil:	She feeds them.
Pupil:	She keeps them warm and protects them from harm.
Teacher:	Yes. She wants them safely in the nest, where she can protect them until they are old enough to take care of themselves. How many of you saw *Disneyland* last week when the picture of *Water Birds* was shown? (Several hands go up and children indicate verbally that they saw the picture.)
Teacher:	Did you see the picture of the little baby tern that wandered away from the nest?
Pupil:	Yes, and his mother got scared.
Teacher:	Indeed she did because she saw danger for the baby. Do you remember what the mother and father tern did? George?
Pupil:	The father sat on the nest while the mother went to find the baby bird.
Pupil:	The mother brought it back to the nest.

Teacher: Yes, you remember the picture very well. When we go out for our physical education period today, would you like to play a game about birds in the nest? The name of the game is Bird Catcher. We need some robins, bluejays, etc. (The teacher uses names that were given by the children and written on the board.)

Teacher: We also need a Mother Bird and a Bird Catcher and I want you to select two members of the class for these parts in the game. Our room is shaped like this. (The teacher makes a sketch on the board while she tells where the nest, bird, cage, forest, etc., will be located. Following this, she explains the entire game to the children, using the illustration on the board.)

Teacher: Now I want you to listen closely as I give you the following directions for playing the game. Remember as much of it as you can.

               A Mother Bird stands in the nest. A Bird Catcher stands between the nest and the cage about here. (Indicates on board.) The rest of you who are in the forest will have names of the different birds we talked about. The Mother Bird calls "Robins," and all of the robins run from the forest to the nest while the Bird Catcher tries to catch them. If he tags a robin, he takes him to the cage. All robins who reach the Mother Bird are safe. The Mother Bird calls another group of birds and the game goes on until all the birds are in the nest or the cage. The winning group is the one that has the largest number of birds safe in the nest. Now we will go out to the playground and I want you to try to play the game from our discussion here. I will give you help if you need it.

               (The game is organized by the children with the assistance of the teacher. They play for a time and she evaluates it with them when they get back to the room.)

Teacher: Now let us review what we learned today. What are some of the things we learned.
Pupil: Names of birds.
Pupil: The Mother Bird protects her babies.
Teacher: Good, Mary, anything else?
Pupil: The little birds should come when the moter calls them.
Pupil: If you don't run to the nest, you will get caught.
Teacher: Did the game do anything for our bodies?
Pupil: It gave us exercise.
Pupil: I like to run and be chased by the Bird Catcher.
Teacher: Did you find that you had to be a good dodger to keep from being tagged? Paul?
Pupil: Yes and I didn't get tagged today.
Teacher: Can you think of any ways in which we might improve the game if we were to play it again?
Pupil: You should run right away when your name is called.
Teacher: Yes, anything else?
Pupil: Don't all stick together to run because more get tagged that way.
Pupil: Don't always run in a straight line for the nest.
Teacher: Yes, those are all good suggestions for improvement. We should remember them when we play the game again.

               One of the important objectives of science education in the elementary school is the development of a scientific attitude. The following procedure illustrates how the game Find the Leader can be used with a fourth-or fifth-grade group as a help toward understanding the meaning and importance of a scientific attitude.

Teacher: Boys and girls, we have a new game to learn today. I think that this game will help you with something that we are trying very hard to develop this year—that is, a scientific attitude. Do you remember some of the things we have said one needs in order to have a scientific attitude?

Pupil: One thing was getting exact information.

Teacher: Yes, Frances, anything else?

Pupil: Observing carefully was one.

Teacher: Good, Bill, and anything else?

Pupil: Learning to solve problems was one, I think.

Teacher: That's right, Bill, Now this game, like so many other games, gives us a problem to solve. Also, in order to solve it, we have to observe very carefully and draw the right conclusions. Let's form a circle around the room. Leave room between your desks and the walls so you can move around a little. We will ask Larry to be the observer. When we are ready to play, Larry will go outside the room and we will choose a leader. The leader starts a motion of some kind, such as skipping, hopping, jumping, marching, or moving some part of the body. Everyone else must do the same thing the leader does. The observer is called back into the room and he tries to find out who the leader is by watching all persons very closely. The leader will change the action frequently, but he must try to make the change while the observer is looking at someone else so as to keep the observer from finding out he is the leader. The observer is given three guesses. If he guesses the leader, he is allowed to choose the next observer. If he does not guess correctly, the leader becomes the observer. Does this game remind you of other games you have played?

Pupil: It's a little like Follow the Leader.

Teacher: Yes, it is something like Follow the Leader. Now, from what you know about the game so far, what are some of the things you can think of already that will help us in playing the game?

Pupil: You shouldn't look at the leader too long or you will give him away.

Teacher: All right. (Writes this on board.)

Pupil: The leader should change often.

Teacher: (Writing this on board.) Yes, this is important to keep the game interesting. These are good suggestions which should help us in playing the game. All right, Larry is the observer. We will also need a leader. Larry, if you will go outside, we will choose a leader. (Observer goes outside the room.) Keith has not been chosen to lead a game for some time, so suppose we have him lead. Who would like to be the messenger? All right, Freddie, you may be the messenger. Will you please tell Larry we are ready for him? (The pupils participate in the game for a time and then the teacher evaluates it with them.)

Teacher: Boys and girls, you did very well with this new game and it is easy to see that you enjoyed it. Can anyone think of something we could do to make it a better game?

Pupil:	It was too easy for the observer to catch the leader, because he made such big changes .
Teacher:	All right. Maybe the leader could make a little change each time instead of a big change.
Pupil:	We looked at the leader too much and the observer could tell by watching us.
Teacher:	Yes, we could probably improve on that as we get more practice. What do we have to know to play this game, particularly in terms of the scientific attitude?
Pupil:	How to be good observers.
Pupil:	How to follow the leader and change actions quickly.
Pupil:	And how to judge the best time for changing actions if you are the leader.
Teacher:	Yes, those things are very important. Do you think you improved any particular ability?
Pupil:	You have to be good at observing.
Pupil:	You have to think.
Pupil:	I was able to change from one thing to another quickly.
Teacher:	Very good. So you see that the scientific attitude is very important in games as well as in other situations.

Some Physical Education Activities Involving Science Concepts

There are many physical education activities in which science concepts are inherent. In some instances a better understanding of a particular topical area of science accrues automatically through participation in certain games, rhythmic activities, and self-testing activities. When there is an awareness that a concept is inherent in a given activity, however, it is more likely the teacher will be able to develop that concept more systematically.

The variety of physical education activities that follow are representative of some of the possibilities of using certain activities to develop science concepts. In the cases that follow it will be noted that specific suggestions are given for developing the concept. However, teachers should use their own ingenuity and creativeness once they recognize a concept as being inherent in a given activity.*

CASE 1: FIRST GRADE

Concept:	Shadows are formed by the sun shining on various objects.
Activity:	SHADOW TAG. The players are dispersed over the playing area, with one person designated as "It." If "It" can step on or

*The interested reader is referred to the following source for a detailed listing of these kinds of activities: James H. Humphrey and Dorothy D. Sullivan, *Teaching Slow Learners Through Active Games* (Springfield, Illinois: Charles C Thomas Publisher, 1970), Chapter Seven.

get into the shadow of another player, that player becomes "It." A player can keep from being tagged by getting into the shade or by moving in such a way that "It" finds it difficult to step on his shadow.

Application: During the Science period the definition of a shadow was given. A discussion led the class to see how shadows are made as well as why they move. The class then went outside the room to the hardtop area where many kinds of shadows were observed. Since each child had a shadow it was decided to put them to use in playing the game.

Evaluation: The children saw how the sun causes shadows. By playing the game at different times during the day they also observed that the length of the shadow varied with the time of day. The activity proved very good for illustrating shadows.

CASE 2: SECOND GRADE

Concept: Moving things slow down before they stop.

Activity: STOP ON A DIME. A perpendicular line is drawn 50 feet from the starting line, with graduations or measurements drawn at one-foot intervals for ten feet beyond the line. Each child begins running when the signal "Go" is given. When he reaches the fifty foot line, the signal "Stop" is given. The intervals past this line show how many feet it took him to stop after he heard the signal.

Evaluation: Each child was able to see that it takes time to stop. All realized that moving objects first slow down and then stop.

CASE 3: FOURTH GRADE

Concept: Each planet travels on its own path called its orbit and is held in place by the sun's gravity.

Activity: MERRY-GO-ROUND. This is a group stunt in which six children lie on their backs with their feet touching in the center. Six more children take positions standing between each two children in the lying position. The children who are standing walk sidewards around the circle, carrying the horizontal children around with them. The heels of the horizontal children move as they are carried around the circle.

Application: This stunt was presented when the class was studying about the sun and the planets, and it was thought that it might be a good opportunity to use it to emphasize the concept. The children first did the stunt as presented and immediately many of them were able to make the transition to using it as a demonstration of the concept. The children on the floor forming the star were the sun. Those standing and holding hands were the planets These "planets" were held to their orbits by the invisible force of the sun called "gravity." As they got into position, those representing the sun were told to hold on tightly and to exert a force pulling the planets toward them while the planets walked around. At a signal from a leader some of these on the outside were to be released by the sun. They were asked to break the fall with their hands. They experienced a falling away tendency which was interpreted as what might happen if the sun's gravity did not hold the planets in place.

Evaluation: The children were very interested and able to make their own deduction. Some of the more advanced ones began to see the beginnings of the concept of centrifugal force—the pull of the planets in their orbits away from the sun, and some very intelligent questions arose and beginnings of a new problem to solve. This appeared very significant to the teacher because it tended to serve as stimulating and interesting introduction to another concept. This had not occurred in other classes when the physical education learning medium had not been used.

CASE 4: FOURTH GRADE

Concept: Things which are balanced have equal weights on either side of their central point.

Activity: RUSH AND TUG. This is a combative activity in which the class is divided into two groups with each group standing behind one of two parallel lines which are about 40 feet apart. In the middle of these two parallel lines a rope is laid perpendicular to them. A cloth is tied to the middle of the rope to designate both halves of the rope. On a signal, members of both groups rush to their half of the rope, pick it up and tug toward the group's end line. The group pulling the midpoint of the rope past its own end line in a specified amount of time is declared the winner. If at the end of the designated time the midpoint of the rope has not been pulled beyond one group's line the group with the midpoint of the rope nearer to its end line is declared the winner.

Application: In performing this combative activity it was decided to have the group experiment with all kinds of combinations of teams such as boys versus boy, girls versus girls, boys versus girls, big ones against little ones, and mixed sizes and weights against the same.

Evaluation: This was a very stimulating experience for the group since it presented to them a genuine problem-solving situation in trying to get the exact combination of children for an equal balance of the two teams. When there was enough experimenting, two teams of equal proportions were assembled and it was found that it was most difficult for either to make any headway. They also discovered that an equal balance depended not only on the weight of their classmates but to a great extent upon their strength.

Other classes where the physical education learning medium had not been used had shown much less interest in this important concept. It was speculated that this was perhaps due to the fact that the procedure presented problem-solving situations that were of immediate interest and concern to the children in a concrete manner.

CASE 5: SIXTH GRADE

Concept: The lever is one of the six simple machines for performing work. There are three "classes" of the lever. In the third-class lever, the effort is placed between the load and the fulcrum. (The forearm is a third-class lever.)

Activity: VOLLEYBALL SERVE. When serving right-handed the ball rests on the palm of the left hand and is held near the right side of the body. The left foot is slightly in advance of the right foot and the knees should be bent slightly. The right arm is swung back and then forward, making contact with the ball that is on the left hand. After contact with the ball, the right arm is extended forward and up in a follow-through motion. The ball should be hit with the heel of the right hand.

Application: The children were told that serving is a basic skill used in the game of volleyball and that for a successful game of volleyball it is necesssary to learn to serve the ball properly. The children were divided into two groups, each group spaced in a pattern on one side of the net facing the other group. After the teacher had demonstrated the serve, each child was given several opportunities to attempt to serve the ball. Some were able to perform rather proficiently but it was obvious that others would need more practice.

Evaluation: After the activity was over they discussed how the arms had acted as levers in this action. Since they had already talked about first-class and second-class levers, the children said they could see how the arm was like a lever also, but that it was a little different. They discussed this difference and the fact that the elbow joint was the fulcrum, the forearm was the effort, and the ball was the load. This led some pupils to suggest other examples that would illustrate this type of lever, i.e., a man swinging a golf club and a boy swinging at a ball with a bat.

Science Concepts in Broad Units of Study

When the history of education is considered over a period of several hundred years, the *unit* may be thought of as a more or less recent innovation. Because of this it is difficult to devise a universal definition for the term "unit." This is due partly to the fact that the term does not at the present time have a fixed meaning in the field of education. Essentially, the purpose of unitary teaching is to provide for a union of component related parts which evolve into a systematic totality. In other words, the unit should consist of a number of interrelated learnings which are concerned with a specific topic or central theme. A variety of types of experiences as well as various curriculum areas are drawn upon for the purpose of enriching the learning medium for all children so that the understandings of the topic in question can be developed.

It will not be the purpose here to consider the advantages or disadvantages of the various types of units that have been discussed in text books and the periodical literature. On the contrary, it will be the purpose of this section of the chapter to discuss the role of physical education as a curriculum area to be "drawn upon for the purpose of enriching the learning medium for all children so that the understandings of the topic in question can be developed."

There is universal agreement among educators that the things children do—the activities—are by far the most important part of the unit. Yet those experiences through which children learn best, that is, play experiences, have been grossly neglected as essential and important activities of the unit. There is, however, an explanation for this paradoxical phenomenon. For example, the classroom teacher, who is in most cases well prepared to guide and direct many learning experiences and activities of the unit, may not feel confident enough to include physical education activities as a means of developing the concepts of the unit. Moreover, when there is a physical education specialist available to assist the classroom teacher, this individual may not be familiar enough with the other curriculum areas to recommend physical education activities that will be of value in developing unit concepts.

In order to show more clearly how physical education can be used as a means of extending the basis for learning in social studies units, a number of concrete examples are submitted at this point. The materials presented include excerpts from social studies units that have been developed by groups of elementary school administrators and teachers under the supervision of the author. Many of the activities have been used with success in developing specific social studies concepts in practical teaching situations.

The first example concerns a major social studies area for the fourth-grade level called "Learning About Our World." The unit is entitled "The Earth and the Sky." It is subdivided into two areas called "Exploring the Earth" and "Exploring the Sky." In this particular unit there are many concepts to be developed. It was found through experimentation that several of the concepts could be further developed through the use of a variety of physical education activities. Following is a sampling of the concepts of the unit and the physical education activities used in their development.

LEARNING ABOUT OUR WORLD

1. Exploring the Earth

Concept: The earth spins around like a top. This concept was further developed through a stunt called The Top. This is an individual activity in which the child stands with his feet close together and his arms at his sides. He jumps into the air and with the use of his arms attempts to turn completely around and land in his original position.

Concept: We learn about changes in the past from the pictures which cave men drew on the walls of their caves and from remains in the earth. This concept was further developed through an activity called Draw-a-Picture Relay. This is a classroom activity in which the children are seated in rows facing the blackboard. The starting signal is the picture which the teacher wants the children to draw. For example, if the teacher calls out "Cat!" the first child in each row goes to the board and draws a part of the cat. The game continues until all have an opportunity to contribute to the drawing. The winner is declared on the basis of where the team finished and a judging of the drawings by the class. Each individual can put only one thing on the board. For example, he can draw a straight line, a curved line, a complete circle, part of a circle, or a dot.

Concept: The earth exerts a force called gravity. This concept was further developed in discussions of those activities that involved throwing an object such as a ball into the air. (Gravity keeps a ball from continuing to go up into the air.)

Concept: "Up" is away from the earth and "down" is toward the earth's center. This concept was further developed through the activity Up-and-Down Relay. In this activity the class is divided into a number of equal groups and each group forms a column. All of the players stoop down in a squatting position. At a signal the last person in each column stands and taps the person in front of him on the shoulder. This person stands and taps the person in front of him on the shoulder. This procedure continues until all persons in the column are standing (up). The procedure is then reversed and the first person in the column turns and taps the person behind him on the shoulder. This person stoops down to his first position. This procedure continues until all persons are in their original position (down).

Concept: Places near the equator usually have hotter summers and warmer winters than those farther away from it. This concept was further developed through a game called Equator Hotter. In this game the members of the class station themselves in a scattered formation within a given area. The teacher places an object (a piece of colored yarn is suitable) on the person of one of the players. The object should not be concealed but small enough so that it can be seen. All of the players except one, who is "It," know where the object is. "It" tries to locate the object and is given clues by the other members of the class. As "It" hunts for the object, the other players call out "Equator" in different tones to show "It" how near or far he is from the object. For example, soft tones mean farther away and loud tones mean nearer. When "It" finds the object he calls out the person's name who has it and all other persons try to get to a previously safe place before being tagged by "It." A point is scored against all caught. The game continues with a new "It."

2. *Exploring the Sky*

Concept:

The sun rises in the east and sets in the west. This concept was further developed through the stunt The Rising Sun. This is an individual activity in which the child sits down with his knees drawn up as close as he can get them to his chest. He clasps his hands together in front of his ankles. He rocks back until his feet are in the air and then he rocks forward until his feet are in the original starting position. (The directions east and west can be indicated.)

Concept:

The length of shadows on the earth vary at different times during the day. This concept was further developed through the game Shadow Tag. In this game the players are dispersed over the playing area, with one person designated as "It." If he can step on or get into the shadow of another player, that player becomes "It." A player may keep from being tagged by getting into the shade or by moving in such a way that "It" finds it difficult to step on his shadow.

Concept:

Tides result from the gravitational pull of the moon and the sun on the earth. This concept was further developed through a game called Pull with the Tides. In this game the group forms a circle and joins hands. A circle is drawn inside the circle of players about 12 inches in front of the feet of the players. At a signal the circle "pulls as tide." Without releasing hands, members try to force other members into the drawn circle. When a player is forced into the drawn circle, a point is scored against him and the game continues. If any of the players release hands, a point is scored against them.

Concept:

Gravity keeps the planets in their elliptical orbits. This concept was further developed through the game Jump the Shot. This game is most successful when played in small groups of from six to ten players. The players form a circle and face the center The teacher or a child selected as the leader stands in the center of the circle. The leader holds the shot in his hand. The shot is a soft object, such as a beanbag or a cloth bag, filled with a soft material and tied on to the end of a length of rope. The leader begins the game by swinging the shot around the circle so that it starts low and reaches a point of about 12 to 15 inches in height. He lets out enough rope so that the shot is near the feet of the players in the circle. Those in the circle try to avoid being hit with the shot by jumping over it as the leader swings it around. If the shot touches the feet of any person in the circle while it is being swung around, a point is scored against him. The game proceeds in this manner and periodically a new leader is selected .

Concept: Air gets less dense as we travel out into space away from the earth. This concept was further developed through a game called Thin Air. The game is played in the same manner as Equator Hotter. When "It" gets close to the object, the players say "The air is getting denser"; and when "It" goes away from the object, the players say "The air is getting thinner." The object may be considered as the earth and the air is densest near the object.

Part Three

Compensatory
Physical
Education

Chapter 14

Meaning of Compensatory Physical Education
Effect of Perceptual-Motor Training on Academic Achievement

The Nature of
Compensatory
Physical Education

As in the case of other terminology used to describe the branches of physical education in this text, the term *compensatory physical education* has perhaps originated with the present author. However, the term *compensatory* as it applies to *education* is not new.

In recent years educators and psychologists in Great Britain have been using the term *compensatory education*. In this regard Morris and Whiting[1] have indicated that the term *compensatory education* now being used tends to replace the former term *re-education*. They contend that the term *re-education* was often misused when standing for compensatory education. Re-education implied educating again (re-educating) persons who had previously reached an educational level and who now for some reason did not exhibit behavior at a level of which they were previously capable. These authors assert that compensatory education implies an attempt to make good a deficiency in a person's earlier education.

The present author uses the term *compensatory physical education* because ordinarily the attempts to improve a deficiency in one's earlier education is likely to take place through the *physical* aspect of the individual's personality.

It is the intent of this chapter to present for the reader:

1. An overview of the meaning of compensatory physical education.
2. A brief review of some representative examples of studies concerned with perceptual-motor training.

[1]P. R. Morris and H. T. A. Whiting, *Motor Impairment and Compensatory Education* (Philadelphia: Lea & Febiger, 1971), p. 9.

3. Some generalizations regarding the effectiveness of perceptual-motor training as far as academic achievement is concerned.

Meaning of Compensatory Physical Education

As stated in the introductory chapter, compensatory physical education seeks to correct various types of child learning disabilities which may stem from an impairment of the central nervous system and/or have their roots in certain social or emotional problems of children.

Perhaps the major thrust of compensatory physical education comes through the medium of *perceptual-motor training*. The term *perception* is concerned with how we obtain information from the environment through the various sensory processes and what we make of it. In the present context the term *motor* is concerned with the impulse for motion resulting in a change of position through various forms of body movement. Espenschade[2] suggests that when the two terms are put together (perceptual-motor) the implication is an organization or interpretation of sensory data with related voluntary motor responses.

Perceptual-motor training is concerned with the correction, or at least some degree of improvement, of certain motor deficiencies, especially those associated with fine coordinations. It has been suggested by Lerner[3] that theorists who stress the importance of perceptual-motor development conclude that when the various sensory-motor and perceptual systems have been fully developed, the child is ready for the next stage of development— concept formation. Concept formation depends upon intact perception which in turn depends upon sound motor development. Motor theorists of learning disabilities caution that a preoccupation with conceptual and cognitive learning may lead to a neglect of the base foundation of motor learning, and that there may be gaps in the developmental sequence which will affect all future learning by either limiting or distorting it. Thus, proponents of this type of training see a need for it with certain neurologically handicapped children who have various types of learning disabilities, that is, identifiable conditions that prevent the adequate accumulation, retention, and utilization of knowledge.

It has been suggested that the child with disorganization in perceptual areas, stemming from an impairment of the central nervous system, may be affected in any of three ways.[4] He may be unable to learn to read, to con-

[2]Anna S. Espenschade, "Perceptual-Motor Development in Children," *The Academy Papers*, No. 1, The American Academy of Physical Education, 1968.
[3]Janet W. Lerner, *Children With Learning Disabilities* (Boston: Houghton Mifflin Company, 1971), pp. 90-116.
[4]Murray M. Kappelman and Robert L. Ganter, "A Clinic for Children with Learning Disabilities," *Children*, July-August, 1970.

ceptualize or reason, or to convert visual impressions into meaningful information. None of these perceptual difficulties is likely to be noticed until the child has been in school long enough for it to show up as a handicap. Diagnosis of the specific types of perceptual difficulty is extremely important as a basis for planning an effective educational program for the child.

Ordinarily, attempts are made to correct or improve fine motor control problems through a sequence of motor competencies, which tend to follow a definite hierarchy of development. Methods of accomplishing this range from highly structured, extremely vigorous, physical exercise programs to unstructured more creative types of programs. Some examples of these programs will be identified in the following chapter.

We should point out that in attempts to make diagnoses of specific difficulties we need to take into account that not all learning difficulties stem from the problems previously suggested. For example, many children suffer emotional problems which encumber their learning ability. Others are lacking in motivation which is often caused by the stilted and sterile conditions of the school itself. The learning of some is influenced by uneven and/or immature development, and of course there are those who simply do not possess sufficient intellectual capacity to learn.

Effect of Perceptual-Motor Training on Academic Achievement

It is the purpose of this section of the chapter to report some of the research that has been conducted on the effect of perceptual-motor training on academic achievement. It should be borne in mind that the studies included represent a small sampling and in no way should they be interpreted as an exhaustive survey.

In attempting to determine the effect of perceptual-motor training on reading achievement in the first grade, Rosen[5] administered to twelve experimental classrooms a twenty-nine day adaptation of the Frostig Program (see following chapter) for the development of visual perception, while thirteen control classrooms added comparable time to regular reading instruction. Pre-and post-testing of experimental and control groups revealed that the former improved in visual perception but not in reading. The investigator felt that the additional time devoted to reading instruction might have been more important for reading achievement than the time devoted to perceptual training. The limitations of the study as seen by the investigator were: the time and nature of the training program, the specific measuring instruments, and differential teacher effects. It was sug-

---

[5]Carl L. Rosen, "An Experimental Study of Visual Perceptual Training and Reading Achievement in the First Grade," *Perceptual and Motor Skills* 22, 1966.

gested by the investigator that it was quite possible that during the course of the school year control pupils through normal growth, development and educational experiences that could not be controlled, acquired many perceptual skills that influenced their reading scores.

In a study using first-grade children, one group received perceptual-motor training exclusively, another just regular physical education activities, and still another group no extra activities at all. The experiment was conducted for two 45-minute periods a week for seven weeks. The groups were tested for academic achievement at the beginning and end of the experiment. The results showed statistically significant gains for the group which received the perceptual-motor training but not for the other two groups. The investigators felt that they could not make any extensive generalizations on the basis of performance of such small groups in only one experiment. They recommended replication of the experiment on at least one other similar group in order to validate the results. They also suggested that they felt that the perceptual-motor group might have improved more than the other groups because of the systematic training in focusing attention and in accurate listening that perceptual-motor training involves.[6]

A study conducted to determine whether children respond with higher scores on the Frostig test of visual perception after completion of the Frostig Visual-Perception Training Program, utilized six schools with large proportions of disadvantaged children. In each of the six schools six classes consisting of two prekindergarten, two kindergarten and two first-grade classes were selected. One class within each grade and each school was selected at random and received the Frostig Program, while other classes were identified as controls. In addition to the Frostig test, kindergarten experimental and control groups were given the Metropolitan Reading Readiness Test before and after the experiment. It was found that children showed greater gains on the Frostig test after having completed the Frostig Program than did the control pupils not receiving the program. However, the kindergarten experimental group which was given the reading readiness test did not show significantly greater gains than the control group in reading.[7]

A study was conducted to find if there was a relationship between performance scores in reading achievement, visual perception, motor development, two perceptual-motor tasks, and eye-hand dominance tests in seventy-five first-and second-grade children. Perceptual development level was evaluated by the Frostig Developmental Test of Visual Perception. Read-

    [6]Clarence C. McCormick, et al., "Improvement in Reading Achievement Through Perceptual-Motor Training," *Research Quarterly,* October 1968.
    [7]James N. Jacobs, "An Evaluation of the Frostig Visual-Perceptual Training Program," *Educational Leadership,* January 1968.

ing level was determined by the Metropolitan Achievement Test. The Lincoln-Oseretsky Motor Development Scale was used to evaluate the level of motor development. The two perceptual-motor tasks were designed by the investigator. Eye-hand dominance was determined by the pencil alignment test and the hole-in-card test. Appropriate statistical methods were used to determine the correlations between the variables and none were high enough for reliable prediction of one variable from another. Also no factors were in evidence that were indicative of interrelationships among the elements of visual, motor, and reading functions.[8]

In an attempt to test the value of providing special perceptual-motor training as part of the general kindergarten curriculum, sixty children designated as low on a school readiness test were randomly assigned to an experimental or control group. The groups were compared for readiness for reading at the end of the year and for reading achievement at the end of the second year. The results showed no significant differences and it was suggested that providing such special training as part of the general curriculum might be seriously questioned. Limitations of the study were: the difference in teaching ability, the number in the sample, the question as to the validity and reliability of the initial screening test, and the difficulty in scoring the tests.[9]

There is much current interest in the use of perceptual-motor developmental methods with elementary-school-age children. It is most important that the reader consider that the many research studies conducted in the area of perceptual-motor training do *not* present clear-cut and definitive evidence to support the notion that such programs result in academic achievement. There are too many other variables that can contribute to academic gains made by children. Such factors as normal maturation, the influence of testing, systematic training in the focus of attention that perceptual-motor training involves, along with the ever-important aspect of teaching ability, certainly need to be considered. Nevertheless, although the findings in support of perceptual-motor training are much more exploratory than definitive, this type of training should be considered in the school curriculum provided there is sufficient supervision and well-qualified personnel. Perceptual-motor training *should not be used in place of* validated teaching procedures, but rather in addition to the regular school curriculum in specific cases where it is warranted.

[8]Ella M. Trussell, "Relation of Performance of Selected Physical Skills to Perceptual Aspects of Reading Readiness in Elementary School Children." *Research Quarterly,* May 1968.
[9]Louis H. Falik, "The Effects of Special Perceptual-Motor Training in Kindergarten on Reading Readiness and on Second Reading Grade Performance," *Journal of Learning Disabilities,* August 1969.

Chapter 15

Perceptual-Motor Skills
Perceptual-Motor Programs

Perceptual-Motor
Development

In this chapter we are concerned with perceptual-motor development as an aspect of compensatory physical education. It will be the purpose of the chapter to:

1. Provide the reader with an understanding of perceptual-motor development.
2. Identify some of the perceptual-motor skills.
3. Identify some perceptual-motor programs.

Perceptual-Motor Skills

There is a considerable amount of agreement among child development specialists that there is no simple distinction between a perceptual skill and a motor skill. This has, no doubt, led to the term *perceptual-motor skills*. In fact, to some extent this term seems to be supplanting such terms as *neuromuscular* and *sensory-motor*.

In general, the current postulation appears to be that if perceptual training improves perceptual and motor abilities, then because of the fact that perceptual and motor abilities are so highly interrelated and interdependent each upon the other, it should follow that training in perception should facilitate perceptual-motor problems. There is abundant objective support of the notion that training of perception can improve perceptual ability. Although there is not a great deal of clear-cut evidence to support the idea that perceptual-motor training does increase the performance ability in perceptual-motor skills, some research, such as the work of Johnson and Fretz,[1] has indicated that certain kinds of perceptual-motor skills can be significantly improved for certain children who take part over a specified period of time in a children's physical development program.

What then are the perceptual-motor skills? Generally, the kinds of skills that fit into a combination of manual coordinations and eye-hand skills may be considered a valid classification.

Visual perception is based on sensorimotor experiences that depend on visual acuity, eye-hand coordination, left-right body orientation, and other visual-spatial abilities including visual sequencing.

Studies have shown a positive correlation between difficulties in visual perception and achievement in reading. Strang cites numerous studies in concluding that, "In general, average and superior readers tend to perform better than retarded readers on tests of perceptual differentiation, tests of closure, and measures of lag in perceptual-motor maturation.[2]

Indications of a child's eye-hand coordination may be observed as he bounces or throws a ball, erases a chalkboard, cuts paper with scissors, copies a design, ties his shoe laces, picks up small objects from the floor, or replaces a cap on a pen. It has been indicated that in reading, the child shows difficulty in eye-hand coordination by his inability to keep his place in reading, to find the place again in the pattern of printed words, and to maintain the motor adjustment as long as is necessary to comprehend word, phrase, or sentence. His tendency to skip lines may arise from inability to direct the eyes accurately to the beginning of the next line.[3]

Depending upon a variety of extenuating circumstances, perceptual-motor skills require various degrees of voluntary action. The basic striking and catching skills are examples of this type and are important in certain kinds of active game activities; that is, receiving an object (catching) such as a ball, and hitting (striking) an object, ordinarily with an implement, such as batting a ball. Other kinds of skills in this category, but not related to game activities, include sorting of objects, finger painting, and bead stringing. There is another group of tasks perceptual-motor in nature which involve such factors as choice, discrimination, and problem solving. These may be found in various types of intelligence tests and the ability to perform the tasks under certain kinds of conditions utilized.

There are certain tasks that are perceptual-motor in character that are done with one hand. At a high level of performance this could involve re-

[1]Warren R. Johnson, and Bruce R. Fretz, "Changes in Perceptual-Motor Skills After a Children's Physical Development Program," *Perceptual and Motor Skills*, April 1967.

[2]Ruth Strang, *Diagnostic Teaching of Reading*, 2d ed. (New York: McGraw-Hill Book Company, 1969), p. 153.

[3]Ibid., p. 61.

ceiving a ball with one hand in a highly organized sports activity such as baseball. At a very low level, in reaching for an object or grasping an object, a baby will do so with one hand.

In some kinds of visual tasks requiring the use of one eye, there appears to be an eye preference. In reading, it is believed that one eye may lead or be dominant. In tasks where one eye is used and one hand is used, most people will use those on the same side of the body. This is to say that there is *lateral dominance*. In the case of those who use the left eye and right hand or the opposite of this, *mixed dominance* is said to exist. Some studies suggest that mixed dominance may have a negative effect on motor coordination, but perhaps just as many investigators report that this is not the case.

Masland and Cratty have summarized the research on the relationship between handedness, brain dominance, and reading ability, and characterize the research as voluminous, often contradictory, and most confusing.[4] The following conclusions are based on their broad review of the research:

1. It has not been demonstrated that laterality of hand or eye dominance or mixed dominance bear a direct relationship to poor reading.

2. There is a very low correlation between handedness or eyedness and brain dominance for language. There is no evidence that changing handedness will influence the lateralization of other functions.

3. There are neither theoretical nor empirical data to support efforts to change handedness or eyedness as a means of improving reading ability.

A condition often related to dominance as far as reading is concerned is that of *reversals*. One type of reversal (static) refers to a child seeing letters reversed such as *n* and *b* apearing as *u* and *d*. In another type (kinetic) the child may see the word *no* as *on*. In some instances it has been found that children with the kinetic type of reversal also have a condition known as "arhythmia" (lack of rhythm). Attempts have been made to provide certain kinds of rhythmic movements for such children in order to correct this condition. It is possible that this approach may have much to commend it and varying degrees of success have been attained with it. More generally, procedures involving kinesthetic techniques of tracing words have been utilized.

At one time reversals were considered as possibly related to dominance. However, later studies negated this earlier view. In more recent years

[4]Richard L. Masland and Bryant J. Cratty, "The Nature of the Reading Process, the Rational Non-Educational Remedial Methods," Eloise O. Calkins, ed. *Reading Forum*, NIMDS, Monograph No. 11, Department of Health, Education, and Welfare, Washington, D.C.

studies tend to support the contention that problems of visual perception, spatial orientation, and recognition of form rather than dominance patterns result in children making reversals.

Perhaps some mention should be made regarding the most satisfactory ways of presenting perceptual-motor skills to children. Although a great deal of evidence has not been accumulated to support one method over another, the work of Smith[5] is of interest.

The purpose of this study was to determine the extent to which kindergarten children were ready for first-grade experiences and to attempt to compare the effects of three methods of presenting perceptual-motor skills on the reading readiness of randomly placed kindergarten children. The results indicated that there was no significant difference between the directed and problem-solving methods of teaching these skills, However, there was a greater mean score gain in the combined directed *and* problem-solving groups when compared with a group where color coded targets were used rather than verbalized directions for the movements. Thus, it was generalized that just doing the movement will not bridge all perceptual-motor learning gaps. It appeared that there is a greater understanding and transfer of learning if the direction of each movement is used to reinforce the movement.

Perceptual-Motor Programs

Most of the perceptual-motor programs are carried on independent of the school and outside the school situation. However, there are some schools that have acquired the services of a perceptual-motor specialist who operates within the framework of the physical education program.

In general, perceptual-motor programs fall into the two broad categories of those that are considered to be *structured* and those that are considered to be *unstructured*. Since there are various degrees of structuring of activities that make up a given program, a considerable amount of overlapping can exist from one program to another. For example, there could be some degree of structuring in a program that for all practical purposes would be classified as unstructured.

The structured program of perceptual-motor training is based on the notion that some form of structured physical activity can contribute to the development of a higher learning capacity for children with certain kinds of learning disabilities.[6] The unstructured type of program tends to be

[5]Paul Smith, "Perceptual-Motor Skills and Readiness of Kindergarten Children," *Journal of Health, Physical Education, and Recreation*, April 1970.

[6]S. Willard Footlik, "Perceptual-Motor Training and Cognitive Achievement: A Survey of the Literature," *Journal of Learning Disabilities*, January 1970.

more creative in nature and is not dependent upon a set of more or less "fixed" exercises.

Play therapists have been aware of the value of the unstructured type of approach for years as shown by the following summary of a study reported by Bills some years ago.[7]

This study was an investigation of the effects of individual and group play on the reading level of retarded readers. As a result of the play therapy experiences it was concluded that (1) significant changes in reading ability occurred as a result of the play therapy experiences; and (2) personal changes may occur in nondirective play therapy in as little as six individual and three group play therapy sessions.

It should be clearly understood that it is *not* the purpose here to either extol or condemn any of the various approaches to perceptual-motor training in the form of organized programs. On the contrary, we simply wish to identify some representative examples of perceptual-motor programs that fall within the range of structuring and unstructuring previously mentioned. Although there are various others, we will confine our identification of such programs to the following. (Sufficient information is provided so that the interested reader can follow up on the original source for more detailed information.)

1. *Glenhaven Achievement Center*

This Center was under the direction of Dr. Newell C. Kephart, one of the early exponents of perceptual-motor training for children with learning disabilities. It is located at Colorado State University, P.O. Box 2153, Fort Collins, Colorado.

This program is based on the theory that the accumulation of motor information is basic to all other perceptual-motor skills. Consequently, with slow-learning children it is often necessary to return to basic motor patterns to allow the child to recapitulate the process of development by which finer and more complex patterns are achieved.

Kephart's treatment techniques tended to focus upon helping the child to operate successfully in his own environment. This takes into account the importance of the child's orientation to gravity as well as awareness of his position in space and time. In addition to the child developing basic control, Kephart believed that the child must develop certain degrees of proficiency in various perceptual-motor skills in order to obtain satisfactory orientation to his environment. He theorized that inability to perform certain perceptual-motor skills results in learning problems for some children. In order to improve such skills Kephart suggested certain kinds of perceptual-motor training.

---

[7]Robert E. Bills, "Nondirective Play Therapy with Retarded Readers," *Journal of Consulting Psychology,* vol. 14, 1950.

2. *Marianne Frostig Center of Educational Therapy*

   This Center is under the direction of Dr. Marianne Frostig and is located at 5981 Venice Boulevard, Los Angeles, California. This program devotes its services to children with learning disabilities. According to its founder, "the physical education programs at the Center are based on research and designed to systematically train children, so that they will no longer find their bodies to be strange obstructive adjuncts, but responsive tools with which to joyfully master the environment."[8]

3. *Reading Research Foundation*

   This program is under the direction of S. Willard Footlik and its main office is located at 814 Diversey Parkway, Chicago, Illinois. One of the stated major goals of this Foundation is to make perceptual-motor training available to as many children as possible who are not achieving their full potential.

   This program conceives perceptual-motor training as a systematic, developmental program of exercises designed to improve the efficiency with which the human machine receives information from the outside world and from within itself, processes or comprehends this information by associating it with past experience, and then utilizes the information to control and guide a purposeful motor response or behavior.

4. *Purdue University Program of Developmental Movement Education*

   This program is coordinated by Dr. Marguerite Clifton, Chairman of the Department of Physical Education for Women, Purdue University, Lafayette, Indiana. The objectives of the perceptual-motor area of this program are: (1) To provide an opportunity for the child to develop a more realistic concept of his own body size and amount of space that his body will require in the performance of varied movement activities; and (2) To encourage the child to seek experiences which require him to process varied sensory information (auditory, tactual, proprioceptive, visual) in order to refine gross motor tasks.

5. *University of Maryland Children's Physical Developmental Clinic*

   This clinic was founded in spring of 1957 by the present Director, Dr. Warren R. Johnson, Professor of Physical Education and Health, University of Maryland, College Park, Maryland. The Clinic was organized in response to a growing need in the Washington, D. C. area for a program which would specialize in improving the physical fitness and/or coordination of sub-fit children—particularly those generally considered in the "special education" category.

   The basic purpose of the Clinic is to improve certain aspects of the "total fitness for living" of children who are referred to it. The approach

---

[8]Marianne Frostig, "Training the Child's Basic Abilities Through Physical Education," *Center Newsletter*, June 1968.

is primarily in terms of physical activity, through which the child may (1) gain greater awareness of the confidence in his body and what he can do with it; (2) acquire and/or improve basic skills which not only increase the range of his movement capabilities and satisfactions, but also heighten his ability to function effectively in the activities of other children, and thus provide a basis for the acquisition of greater social skill; and (3) increase the basic efficiency, stamina, and power of his body-machine.

All of the programs identified here, as well as numerous others, have their enthusiastic supporters. These programs utilize a variety of approaches in attempting to solve learning problems of children. Regardless of the approach used and the degree of structuring in executing the approach, any program should take into account the total personality development concept.

Chapter 16

Standard
    Game Activities
    Rhythmic Activities
    Stunts and Tumbling
    Trampoline
    Balance Beam
    Ball Handling Activities
Specialized

Perceptual-Motor
Media

When thought of as an educational term, "media" has been defined by one source as "printed and audiovisual forms of communication and their accompanying technology."[1] As far as perceptual-motor media are concerned, the meaning of media needs to be extended to include the various types of instruments, machines, and apparatus used to promote perceptual-motor development, in addition to all forms of auditory and/or visual input. And above all, the vastly important movement experiences of children should be considered as an essential medium.

It is the major function of this chapter to:

1. Familiarize the reader with some representative examples of perceptual-motor media.
2. Make suggestions with regard to the purpose of the media and how they might be applied.
3. Emphasize how perceptual-motor abilities can be improved through regular physical education activities.

For our purposes here we will arbitrarily classify media as either *standard* or *specialized*. "Standard" means those kinds of media that are used in various other situations not specifically concerned with perceptual-motor training. "Specialized" means those kinds of media that have been pretty much designed especially for use in perceptual-motor training.

[1]American Library Association, *Standards for School Media Programs,* 50 Huron Street, Chicago, Illinois, 1969.

Standard

These kinds of media represent a near absolute form of compensatory physical education because they involve standard types of physical education activities that are included in a well-balanced elementary school physical education program. This is to say that inherent in these media are natural ways in which perceptual-motor ability can be improved. It is interesting to note, however, that a paradoxical phenomenon exists in that many physical education teachers in the elementary schools are not aware of this. When physical education teachers do become alerted to the fact that many types of regular physical education activities can provide an excellent medium for perceptual-motor training, perhaps then many of the perceptual-motor needs of children can be cared for as a part of the regular physical education program. Ideally, this could obviate the need for specialized highly structured perceptual-motor programs.

One recent study places some credence in this point of view. This investigation compared a group of children who received systematic perceptual-motor training through a specialized program with a group participating in active games containing the same aspects of perceptual-motor development. There was no significant differences between the groups as both groups achieved equally as well academically following the experience.[2]

Game Activities

According to some authorities, disturbances in body image or lack of body awareness, and not lack of movement skills, are a possible cause in some disturbances of visual perception.[3] Thus, it could be reasoned that improvement of body image could have a positive effect on visual perceptual ability of children. An example of a game that can contribute to the development of body image is one called *Busy Bee*. In this game the children are in pairs facing each other and dispersed around the activity area. One child who is the *caller* is in the center of the area. He makes calls such as "shoulder to shoulder," "toe to toe," or "hand to hand." (In the early stages of the game it might be well to have the teacher do the calling.) As the calls are made, the paired children go through the appropriate motions with their partners. After a few calls, the caller will shout, "Busy Bee!"

[2]Joy Schwab, Comparison of Effects of Frostig Move-Grow-Learn and Selected Game Activities, Master's thesis, University of Maryland, College Park, Maryland, 1973.

[3]A. Jean Ayres, "Summary of Presentations to Los Angeles County Elementary Guidance Association: Types of Perceptual-Motor Deficits in Children with Learning Difficulties," April 1964.

This is the signal for every child to get a new partner, including the caller. The child who does not get a partner can become the new caller.

This game has been experimented with in the following manner: As the children played the game, the teacher made them aware of the location of various parts of the body in order to develop the concept of full body image.

Before the game was played, the children were asked to draw a picture of themselves. Many did not know how to begin, and others omitted some of the major limbs in their drawings. After playing Busy Bee, the children were asked again to draw a picture of themselves. This time they were more successful. All of the drawings had bodies, heads, arms, and legs. Some of them had hands, feet, eyes, and ears. A few even had teeth and hair.[4]

Another example of how certain games can help children with learning difficulties is seen with children with slow reaction time. This is the amount of elapsed time that it takes a person to get an overt response started after receiving a stimulus, or the stimulus to response interval. Such children ordinarily have difficulty in processing input from an auditory and/or visual stimulus. When this occurs some teachers tend to feel that the child is not interested and lacks enthusiasm. This condition can be improved over a period of time by games requiring auditory and/or visual input as a starting signal. One such game is *Crows and Cranes* which involves auditory input. The game is played in the following manner.

The playing area is divided by a center line. The group is divided into two teams. The children of one team are designated as Crows and take positions on one side of the area, with the base line on their side serving as their safety zone. The members of the other team are designated as Cranes and take positions on the other side of the area, with their base line as a safety zone. The teacher stands to one side of the area by the center line. The teacher then calls out either "Crows" or "Cranes." If the teacher calls the Crows, they turn and run to their base line to avoid being tagged. The Cranes attempt to tag their opponents before they cross their base line. The Cranes score a point for each Crow tagged. The Crows and Cranes then return to their places, and the teacher proceeds to call one of the groups; play continues in the same manner. As the teacher observes certain children reacting slowly they can be grouped together.

The game of *Black and White* is played in the same manner but uses visual input. One team is the Blacks, and the other the Whites. An object,

[4]James H. Humphrey and Dorothy D. Sullivan, *Teaching Slow Learners Through Active Games* (Springfield, Illinois: Charles C Thomas Publisher, 1970), p. 20.

black on one side and white on the other, is tossed into the air. If it comes down on the black side, the Blacks run for their base line, and vice versa.

Rhythmic Activities

In reporting about neurological dysfunctioning in the visual-perceptual-auditory-motor areas, McClurg implied that disabled readers frequently lack coordination in such basic motor movements as walking and running. And further, that motor *rhythm* is often lacking in persons with reading, writing, and spelling problems.[5]

It will be recalled that the condition of *reversals* was mentioned in the previous chapter, and further that in some instances it has been found that children with the kinetic type of reversal also have a condition known as *arhythmia,* or lack of rhythm. It is interesting to note that in this general connection, Drake found that by working with dyslexic children in fine motor skills such as handwriting, and patterned motor skills—especially folk dancing—improvement in reading was in evidence.[6]

It appears logical to assume that rhythmic activities can be a very important medium in perceptual-motor training. Perhaps for most children the most successful type to use would be creative rhythms, where the child responds by expressing himself in a way that the rhythmical accompaniment makes him feel. When the child is able to use his body freely, there is a strong likelihood that there will be increased body awareness. Creative rhythms will also give the child free self-direction in space, as well as self-control, in that he is not involved with a partner in a more formalized rhythmic activity. In this regard it should be mentioned, however, that there is also merit in some cases in performing the activity within the framework of an established pattern. This is particularly true as far as emotional release is concerned. Mental hygienists know that some persons can express themselves with more spontaneity in a relatively structured situation than in one where they have more freedom (possibly a factor in the work reported by Drake above). Such persons, when they skip, dance, clap, and whirl to the rhythm of the music may be expressing themselves with an abandon that is not possible when they are free to express themselves in any way they wish.[7]

[5]William H. McClurg, "The Neurophysiological Basis of Reading Disabilities," *The Reading Teacher,* April 1969.

[6]Charles Drake, "Reading, 'Riting, and Rhythm," *The Reading Teacher,* December 1964.

[7]Emma M. Layman, in *Science and Medicine of Exercise and Sports,* 2d ed., ed. W. R. Johnson and E. R. Buskirk, (New York: Harper and Row Publishers, 1973).

Stunts and Tumbling

Certain stunt and tumbling activities can be of value in providing for perceptual-motor development. For example, since reading is a perceptual skill involving bilateral movement, certain stunts involving such movement might be used to advantage. It has also been found that certain stunts are useful in helping to improve body awareness. Stunts which alert the child to the movement of certain muscle groups when he presses against something can be of value for this purpose. Such a stunt is the *Chinese Get Up* explained and illustrated in Chapter 9.

In tumbling activities involving some of the simple rolls there is an opportunity to use those parts of the body, for example the torso, which is less sensitive to *tactile* perception than other parts of the body. An example is the *Log Roll*, also explained and illustrated in Chapter 9.

Trampoline

The trampoline can be particularly useful in developing better awareness of self and concepts of spatial relationships. Kephart,[8] one of the early exponents of the value of the trampoline in perceptual-motor training, suggests that not only must the child learn a dynamic relationship to the center of gravity and maintain a dynamic balance, but he must maintain these coordinations under changing relationships. In addition, the changes in these relationships are not the result of his own effort directly, but are dependent in a large part on the trampoline and its functions. Thus, the timing and rhythm of his activity are dictated by the spring of the trampoline rather than directly determined by his own movements. In activities on the surface area, the child can adjust his movements to the rhythm pattern of his muscles. Thus, if the neurological innervation to one or more muscle groups loses its rhythm, he merely adjusts his movements to this change. On the trampoline, such adjustment is not possible, since the rhythm is dictated by the device. Therefore, he must learn to maintain adequate and constant rhythms in his neuromuscular coordination which are demanded in few other activities. Thus, mere activity of bouncing on the trampoline contributes to body image and spatial relationships within the body.

Some research has been conducted in connection with the benefits to be derived from the use of the trampoline as a perceptual-motor medium. An

[8]Newell C. Kephart, *The Slow Learner in the Classroom* (Columbus, Ohio: Charles E. Merrill Books, 1960).

example is the work of McCants.[9] In a controlled study to determine the effects of an eight-week instructional program of trampolining upon selected measures of the physical fitness of mentally retarded and emotionally disturbed children in a special school it was found that the experimental group improved significantly on all tests. It was also observed that there were other improvements in the experimental group in the way of classroom performance, social adjustment, morale, and confidence. An interesting aside to this study was that the investigator was employed immediately to continue the program for the rest of the children in the school.

Some perceptual-motor specialists have developed a series of trampoline activities. One such progressive sequence has been developed and published by Lyle K. Trexler.[10] The sequence of activities is accompanied by directions for their use.

Balance Beam

Activities on the balance beam can help the child maintain his relationship to gravity, and at the same time help to develop space awareness and directionally related movements. With regard to the use of the balance beam Smith[11] observes that autokinetic movement, the visual illusion that gives one the impression that a stationary object is in motion, occurs during prolonged periods of constant visual focus on an object. Because of this she suggests that when teaching activities requiring children to maintain continuous and prolonged focus on stationary object or spot (such as balance beam exercises demand), the child should be encouraged to occasionally shift his visual focus by a few degrees right or left. It may be helpful to provide some focal point that is in constant slight motion. For beginners, a blinking light might be provided on standards at each end of the beam. Such a teaching aid may produce more efficient motor response in balance activities.

Attempts to study the relationship between reading and ability to perform dynamic balance have yielded varying results. In one such study Walker[12] compared balance beam walking test scores with reading readiness test scores of 162 first-grade children. On the basis of his data he gen-

---

[9]Robert McCants, Effects of an Eight-Week Trampoline Instruction Program on Certain Measures of the Physical Fitness of Retarded Children, Master's thesis, University of Maryland, College Park, Maryland, 1962.
[10]Lyle K., Trexler, "The Trampoline: A Training Device for Children with Perceptual-Motor Problems," *Academic Therapy*, Winter Issue, 1969-70.
[11]Hope M. Smith, "Implications for Movement Education Experiences Drawn from Perceptual-Motor Research," *Journal of Health, Physical Education, and Recreation*, April 1970.
[12]James Walker, A Comparison of Lee-Clark Reading Readiness Scores with a Test of Balance Using Selected First Grade Children, Master's thesis, University of Maryland, College Park, Maryland, 1963.

eralized that (1) there seemed to be a tendency for first-grade children scoring high or low on the reading readiness test to score respectively high or low on the balance beam walking test; (2) there seemed to be a much greater relationship between balance beam walking test scores and reading readiness test scores exhibited by girls than boys; and (3) girls tended to score higher than boys on the balance beam walking test. It is important to recognize that these are not cause and effect relationships but coexisting behaviors.

Ball Handling Activities

Such skills with inflated balls as tapping (bouncing), throwing to a partner or target, and catching can often be useful in helping children develop eye-hand coordination, timing, and bilaterality.

Ordinarily, children with eye-hand coordination problems have difficulty catching a ball, not necessarily because of a motor response, but perhaps more likely because of slowness in eye movement. It may be a good practice with some children to simply roll the ball slowly across the surface area and have them follow it with their eyes. Several children can sit in a circle and roll the ball back and forth to each other. Later they can work on catching a ball at a short distance in the air. A beach ball or even a balloon may be good to begin with because the lighter weight of this type of object will cause it to move more slowly through the air. Under these conditions of being able to follow the object visually, the child should be more successful in catching it.

Bouncing a ball can be used to advantage to improve timing. Sometimes it is helpful to accompany bouncing with some sort of rhythm. Many children in their first experience with ball bouncing tend to "slap" the ball hard, causing it to rebound in a way that is difficult to control. One way to help to avoid this is to suggest that the ball is a friend and should be treated as such ("as you might pat your puppy dog").

It should be understood that the physical education activities that have been suggested here for use as perceptual-motor media are merely representative examples and in no sense of the word exhaust the possibilities. The creative and imaginative teacher will think of many forms of physical education activities that have value in perceptual-motor development.

Specialized

Examples of specialized media for perceptual-motor training used in two different programs will be presented here. These are the Perceptual-Motor Training Laboratory, which is a part of the movement education program for children at Purdue University mentioned previously and the Children's Physical Developmental Clinic at the University of Maryland.

The objectives of the perceptual-motor area of the Purdue program are stated as follows by the Coordinator, Dr. Marguerite Clifton.[13]

1. To provide an opportunity for the child to develop a more realistic concept of his own body size and the amount of space that his body will require in the performance of varied movement activities.

2. To encourage the child to seek experiences which require him to process varied sensory information (auditory, tactual, proprioceptive, visual) in order to refine gross motor tasks.

A series of 17 perceptual training tasks have been devised, and each emphasizes the use of a particular perceptual mode, but not always to the exclusion of other modalities. Each of the tasks utilizes an original piece of equipment designed specifically for this program. Accomplishment of a given task requires a child to employ the appropriate perceptual modality or combination of modalities.

The "bedspring walk" is an example in which the child is required to attend to proprioceptive input in order to accomplish any one of several tasks, and particularly when his eyes are closed. The equipment is simply a double set of old-fashioned bed springs covered with canvas. (Specifications for the equipment used to accomplish the various tasks have been published by Jacqueline Herkowitz)[14]

The final example of specialized perceptual-motor media reported here is concerned with those designed and developed by Dr. Warren R. Johnson, Director of the Children's Physical Developmental Clinic at the University of Maryland. These media are produced by Medical Motovation Systems, Inc., Research Park, State Road, Princeton, New Jersey, under the name of *NPO Equipment* (Neuromuscular Perceptual Organization).

The equipment consists of the NPO Balance Beam, NPO Kick-Throw Rebounder, and NPO Footprint Guide, the first of which will be described here.

The NPO Balance Beam beckons the learner forward. The child steps onto the lighted starting target, thereby causing the first panel or target of the balance beam to light up. Each target is different in color and each successful step causes the next one to light—inviting the child to the next correct move. This beckoning technique has been found to hold the atten-

---

[13]Marguerite Clifton, "A Developmental Approach to Perceptual-Motor Experiences," *Journal of Health, Physical Education, and Recreation,* April 1970.

[14]Jacqueline Herkowitz, "A Perceptual-Motor Training Program to Improve the Gross Motor Abilities of Preschoolers," *Journal of Health, Physical Education, and Recreation,* April 1970.

tion even of individuals of diagnosed short attention span—to achieve repetition of effort and to create rapid progress in balance and coordination. Completion of the balanced walk brings an acknowledging buzzer to signal success and reward the effort. The task may be made more difficult by simply turning the beam over to its narrower side. And, it is possible to measure progress in the time needed to accomplish the task and in correctness of walking either forward or backward.

A film with children actually using the equipment is available to assist in the training of aides and volunteers who supervise children. The objectives of using NPO Equipment are explained and a variety of uses for each unit are shown.

It is appropriate in closing this Chapter to reemphasize caution and restraint in the use of perceptual-motor training. While under adequate supervision and with properly prepared personnel, many of the types of experiences referred to can be of value. Nevertheless, the "bandwagon" syndrome connected with any relatively new approach to dealing with behavior of children needs to be taken into account.

Appendix

Characteristics of Children of Elementary School Age

Perhaps the best source of *needs* and *interests* of children is their inherent physical, social, intellectual, and emotional characteristics. The material that follows is provided as a possible guide for the selection of physical education activities based on the needs and interests of children.

It will be noted that the characteristics are presented in terms of age levels. This procedure seems essential for a more complete understanding of the characteristics of average children at a given grade level. This implies that during the course of a school year a child will move from one age level to another. For instance, in general the child starts in the first grade approximately at the age of 6 years and at the completion of his first year of school he is approaching or has reached the age of 7 years. Similarly, the second-grader is approximately 7 years of age at the start of his second year in school and is approaching or has reached the age of 8 years when the school year closes. The following scale is based on the age-and grade-level assumption made here:

Grade in School	Age Level
Kindergarten	5-6
First grade	6-7
Second grade	7-8
Third grade	8-9
Fourth grade	9-10
Fifth grade	10-11
Sixth grade	11-12

The detailed description of the characteristics which is given here includes the age levels from 5 through 12. In examining the characteristics, teachers will no doubt profess greatest interest in those age levels which pertain most specifically to the grade level at which they are teaching or expect to teach. It is recommended, however, that consideration be given to the age levels that are on either side of the teacher's specific interest. In other words, it seems essential that the teacher have a full understanding of the characteristics of the children at the preceding grade level and a knowledge of the changes that will be inherent in characteristics at subsequent grade levels. Ideally, each elementary school classroom teacher should possess a general knowledge of the characteristics of children at all age levels of the elementary school, regardless of the specific grade level taught. The teacher is then in better position to see the development of the elementary school child at his or her specific grade level as a part of his or her total growth pattern. The physical education specialist who teaches at all levels of the elementary school perhaps has little alternative but to develop a thorough understanding of the characteristics of the entire age span of elementary school children. This knowledge appears to be essential if the specialist is to do an adequate job of guiding, directing, and supervising physical education learning experiences.

The characteristics of children from ages 5 through 12 included in the following pages have been developed through a documentary analysis of over a score of sources that have appeared in the literature in recent years. It should be understood that these characteristics are suggestive of the behavior patterns of the so-called normal child. This implies that if a child does not conform to these characteristics, it should not be interpreted to mean that he is seriously deviating from the normal. In other words, it should be recognized that each child progresses at his own rate and that there will be much overlapping of the characteristics listed for each age level.

Characteristics of the 5-Year-Old Child

PHYSICAL CHARACTERISTICS

1. Boys' height 41.9—45.9 inches, weight 37.7—48.7 pounds; girls' height 41.6—45.6 inches, weight 36.1—47.9 pounds.[1]
2. May grow two or three inches and gain from three to six pounds during the year.
3. Girls may be about a year ahead of boys in physiological development.
4. Beginning to have good control of body.

[1]Heights and weights are based upon computed means from *Basic Body Measurements of School Age Children*, U. S. Department of Health, Education, and Welfare, Office of Education, June, 1953.

5. Can ride a tricycle and climb well.
6. The large muscles are better developed than the small muscles that control the fingers and hands.
7. Usually determined whether he will be right-or-left-handed.
8. Eye and hand coordination is not complete.
9. May have farsighted vision.
10. Vigorous and noisy, but activity appears to have definite direction.
11. Tires easily and needs plenty of rest.
12. Can wash and take care of toilet needs.
13. Can use fork and spoon and may try to use knife.
14. May or may not dress himself.
15. Stomachaches may be common.

Social Characteristics

1. Interested in neighborhood games which involve any number of children.
2. Plays various games to test his skill.
3. Enjoys other children and likes to be with them.
4. Interests are largely self-centered.
5. Seems to get along best in small groups.
6. Shows an interest in home activities.
7. Imitates when he plays.
8. Gets along well in taking turns.
9. Respects the belongirgs of other people.

Intellectual Characteristics

1. Enjoys copying designs, letters, and numbers.
2. Interested in completing tasks.
3. May tend to monopolize table conversation.
4. Frequently bothered by frightening dreams.
5. Memory for past events good.
6. Looks at books and pretends to read.
7. Likes recordings and words and music that tell a story.
8. Enjoys counting objects.
9. Slightly over 2,000 words in vocabulary.
10. Can speak in complete sentences.
11. Can sing simple melodies, beat good rhythms, and recognize simple tunes.
12. Daydreams seem to center around parties and make-believe play.
13. Attention span increasing up to over 20 minutes in some cases.
14. Is able to plan activities.
15. Enjoys stories, dramatic plays, and poems.

16. Enjoys making up dances to music.
17. Pronunciation is usually clear.
18. Is able to express his needs in words.

EMOTIONAL CHARACTERISTICS

1. Seldom shows jealousy toward younger siblings.
2. Usually sees only one way to do a thing.
3. Usually sees only one answer to a question.
4. Inclined not to change plans in the middle of an activity, but would prefer to begin over.
5. May fear being deprived of mother.
6. Some definite personality traits evidenced.
7. Is learning to get along better, but still may resort to quarreling and fighting.
8. Likes to be trusted with errands.
9. Enjoys performing simple tasks.
10. Wants to please and do what is expected of him.
11. Is beginning to sense right and wrong in terms of specific situations.

Characteristics of the 6-Year-Old Child

PHYSICAL CHARACTERISTICS

1. Boys' height 44–48.2 inches, weight 41.3–53.9 pounds; girls' height 43.7–47.9 inches, weight 39.6–53.2 pounds.
2. Growth is gradual in weight and height.
3. Milk teeth shedding and first permanent molars emerging.
4. Good appetite and wants to eat between meals.
5. Needs good supply of energy.
6. Marked activity urge absorbs him in running, jumping, chasing, and dodging games.
7. Muscular control becoming more effective with large objects.
8. Endurance is low and heart is small.
9. Has a low visual ability to focus on small fast-moving objects.
10. There is a noticeable change in the eye-hand behavior.
11. Legs lengthening rapidly.
12. Big muscles crave activity.
13. Enjoys stunts involving total body movement.

SOCIAL CHARACTERISTICS

1. Self-centered and has need for praise.
2. Likes to be first and likes to win.

3. Indifferent to sex distinction.
4. Enjoys group play when groups tend to be small.
5. Likes parties but behavior may not always be decorous.
6. The majority enjoy school association and have a desire to learn.
7. Interested in conduct of his friends.
8. Boys like to fight and wrestle with peers to prove masculinity.
9. Shows an interest in group approval.

INTELLECTUAL CHARACTERISTICS

1. Vocabulary upwards of 2,500 words.
2. Interest span inclined to be short.
3. Knows number combinations making up to ten.
4. Knows comparative values of the common coins.
5. Can define simple objects in terms of what they are used for.
6. Knows right and left sides of the body
7. Has an association with creative activity and motorized life experience.
8. Drawings are crude but realistic and suggestive of early man.
9. Will contribute to guided group planning.
10. Conversation usually concerns his own experiences and interests.
11. Curiosity is active and memory is strong.
12. Identifies himself with imaginary characters.

EMOTIONAL CHARACTERISTICS

1. Restless and may have difficulty in making decisions.
2. Emotional storms, such as temper tantrums, may be difficult to control at times.
3. Behavior patterns may often be explosive and unpredictable.
4. Jealousy toward siblings at times; at other times takes pride in siblings.
5. Greatly excited by anything new.
6. Behavior becomes susceptible to shifts in direction, inwardly motivated and outwardly stimulated.
7. May be self-assertive and dramatic.

Characteristics of the 7-Year-Old Child

PHYSICAL CHARACTERISTICS

1. Boys' height 46–50.4 inches, weight 45.4–59.6 pounds; girls' height 45.7–50.1 inches, weight 43.7–58.7 pounds.
2. "Big-muscle" activity predominates in interest and value.
3. More improvement in eye-hand coordination.

4. May grow two to three inches and gain three to five pounds in weight during the year.
5. Tires easily and shows fatigue in the afternoon.
6. Has slow reaction time.
7. Needs to sleep approximately 11 hours daily.
8. May have to be reminded at times about control of elimination.
9. Heart and lungs are smallest in proportion to body size.
10. General health may be precarious with susceptibility to disease high and resistance low.
11. Endurance is relatively poor.
12. Coordinations are improving, with throwing and catching becoming more accurate.
13. Whole-body movements are under better control.
14. Small accessory muscles developing.
15. Displays amazing amounts of vitality.

SOCIAL CHARACTERISTICS

1. Wants recognition for his individual achievements.
2. Sex differences are not of too great significance.
3. Not always a good loser.
4. Conversation often centers around family.
5. Learning to stand up for his own rights.
6. Interested in friends and is not influenced by their social or economic status.
7. May have nervous habits such as nail-biting, tongue-sucking, scratching, or pulling at ear.
8. Attaining orientation in time.
9. Gets greater enjoyment from group play.
10. Shows greater signs of cooperative efforts.

INTELLECTUAL CHARACTERISTICS

1. Abstract thinking is barely beginning.
2. Is able to listen longer.
3. Reads some books by himself.
4. Is able to reason, but has little experience upon which to base judgments.
5. The attention span is still short and retention poor, but repetition is enjoyed.
6. Reaction time is still slow.
7. Learning to evaluate the achievements of self and others.

8. Concerned with own lack of skill and achievement.
9. Becoming more realistic and less imaginative.

EMOTIONAL CHARACTERISTICS

1. Curiosity and creative desires may condition responses.
2. May be difficult to take criticism from adults.
3. Wants to be more independent.
4. Reaching for new experiences and trying to relate himself to enlarged world.
5. Overanxious to reach goals set by parents and teachers.
6. Critical of himself and sensitive to failure.
7. Tantrums are vanishing.
8. Becoming less impulsive and boisterous in actions than at age 6.

Characteristics of the 8-Year-Old

PHYSICAL CHARACTERISTICS

1. Boys' height 48.1–52.7 inches, weight 49.5–66.9 pounds; girls' height 47.7–52.3 inches, weight 47.5–66.3 pounds.
2. Interested in games requiring coordination of small muscles.
3. Arms are lengthening and hands are growing larger.
4. Eyes can accommodate more readily.
5. Some develop poor posture.
6. Accidents appear to occur more frequently at this age.
7. Fewer communicable diseases.
8. Appreciates correct skill performance.

SOCIAL CHARACTERISTICS

1. Girls are careful of their clothes but boys are not.
2. Leaves many things uncompleted.
3. Has "special" friends.
4. Has longer periods of peaceful play.
5. Does not like playing alone.
6. Enjoys dramatizing.
7. Starts collections.
8. Enjoys school and dislikes staying home.
9. Likes variety.
10. Recognition of property rights is well established.
11. Responds well to group activity.
12. Interest will focus on friends of own sex.
13. Beginning of the desire to become a member of the club.

Intellectual Characteristics

1. Can tell day of month and year.
2. Voluntary attention span increasing.
3. Likes to read.
4. Interested in far-off places, and ways of communication now have real meaning.
5. Aware of adult world and his place in it.
6. Ready to tackle almost anything.
7. Shows a capacity for self-evaluation.
8. Likes to memorize.
9. Likes to go to Sunday School.
10. Not always too good at telling time, but very much aware of it.

Emotional Characteristics

1. Dislikes taking much criticism from adults.
2. Can give and take criticism in his own group.
3. May develop enemies.
4. Does not like to be treated as a child.
5. Has a marked sense of humor.
6. First impulse is to blame others.
7. Becoming more realistic and wants to find out for himself.

Characteristics of the 9-Year-Old Child

Physical Characteristics

1. Boys' height 50–54.8 inches, weight 54.6–74.2 pounds; girls' height 49.6–54.4 inches; weight 51.9–74.1 pounds.
2. Increasing strength in arms, hands, and fingers.
3. Endurance improving.
4. Needs and enjoys much activity; boys like to shout, wrestle, and tussle with each other.
5. A few girls are nearing puberty.
6. Girls' growth maturity gaining over boys' up to two years.
7. Girls enjoy active group games, but are usually less noisy and less full of spontaneous energy than boys.
8. Likely to slouch and assume unusual postures.
9. Eyes are much better developed and are able to accommodate to near work with less strain.
10. Needs 10–11 hours sleep; is a good sleeper, but often does not get enough sleep.
11. May tend to overexercise.

12. Sex differences appear in recreational activities.
13. Interested in own body and wants to have questions answered.

Social Characteristics
1. Wants to be like others, talk like others, and look like them.
2. Girls are becoming more interested in their clothes.
3. Is generally a conformist and may be afraid of that which is different.
4. Able to be on his own.
5. Able to be fairly responsible and dependable.
6. Some firm and loyal friendships may develop.
7. Increasing development of qualities of leadership and followership.
8. Increasing interest in activities involving challenges and adventure.
9. Increasing participation in varied and organized group activities.

Intellectual Characteristics
1. Individual differences are clear and distinct.
2. Real interests are beginning to develop.
3. Beginning to have a strong sense of right and wrong.
4. Understands explanations.
5. Interests are closer to 10- or 11-year-olds than to 7- or 8-year-olds.
6. As soon as a project fails to hold interest, it may be dropped without further thought.
7. Attention span is greatly increased.
8. Seems to be guided best by a reason, simple and clear-cut, for a decision which needs to be made.
9. Ready to learn from occasional failure of his judgment as long as learning takes place in situations where failure will not have too serious consequences.
10. Able to make up own mind and come to decisions.
11. Marked reading disabilities begin to be more evident and may tend to influence the personality.
12. Range of interest in reading in that many are great readers while others may be barely interested in books.
13. Will average between six and seven words per remark.

Emotional Characteristics
1. May sometimes be outspoken and critical of the adults he knows, although he has a genuine fondness for them.
2. Responds best to adults who treat him as an individual and approach him in an adult way.

3. Likes recognition for what he has done and responds well to deserved praise.
4. Likely to be backward about public recognition, but likes private praise.
5. Developing sympathy and loyalty to others.
6. Does not mind criticism or punishment if he thinks it is fair, but is indignant if he thinks it is unfair.
7. Disdainful of danger to and safety of himself, which may be a result of increasing interest in activities involving challenges and adventure.

Characteristics of the 10-Year-Old Child

PHYSICAL CHARACTERISTICS

1. Boys' height 51.8–56.8 inches, weight 59.2–82.2 pounds; girls' height 51.6–56.8 inches, weight 57.1–83.5 pounds.
2. Individuality is well defined and insights are more mature.
3. Stability in growth rate and stability of physiological processes.
4. Physically active and likes to rush around and be busy.
5. Before the onset of puberty there is usually a "resting period" or "plateau," during which the boy or girl does not appear to gain in either height or weight.
6. Interested in the development of more skills.
7. Reaction time is improving.
8. Muscular strength does not seem to keep pace with growth.
9. Refining and elaborating skill in the use of small muscles.

SOCIAL CHARACTERISTICS

1. Begins to recognize the fallibility of adults.
2. Moving more into a peer-centered society.
3. Both boys and girls amazingly self-dependent.
4. Self-reliance has grown, and at the same time intensifed group feelings are acquired.
5. Divergence between the two sexes is widening.
6. Great team loyalties are developing.
7. Beginning to identify with one's social contemporaries of the same sex.
8. Relatively easy to appeal to his reason.
9. On the whole he has a fairly critical sense of justice.
10. Boys show their friendship with other boys by wrestling and jostling with each other, while girls walk around with arms around each other as friends.

11. Interest in people, in the community, and in affairs of the world is keen.
12. Interested in social problems in an elementary way and likes to take part in discussions.
13. Girls and boys are definitely separating in their interests, boys preferring rough-and-tumble games and girls usually preferring quieter games.
14. As one of the gang, he has the feeling of the need of belonging and being liked by others; boys keep the gang interest longer than girls.
15. Girls are more aware of interpersonal relationships than boys.
16. Boys have a high degree of interest in team games.

Intellectual Characteristics

1. Works with executive speed and likes the challenge of arithmetic.
2. Shows a capacity to budget his time and energy.   .
3. Can attend to a visual task and at the same time maintain conversation.
4. Some become discouraged and may give up trying when unsuccessful.
5. The attention span has lengthened considerably, with the child able to listen to and follow directions and retain knowledge more easily.
6. Beginning understanding of real causal relations.
7. Making finer conceptual distinctions and thinking reflectively.
8. Developing a scientific approach.
9. Better oriented with respect to time.
10. Ready to plan his day and accept responsibility for getting things done on time.

Emotional Characteristics

1. Increasing tendency to rebel against adult domination.
2. Capable of loyalties and hero worship, and he can inspire it in his schoolmates.
3. Can be readily inspired to group loyalties in his club organization.
4. Likes the sense of solidarity which comes from keeping a group secret as a member of a group.
5. Girls dramatize with paper dolls many life situations in whispered secrets or in outspoken dialogue.
6. Boys have an increasing tendency to show lack of sympathy and understanding with girls.
7. Girls have an increasing tendency to show lack of sympathy and understanding with boys.
8. Boys' and girls' behavior and interests becoming increasingly different.

Characteristics of the 11-Year-Old Child

PHYSICAL CHARACTERISTICS

1. Boys' height 53.6–58.8 inches, weight 64.5–90.7 pounds; girls' height 53.7–59.3 inches, weight 63.5–94.5 pounds.
2. Marked physical changes are taking place which for the time being cut down the amount of energy a child can put on activities.
3. Marked changes in muscle system tend to awkwardness and habits distressing to the child.
4. Shows fatigue more easily.
5. Some girls and a few boys suddenly show rapid growth, evidence of the approach of adolescence.
6. In general, this is a period of good health, with fewer diseases and infections.
7. Girls may often be taller and heavier than boys.
8. Uneven growth of different parts of the body.
9. Rapid growth may result in laziness of the lateral type, and fatigue and irritability of the linear type.
10. Willing to work hard at acquiring physical skills, and emphasis is on excellence of performance of physical feats.
11. Boys are more active and rough in games than girls.
12. Eye-hand coordination well developed.
13. Bodily growth is more rapid than heart growth, and lungs are not fully developed.
14. Boys develop greater power in shoulder girdle muscles.

SOCIAL CHARACTERISTICS

1. Internal guiding standards have been set up and, although guided by what is done by other children, he will modify his behavior in line with those standards already set up.
2. Does a number of socially acceptable things not because they are right or wrong.
3. Although obsessed by standards of peers, he is anxious for social approval from adults.
4. Need for social-life companionship of children of own age.
5. Liking for organized games more and more prominent.
6. Girls are likely to be self-conscious in the presence of boys and are usually much more mature than boys.
7. Team spirit is very strong.
8. Boys' and girls' interests are not always the same and there may be some antagonism between the sexes.

9. Often engages in silly behavior, such as giggling and clowning.
10. Girls are more interested in social appearance than are boys.
11. Boys more interested in approbation of other boys than of girls.

Intellectual Characteristics

1. Increasing power of attention and abstract reasoning.
2. Able to maintain a longer period of intellectual activity between first-hand experiences.
3. Interested in scientific experiments and procedures.
4. Can carry on many individual intellectual responsibilities.
5. Able to discuss problems and to see different sides of questions.
6. May lack maturity of judgment.
7. Increased language facility.
8. Attention span is increasing and concentration may be given to a task for a long period of time.
9. Level of aspiration has increased.
10. Growing in ability to use several facts to make a decision.
11. Insight into causal relationships is developing more and is manifested by many "why" and "how" questions.

Emotional Characteristics

1. If unskilled in group games and game skills, he may tend to withdraw.
2. Boys may be concerned if they feel they are underdeveloped.
3. May appear to be indifferent and uncooperative.
4. Moods change quickly.
5. Wants to grow up, but may be afraid to leave childhood security behind.
6. Increase in self-direction and in a serious attitude toward work.
7. Need for approval to feel secure.
8. Beginning to have a fully developed idea of own importance.

Characteristics of the 12-Year-Old Child

Physical Characteristics

1. Boys' height 55.3–61.1 inches, weight 69.8–101.4 pounds; girls' height 56.1–61.9 inches, weight 71.9–107.5 pounds.
2. Becoming more skillful in the use of small muscles.
3. May be relatively little body change in some cases.
4. Sex interests are at a very low ebb.
5. Ten hours' sleep is considered average.
6. Heart rate at rest is between 80 and 90.

SOCIAL CHARACTERISTICS

1. Increasing identification of self with other children of his own sex.
2. Increasing recognition of fallibility of adults.
3. May see himself as a child and adults as adults.
4. Getting ready to make the difficult transition to adolescence.
5. Pressure is being placed on individual at this level to begin to assume adult responsibilities.

INTELLECTUAL CHARACTERISTICS

1. Learns more ways of studying and controlling the physical world.
2. The use of language (on many occasions his own vocabulary) to exchange ideas or for explanatory reasons.
3. More use of reflective thinking and greater ease of distinction.
4. Continuation in development of scientific approach.

EMOTIONAL CHARACTERISTICS

1. Beginning to develop a truer picture of morality.
2. Clearer understanding of real causal relations.
3. The process of sexual maturation involves structural and physiological changes, with possible perplexing and disturbing emotional problems.
4. Personal appearance may become a source of great conflict, and learning to appreciate good grooming or the reverse may be prevalent.
5. May be very easily hurt when criticized or made the scapegoat.
6. Maladjustments may occur when there is not a harmonious relationship between child and adults.

Index